Wellbeing in Interiors

Philosophy, Design and Value in Practice

BY ELINA GRIGORIOU

RIBA Publishing

This book is dedicated with love to all of my brilliant family, without whom I would not love all the things that have led me to make every effort for Wellbeing and the betterment of life in this world.

Also to my Philosophy tutors and groups over the years who have given me guidance, pushed me to ask questions, and encouraged me to keep looking and finding meaning in life.

And to my Friends, for the same reasons as C.S Lewis.

© RIBA Publishing 2019

Published by RIBA Publishing, 66 Portland Place, London, W1B 1NT

ISBN 978 1 85946 579 0

The right of Elina Grigoriou to be identified as the Author of this Work has been asserted in accordance with the Copyright, Designs and Patents Act 1988 sections 77 and 78.

All rights reserved. No part of this publication may be reproduced, stored in a retrieval system, or transmitted, in any form or by any means, electronic, mechanical, photocopying, recording or otherwise, without prior permission of the copyright owner.

British Library Cataloguing-in-Publication Data
A catalogue record for this book is available from the British Library.

Commissioning Editor: Elizabeth Webster
Production: Jane Rogers
Designed and typeset by John Round Design
Printed and bound by Page Bros, Norwich
Cover image: Shutterstock.com

While every effort has been made to check the accuracy and quality of the information given in this publication, neither the Author nor the Publisher accept any responsibility for the subsequent use of this information, for any errors or omissions that it may contain, or for any misunderstandings arising from it.

www.ribapublishing.com

Acknowledgements

This book's original format was the brainchild of RIBA Publishing commissioning editor Sharla Plant, without whom it would not have got off the ground. She was inspired by a series of talks on evidence-based design for Wellbeing organised by the Feeling Good Foundation and The Building Centre Trust.

A number of expert contributors were originally involved in the book, to whom I am grateful for their contributions and thank for their specialist work to promote the agenda of Wellbeing in their respective fields. These are Briony Turner, Derek Clements-Croome, John Mardaljevic, Maro Puljizevic, Bridget Juniper, Victoria Hume, Sarah Hewitt, Lily Bernheimer, Roberto Serra, Angela Wright, Katie Livesey and Derrick Crump.

Richard Francis was a joint editor of the book's original draft, and was always a great support for discussing ideas and promoting Wellbeing. I am grateful for all his support and encouragement along the way. I'm also grateful to Richard for providing me with the concept of 'believers'. It has helped me identify who I should spend time with (and effort on), and who to leave until their time is right.

Managing the renewed book's direction and purpose was in the diplomatic and caring hands of my second commissioning editor, Elizabeth Webster; thank you Liz! She then passed me on to my third and final editor, Susannah Lear, whom I thank for her fresh outlook on the manuscript's composition, and her combination of steady nudging and understanding every time I gave her a deadline and waved at it as it went flying past. Each editor has, in my experience, been perfect for the stage the book was at, and contributed their skill to shaping the manuscript into something akin to a half-readable book. This being my first book, I have needed a fair amount of guidance, and learned a huge amount from the process. Thank you to the whole team at RIBA Publishing for picking up this book and running with it.

Thank you also to all those who, through small or large efforts, further good design; design that supports Wellbeing and the wider sustainability agenda. There are many unsung heroes who are the real cogs of change, and I'm grateful to the hundreds of sources I have been able to tap into over my career, both academic and professional, who will never get their name in lights, but will have contributed to those who have.

Thank you also to the Grigoriou Interiors team – Amy Bettison, Maria Popova and Nicole Floss – who have been such superstars, helping to drive sustainability and Wellbeing into industry and society through every project they work on, piece of research they undertake, and smile or funky card they share with the team. Thank you for being such great supporters and making a great team!

My final thank you goes to my sister, friend and business partner Angeliki, for sharing in the effort to enable Wellbeing. Also, for her support in the writing of this book – she would have loved to have spent three months correcting this manuscript if she could, and you would all have benefited from it! My name goes on the cover and in articles, but Angeliki is always part of it.

Contents

Acknowledgments
iii

Preface
vi

Introduction
viii

General approach of the book
viii

What to expect in each part
x

Defining wellbeing
xii

Part 1
Philosophy: prerequisites and outputs of wellbeing
1

Chapter 1
Prerequisites of wellbeing
2

Beauty
3

Comfort
7

Chapter 2
Outputs of wellbeing 9

Relationship of comfort and performance
10

Occupant performance affected by interiors
11

Wellbeing and productivity link
12

Harmony
13

Part 2
Design in practice: delivering a design for wellbeing
17

Chapter 3
Knowing the users
18

The User Profile
19

Empathy
28

Environmental psychologists
30

A specialist explaining things in their own words...
32

CASE STUDY: Huckletree co-working workplace
36

Chapter 4
Existing buildings and priorities
39

Selecting and working with existing buildings
40

Prioritising issues
41

Chapter 5
Designing user experience
43

User experience through spaces
44

Entering into a building
46

Multi-sensory design
47

Biophilia
48

Chapter 6
Design characteristics and issues affecting wellbeing
50

Part 3
Design in practice: aesthetic issues affecting wellbeing
55

Chapter 7
Elegance/Elegant
57

Chapter 8
Balanced or symmetrical
60

The relationship of nature, proportion and symmetry
65

Chapter 9
Colour and the psychology behind it
67

Introduction to colour psychology
68

The impact of colour
69

Use of colour in interiors
70

The psychological properties of the main hues
70

Process of colour selection
73

The four colour groups
74

The interdependence of shape, size and colour
75

Chapter 10
Repetition and patterns
77

Chapter 11
Shapes, volumes and proportions
80

Shapes
81

Contours and angles
81

Symbolism of shapes
84

Proportion of shapes and patterns
86

Fibonacci sequence and the golden ratio
89

Volumes of space
91

Ceiling height
92

Chapter 12
Symbolism
94

Chapter 13
The use of artwork in interiors
97

A specialist explaining things in their own words...
100

Chapter 14
Materials and textures
108

Materials
109

Textures
110

Measuring the effect and amount of texture
115

Part 4
Design in practice: physical issues affecting wellbeing
117

Chapter 15
Interior atmosphere
120

Air quality overview
121

Thermal comfort
121

Humidity
127

Fuel for the mind
128

Air health
129

Specifying products and materials
131

Study highlights of indoor air quality testing outcomes in occupied spaces
133

Chapter 16
Illumination and light design
135

Visual and non-visual impacts on humans
137

Lighting for meaning and emotional expression
138

Working with daylight
139

Strategies to integrate in design
139

Artificial light
142

Light source types
142

Impacts to colour and texture
144

Task and ambient lighting
145

Chapter 17
Space planning
147

Contemplation and communal spaces
150

Furniture
152

Views out and lines of sight
154

Harmonising interior layout with occupier culture or needs
155

Security and interiors
157

Chapter 18
Acoustic design
159

Designing for good acoustics
160

Sound treatment and design thinking
163

Chapter 19
Operational issues
166

Controllability
167

'SoftLandings' process
168

The landlord, facilities manager and tenant opportunities
168

Occupancy surveys
169

Part 5
Value in practice: measuring wellbeing
173

Chapter 20
Identifying and managing value
174

Measuring wealth
176

A better place
177

Defining project KPIs and UPAs
178

Performance of space
184

Strategy, clarity and measurement of value
184

Chapter 21
Measuring value
186

Measuring wellbeing
187

CASE STUDY: Measuring wellbeing in a call centre
187

Measuring productivity and SROI
190

Conclusion
192

Refereneces
196

Index
201

Image credits
206

Preface

> *May all be happy.*
> *May all be without disease*
> *May all creatures have wellbeing*
> *And none be in misery of any sort.*
> VEDIC PRAYER

What is 'good' interior design? How can it enhance wellbeing and user experience? And how can I, as a designer, enable it? These are the questions that have followed me throughout my career.

The seeds were sown from my earliest days. Even though I always had an instinctive insight into why some interior features worked well together (and some did not), I was not able to articulate this to project teams, or demonstrate impacts to support project outcomes. This frustration set me on a path of discovery – a path that, in attempting to answer the above questions, first involved seeking a deeper understanding of my own instinctive creativity, and using that understanding to constantly improve and refine my skill. Gaining this understanding enabled me to then share these insights with my own design team, this in turn enabling clients to understand the reasoning behind my (and other interior designers') choices.

At Grigoriou Interiors – a company I run with my sister and business partner Angeliki – we aim to create good, sustainable spaces that care for the environment and support human flourishing. Every day we champion in our projects the idea that a sustainable result includes human prosperity as well as environmental and economic prosperity. Much of the knowledge in this book derives from our own projects, research and learnings. One of the simplest learnings is about making a choice: a conscious choice to actively support people's wellbeing and create a sustainable interior. It has become more and more evident through our work and that of the wider business and public world, that space is too often seen as just another tool which we use to conduct business with, another tool we use to socialise and live our lives through. Space, of course, is only one of a number of issues that impact and contribute towards supporting occupant wellbeing, and at Grigoriou Interiors we have evolved to seeing space as an active contributor to supporting wellbeing, to supporting a valuable life rather than being of primary value in itself.

Understanding *what* affects us as users of interiors, and *how* it affects us, is the focus of this book's content. Aimed primarily at interior designers and architects, as well as fellow project consultants involved in the design process, the book helps them to explain their approach to clients, and gain respect for their work. For the client, the book enables an understanding of what good design is, and how the client can extract best value from a design and project. For the wider interiors community, the book offers insight into professional skills, and how these overlap in different roles, encouraging a collaborative approach and mindset. Most importantly, I hope this book gives designers the ability to use the tools at their disposal in an informed manner to enable good design for people's wellbeing. As designers, our journey should be towards 'good'; towards making good decisions consciously; towards creating good design and spaces that allow us all to flourish. This, after all, is what this book is about.

I wish you an enjoyable and enlightening read, drawing as it does not just on my experience, but the experience and insights of various experts and practitioners in the field. Most of all, I hope you get many opportunities to put the knowledge and understanding contained in this book into practice. With wellbeing in our hearts, minds and fingers, let's get started!

ELINA

Introduction

You walk into a coffee shop, passing the busy serving counter. You move deeper into the interior looking for a seat, and hopefully a table, too. Your eyes quickly scan the room, taking note of the people already seated, and you clock the vacant seats. You make a decision about which seat you will sit in within seconds. As an experienced interior designer, I'm pretty sure I know which seat you will choose.

You will either feel uncomfortable about this, or happy; and it depends on whether you believe I, as a designer of spaces such as coffee shops, am intending and ensuring you are happy and comfortable in such spaces. That is the power of good design – to knowingly influence a person's experience and quality of life; to influence behaviour and the decisions people make; or to simplify life and introduce harmony. This is not a magical power, but with some experience and the knowledge in this book, a semblance of magic may be achieved.

Good design is not an end result, but a systematic process where thought has been applied to the selection of each action, where problems are designed out and simplicity rules. It is not a luxury but a reasoned approach towards achieving the best outcomes for a space, ensuring it is an active or passive tool for a good life.

General approach of the book

This book supports a design process based upon evidence-based design (EBD). EBD (which started primarily in the healthcare sector) is a way of approaching the design process that allows designers, consultants and clients to understand, and then support, design proposals, based upon data and reason.

'Evidence-based design is a key component in developing better things. It's a philosophy that's critical for ensuring the team have a common objective and rationale for decision making when working in large multidisciplinary teams. Measurement is a critical part of this.'[1] Design Council, 2015

Of course, it is worth noting that metrics and research results will be based on a particular set of conditions that will never be identical in any one project, so it is vital that project teams make decisions on facts that include local and current conditions to create pragmatic expectations. Whatever the situation, the way an issue impacts the ability to support wellbeing depends upon the designer understanding the occupants, and how people are affected by interior design. The actual context a person will be in – at work, in a restaurant, in a shop or at home – may change, but all will be affected by good – or bad – design.

Throughout, the book asserts that the responsibility of driving the wellbeing agenda lies with everyone in the project team. It starts with the client team, runs through the design team members, all the way to the sub-contractors and suppliers of each project. Clients need to understand why wellbeing is important, and how they will be responsible for using the interiors they are responsible for in a responsive way. The design team needs to ensure that decision making at all levels supports occupant wellbeing, acting as gatekeepers on behalf of the client when difficulties arise in implementation. Sub-contractors and suppliers need to not just deliver to specifications, but ensure they are looking after their teams in what can be often a difficult and stressful environment. The wellbeing agenda must literally be on the agenda, at project meetings; it must be an ongoing part of the conversation.

The structure of the book
What is good interior design? How can it enhance wellbeing and user experience? How can I, as a designer, enable it? Providing answers without first understanding the question will have limited value, so the book begins by exploring the nature and philosophy of wellbeing itself. A doctor can treat a patient, but unless the cause of ill health has been understood, the effects will keep on coming. Similarly, a designer can design an interior for wellbeing, but unless the philosophy of wellbeing has been understood, the design will not achieve its objective.

The book then moves on to the theory that links the philosophy to the practice, and then onto the practice – and practical application – itself.

Divided into five parts, the book is split into 21 chapters, each containing the theory and principles behind how wellbeing is put into practice. Where appropriate, each chapter concludes with key activities that can be implemented on projects immediately – putting design for wellbeing into practice.

Some of the design interventions described in this book are large, some small; some come with considerable cost, some with little or none. Of course, it is always worth being mindful of the costs involved in bad design thinking and inadequate design process; these invariably have a compounding effect during the operation of the space, reducing value to the user.

Whatever the cost of the design intervention, however, all look to inform the practical application of the philosophy and theory discussed in the book.

You can read this book from cover to cover, or dip into parts or chapters as issues arise on projects. However, I would recommend starting with Part 1 on the philosophy, as it will provide the context with which to understand how to adapt the data and knowledge applications of Parts 2, 3 and 4 on Design in Practice, and contextualise Part 5, Value in Practice, at the end.

What to expect in each part

Part 1 of this book explores the nature and philosophy of wellbeing, its prerequisites (including beauty) and outputs (including occupant performance). The aim is to understand how and why wellbeing matters to life and people, and why it needs to be provided for in a design approach that is described as 'good'. The philosophy behind the theory and implementation is vital, as without it, design for wellbeing becomes something of a game of risk, especially around cognitive and emotional wellbeing, as decisions are being made blindly.

Part 2 delves into the delivery process itself, and what tools are required as part of the design process, especially the use and creation of User Profiles – which are a core tool in designing for wellbeing, for achieving 'good design'. The part concludes with a list of Design Characteristics all projects need to define as part of the briefing stage to ensure occupant wellbeing can be achieved, and how these characteristics can be applied and enhanced to address the aesthetic and physical issues that form part of the design process itself. Each decision, whether about lighting or acoustic design, about colour, ceiling heights or floor textures, can be kept on track through the work done on defining the Design Characteristics and creating the User Profiles.

Parts 3 and 4 explore these aesthetic and physical issues in more detail, recognising that most issues overlap and influence each other to some extent. These parts can be dipped into during projects, and used as a reference manual. Having understood Part 1, and adopted the tools of Part 2, Parts 3 and 4 should be easy to integrate into a fluid process.

Finally, Part 5 focuses on the need to identify the real value of approaching project targets, one of them being occupant wellbeing. Even if a client and design team are all on board to support occupant wellbeing, how far is it sustainable to do so within the project parameters? If existing features don't support occupant wellbeing, what impact will they have (or have already), and how do you know what investment to make? This part provides insight into how to approach these questions both theoretically and practically, seeking clarity and measurement through a methodology and weighting approach.

Part 5 is also important in relation to contextualising the impact of interiors. They are just one aspect of life that affects how well we live, and how much of our life is spent happily. Many issues will affect us – from nutrition to education – and the built environment we inhabit is just one of the cogs in our system which we can refine to ensure we align with broader life and society objectives for a good life.

We tend to spend a significant part of our time indoors, using external spaces to travel from one building and its interior to another during the course of a day, especially in urban settings. So the effect interiors have on us is intensified as a result of time exposure. If we all wish to live in communities and societies that flourish, the social return on investment (SROI) measurement and integration in projects is of high importance.

Defining wellbeing

The World Health Organization's definition of health is *'a state of complete physical, mental and social well-being and not merely the absence of disease or infirmity.'*[2] This statement outlines the three parts of a person's being that are active in any given moment, and to which we need to respond, to ensure their wellbeing. What is a little vague in this definition is the distinction between 'health' and 'wellbeing' – as it would seem to place them on the same line. As health is taken to be lack of illness, this would assume a neutral state of existence (zero), whereas wellbeing is a quantified state of wellness and happiness, so can't be neutral and thus an improvement on it.

Occupant wellbeing is supported by designs that capture the needs of the physical body, the mind and the emotions of occupants in any given space. There is no single generic interior design solution that will support occupant wellbeing in every space; each design proposal needs to adapt its details to suit individual people and tasks. But ultimately, and this is extremely important to be acknowledged when designing for wellbeing, we cannot *give* wellbeing to anyone else other than ourselves. A person, as a free-willed being, will choose to be well or not. We can design spaces to the nth degree with the latest supportive settings and composition, yet if a person chooses not to be happy on any given day for whatever reason, they will not experience wellbeing.

Wellbeing is a choice, not a given.

But what actually *is* wellbeing? Whether we are discussing it in relation to space, nutrition or poetry, what do we mean? Advaita, a school of Indian philosophy, with its description of the types of energy on which all existence is lawfully acting upon, provides the closest description to wellbeing so far. One of the energies, which balances human behaviour and is called 'Sattwa', is also referred to as 'light'. It can also be considered as the application of reason when blending logic and emotion. Sattwa is described as the predominant acting energy that allows a state where knowledge for what is needed in life is available, and where responses to problems become apparent. The following adapted description, which is based on text provided by the School of Philosophy and Economic Science, articulates a perfectly balanced and flourishing human state as:

Wellbeing is a state where there is a feeling of wellness and happiness in all three parts of the self. Wellbeing is where:

- The body feels light, healthy, refreshed, agile, alert and at ease.

- The mind is clear, bright, perceptive and efficient, information and analysis can happen easily, learning is effortless, we have the ability to use our faculty of reason effectively and our memory is fresh.

- The emotions are clear, we respond to others around us, where generosity, positivity and a sense of unity exists, where love and care occur naturally without expecting a return.[3]

Wellbeing is a human state affected by a wide variety of physical, emotional and transactional issues. It is an experience, and not a design description, so an interior design is able to *support* the wellbeing of occupants but not *provide* it. This being said, designing for wellbeing in interiors – designing 'good' interiors – remains a valuable, and potentially life-changing, endeavour.

PART 1

Philosophy: Prerequisites and Outputs of Wellbeing

Chapter 1: Prerequisites of wellbeing 2 • Chapter 2: Outputs of wellbeing 9

CHAPTER 1
Prerequisites of wellbeing

Beauty 3 • Comfort 7

In this chapter we will consider some prerequisites of design thinking which will support the direction a project will take. We will discuss the need for beauty, the aims to achieve comfort in design, and tackle the issue of performance and productivity links to the design.

We achieve wellbeing through our experience of beauty in the physical, emotional and spiritual realms. We support wellbeing in design by ensuring we are not removing comfort, and we are aiming for beauty. Our experience will be fully enabled only if we are comfortable. We are comfortable if there is harmony between the parts that make up the physical and emotional aspects of the space and ourselves, its occupants.

Once harmony is present then the expected and required results are produced. Whatever is defined as a task output, whether that is to sleep, eat, sell, meet, fix, create or write,

'Human perception works with the aim of making the surrounding world complete, stable and apprehensible. Aesthetic experiences fulfil the same purpose. In aesthetic experience we consciously attend to our spontaneous perceptual process of understanding; attending to aesthetic qualities in art and design – or in the world around – means that we open up for reflection on experiences as such. What we attend to is the perceptual qualities – for example colour and light qualities – not the physical thing.'[1] Ulf Klarén

a harmonious design will ensure a task's output is done to the best of the ability of that individual or group. So productivity and effectiveness will be the logical result.

So let's see how this all makes sense and open up the issues for exploration. What is beauty and what does it have to do with wellbeing?

Beauty

Beauty is an experience, it's not the property of an object. Sit with this one for a while if you're not ready to accept this as true. You don't need to accept or reject it at this stage.

Beauty is not a permanent state but the response a person will have to something, to another person, an action, a feeling, an object, and so on. We can all experience beauty through our eyes, ears, skin, and hands; basically through our senses; but we also experience it through our minds and our feelings. A mathematical equation can be beautiful, as can be a person's behaviour. In our living environment it has become a dominant quality through its visual representation, but this is restricting it to just one of our physical senses. Spaces have been designed with an imbalance of importance on what the eyes see, which has caused other important details and cognition to be forgotten. For example, feature wall colours absorb design time on the selection of the colour or wall finish without considering how thermal comfort may impact a user's experience because of the colour and the other way around. Humans find comfort through all of our senses, not just through the eyes, but also through an experience of being.

Let's delve into this philosophical idea though deeper and build it up from the basics, as it is core to contextualising design approaches on every project. Sir Christopher Wren is quoted as saying in his book *Parentalia*, *'There are two causes of beauty – natural and customary. Natural is from geometry consisting in uniformity, that is equality, and proportion. Customary beauty is begotten by the use, as familiarity breeds a love to things not in themselves lovely. Here lies the great occasion of errors, but always the true test is natural or geometrical beauty. Geometrical figures are naturally more beautiful than irregular ones: the square, the circle are the most beautiful, next the parallelogram and the oval. There are only two beautiful positions of straight lines, perpendicular and horizontal; this is from nature and consequently necessity...'*[2]

FIGURE 1: 01
A beautiful idea in the V&A Museum lobby in London

FIGURE 1: 02
Beauty in the fine craftsmanship and pattern arrangement of a Chinese textile piece

FIGURE 1: 03
Furniture showroom in London; beauty in simplicity and silence

His case is that nature is beautiful and all areas of life where harmony with her systems and proportions exist, such as music, architecture, poetry or design, will be beautiful. Perceptions of beauty linked to habit or social norms will be in absolute terms not true and not lasting. But we can't ignore these perceptions, so the question we need to respond to is: is there a place for both in our approach to design with the aim of wellbeing? Is a client who has been raised with certain social norms to be overruled when they show us their perception of beauty when it does not fall under nature's terms? How does a designer work with a client and their perception of beauty to ensure they have provided knowledgeable advice, understood the client and occupants and driven the project towards their wellbeing as the aim? Do designers' own perceptions of beauty fall under the Natural lawful type or are they following social norms and does it matter? Understanding what beauty is, and why it is important in the conversation of wellbeing, is core.

Further on in this book, within case studies that showcase natural and customary design approaches, such as biophilia, user controllability and contour bias, it is suggested that there is a marriage of natural and customary issues within a design approach that eventually ensures a space is indeed designed for wellbeing and achieves beauty. The link between beauty and wellbeing is found in two main issues; first, along the Platonic and classical philosophy terms, where if something is considered beautiful we instinctively know it is so as it reflects our human self and reminds us of our own existence. It makes us mindful and fully present, and when we are in these states of awareness we are happier than when living in a dream. Secondly, beauty is also a tool to identify if an action, an idea or an object is appropriate to us or to the occupiers of the interior. The existence of beauty represents an ideal we aspire to as individuals to live up to and as societies.

It is a philosophical truth that beauty exists within a person and not the object or idea that is seen. So as beauty exists within the human being and not the object, knowing which object or idea that is able to stimulate beauty in another human or group of humans, is key to offering this experience and getting the design right. Part of the benefits of experiencing beauty is that it allows love, knowledge, measure (balance) and truth to be brought into the mix and this immediately means a conversation that includes emotions and connection between people rather than living in isolation. The second link between beauty and wellbeing is that proportions and performance settings of spaces that are considered over millennia to be attractive and pleasurable, follow certain proportions, certain dimensions and settings that when considered against the health of a human being, can be seen to be the ideal settings and provision to sustain a human. So it would seem that if we consider the settings and provisions from a scientific point and with only health in mind, we will find that these will also be considered as beautiful.

Beauty is explored, and its importance to humans analysed, by the modern-day philosopher Alain de Botton in his book *The Architecture of Happiness*. It is also captured by earlier philosophers such as R.W Emerson in his essay 'The Poet', and artists such as Mark Rothko in his book *The Artist's Reality*. They all approach the issue from different perspectives but their insights are comparable; when something is considered 'beautiful' by any one of us, it is answering our own internal state of existence.

Our attraction to beauty is an internal quest for what is true, what is yearned for by us in our life's journey to achieve what is referred to many times as 'inner peace', also known as 'completeness'. So the experience of completeness, of truth, is known through the experience of beauty. Philosophers would say that we experience beauty when we are partaking of truth – a high project and life objective for sure – and, no less important or 'right' to aim for it. For day-to-day life we could consider the use of beauty as a tool to test whether an experience, an idea, or an object, is created authentically and following a natural and lawful process. As, if it has, it will hold beauty in it for us, and if not, we need to work on it until it does.

Looking back at the description of what wellbeing is we saw that ease, calm and a sense of inner and outer fluidity are very much key aspects. So, if those are the effects of beauty then it makes sense to ensure it forms a part of a design's effect on people.

If an interior has been designed with the aim of finding and expressing what is true at that particular time and that aims to be part of the occupants' search for truth and completeness, then it will be considered to have beauty.

In the case of designing interiors we could seek beauty in two main ways: the way a space will influence behaviour and enable a particular way of life within it (links creating an experience), and the way we create the physical forms themselves (individual stimulus). We must question the presence of beauty in both the experience of life that users will be provided in the space, and the harmony of shapes, patterns, colours, air quality etc on our nature individually that then will form the whole effect.

Through a physical form or action, we see a promise and the answer of what is missing within us, to complete ourselves and our life. Logos, brands and advertising work in exactly the same way: the colours of a logo will promise you either calm or animation if you buy the object advertised or interact with the brand. We react to the ideals and characteristics we see things represent and a way of life they symbolically aspire us to follow. The one we are drawn to is the something missing from us.

We need to develop the conversation and knowledge in our industry and wider society to bring the idea of beauty, and wider meanings, to the fore. Until project teams add such topics to meeting agendas and they are discussed throughout design and delivery, the understanding of beauty and its importance to humankind, will remain incomplete in definition and understanding, and most importantly, designs will fall short of supporting wellbeing.

The art historian Wilhelm Worringer as a student in 1907 wrote his thesis titled 'Abstraction and Empathy: a Contribution to the Psychology of Style', which has become a seminal piece in art history and revolutionised art thinking. In it he proposes that the psychology of societies, based on their circumstances at any given time, affects their preferences on what they find to be aesthetically pleasing, what is considered beautiful. He noted two main artistic preferences society chooses to follow, the 'abstract' and 'realistic'. He observed that the preference of a society for one or the other style was a reflection of their political and societal structure, and in their lack of something. Societies with less autocratic approaches or disharmony preferred artistic expressions with order and clarity (realistic), and societies with organised structure and a certain routine, would seek an experience beyond the ordinary and to be in contact again with strong feelings and for their entire nature to feel alive (abstract). In both cases, people are looking to fill gaps that provide a sense of completeness and to re-balance things. This can also be reflected in family homes and corporations; if large changes and upheavals have either recently occurred or are going to be introduced over the next few years, the design intent can consider this as part of its strategic direction. In this way, the design will be found beautiful by occupants and support their wellbeing.

The description of 'functional' has been unjustly set as an opposite to 'beauty', as functional can be beautiful too. In fact, if the design of an interior does not function beautifully, in the eyes of the users it will lack real beauty as it will not achieve the aspired ideals that are missing. So many images of attractive interiors or eye-catching photos can be found in magazines or design books, only to then realise in real life that the beauty was not in the space itself but in the photo. beauty in the built environment must be found in the way interiors make us feel and the way we interact with them – what inner questions it answers for us and how it supports our life's objectives. The experience of entering, moving through and staying for a length of time in one area to conduct a task, must give us the feeling that we are experiencing something beautiful if we are to support occupant wellbeing.

In the inspirational Living Building Challenge (LBC) sustainability standard[3] there is a point awarded for efforts made towards creating aesthetically beautiful buildings and spaces. As the scheme acknowledges, this will be a hard call to make as it will

FIGURE 1: 04 AND 1: 05
Examples of 'abstract' and 'realistic' approaches with interior finishes

be project specific, but beauty is a key requirement of a sustainable result. This requirement neatly explains LBC's vision to nurture designs that do not just elevate, but celebrate people's spirit and inspire everyone to 'be' and do better. The LBC website contains some informative project case studies that can assist in insights of designing broader wellbeing into spaces.

Our search for wellbeing is given reason through the existence of beauty. We live well to experience beauty, to find the answers we seek. But beauty also works in sustaining life. It's natural.

David Wade, an expert researcher and writer of a number of books on world shapes and geometry, in his online website, under the Philosophical and Scientific section, shares thoughts from historic sources, and includes rather succinctly Plato's thoughts with this quote: 'For Plato, the truly beautiful could not be conveyed by any work of representation or imagination; at best these could only ever be conditionally beautiful. True beauty had to express at least some of the eternal quality of his "Forms", the terms of which he seems only to have found in geometry.' Plato, whose work underpins most of European and Western thinking and culture, delved deeper, analysed and reflected the links between the human 'spirit' and the physical world.

He explored the opportunity of achieving harmony in the symbiosis of the human existence with the physical world we live in, which is the utopia of designing for wellbeing. It is where the body feels light, refreshed and at ease, where the mind is clear, perceptive, agile and reasoned, where our emotions are clearly responsive to others, are open, generous and we feel a sense of unity. This could be in the form of relaxing in a space that is made up of curved shapes, or trying to concentrate on proofreading a report with straight and angular shapes around us.

FIGURE 1: 06
Travelling up the interior spaces of Westminster underground station in central London is an experience of function in motion. Travellers flow through the space and 'up towards the top light'

Comfort

We are able to *choose* to be well, when our emotional state, our mind and our body are all healthy. As proposed in the Introduction, in the outline of what wellbeing is and what it is not, as a minimum we must be healthy and in a state of comfort.

The Cambridge online dictionary defines comfort as 'comfort (NO PAIN): a pleasant feeling of being relaxed and free from pain.' Comfort is a subjective and self-declared state that can only be defined by a person's own reflections. The dictionary description refers to a lack of something, and the result of being relaxed, it does not actually provide information on the presence of whatever is happening that will define comfort. On this basis, designers need to define what actually it is that we need included in an interior design to ensure comfort is achieved.

Based on the earlier definition of what health and wellbeing are, where health is zero and wellbeing is a state of +1, we will place comfort above health and below wellbeing. This is because someone can be in a momentary state of physical pain but still be healthy, think efficiently and feel happy emotions – but because of their discomfort, the other physical and mental states will be relied upon to maintain a temporary balance, so not allowing to move up towards a state of wellbeing, but also not quite back down to going below zero. So continuing our mathematical approach we propose this equation: health is equal or < comfort is equal or < wellbeing.

From prolonged experiences within a state of wellbeing, where a person in thinking clearly, has a physical lightness and feels emotionally open, they will develop a reserve of strength and a coping capacity that is referred to as resilience – resilient to difficulty and discomfort. If a person has low resilience they will not cope easily through difficult times, if they have good or high levels of resilience they will be drawing upon that to see them through times when they find themselves in temporary discomfort or bad health. So resilience is a mechanism that people use to maintain a level of comfort for a period of time, or allows them to regain health faster.

Comfort can come and go in short cycles as we live in a constantly moving world, both physically, mentally and emotionally. Our link with comfort should be seen as an interactive relationship. If a room's temperature is not appropriate for our skin's comfort then we usually ask for the heating or cooling system/windows to be adjusted and everyone else in the same space needs to adjust too. Interactive comfort means that we first remove or add a piece of clothing that starts developing a conversation between the space and its users which can be sustained for longer periods in multi-occupied spaces, and that also considers environmental impacts.

There are many occasions in western style workplace cultures where broadly clothing styles prescribe the interior air temperatures. In the middle of a warm summer, traditional female office or retail workers often wear light summer clothing, and male workers wear shirt and tie – this imbalance in dress approach, let alone the nature of the genders' physique, creates an impossible goal in targeting universal 'comfort'. It typically results in air conditioning temperatures and flows remaining fixed and female workers feeling cold, some of which will start then keeping additional clothing at work to combat the uncomfortable air conditioning settings. However, with recent workplace cultures evolving and a more casual dress code being introduced, it tends to create a narrowing in dress code differences that supports a common ground on heat settings and occupant response.

According to the UK's Health and Safety Executive, 'thermal comfort' is defined in British Standard BS EN ISO 7730 and expanded further as: *'that condition of mind which expresses satisfaction with the thermal environment. ...So the term "thermal comfort" describes a person's psychological state of mind and is usually referred to in terms of whether someone is feeling too hot or too cold.'*

The definition of 'comfort' also needs defining in the context of other human preferences that are affected through an interior's design. For example, introduce benchmarks that describe the way someone is feeling *colour comfort*, *shape comfort*, *spatial volume and material comfort*, *layout comfort*, *visual comfort*, etc.

If for example there is bad lighting design and no glare protection on external windows, occupants' eyes will have mild discomfort or will actually hurt. If acoustics are not considered and sound levels are too high in a school, it will create noise and high reverberation in classrooms, resulting in hard hearing and low learning as well as physical exhaustion in the effort to do so. If colours are too bright, contrasting or stimulating they will exhaust eyes and tire our mental capacity to pay attention. The following chapters in this book tackle the levels or approach required for each design issue to include comfort as the end result.

CHAPTER 2

Outputs of wellbeing

Relationship of comfort and performance 10 • Occupant performance affected by interiors 11 • Wellbeing and productivity link 12 • Harmony 13

Relationship of comfort and performance

The link between Comfort and performance is important and is clear to see in task-based spaces such as workplaces, learning spaces, healthcare and public institutions. The example of how noise will interrupt the concentration of a task and the time it takes someone to re-engage and eventual finish it makes a relatable and strong example of slower productivity and deterioration of work quality. Many organisations and workers themselves are naturally keen to perform to their highest productivity levels. Schools and universities wish students to perform to their highest learning ability – and many students demand this of themselves too.

So designers need to start looking at the points of design which support Comfort but also allow us to perform at the best of our ability the tasks that we are doing. To find a relevant vocabulary and link in the work performance field, I have turned to the work of Alasdair White[4], a management performance consultant. He refers to three states: the comfort zone, the optimal performance zone and the danger zone. The most useful description of the comfort zone which turns into performance, is as follows:

The comfort zone is a behavioural state within which a person operates in an anxiety-neutral condition, using a limited set of behaviours to deliver a steady level of performance, usually without a sense of risk.

And he unpicks the definition further to say:

This implies that, providing there is no change in the 'anxiety' or the skills applied, the level of performance will remain constant. Equally, if there is a change in the 'anxiety' or the skills applied then a change in the level of performance will result – either upwards or downwards.

To offer some definitions which we can refer to in relation to proposed performance levels of interior design features, we adopt White's with a small twist, and refer to a 'comfort zone', a 'high performance zone' and an 'anxiety zone'.

Placing this principle in interior environments, 'anxiety' can be understood as the state a person is taken to, out of their comfort, through high or low temperature, too intense colours, bad air and material toxins, high CO_2 levels, daylight presence or ergonomics and so on. The mind and emotions will also be in a state of anxiety if there is a perception of or lack of security through the interior layout, lack of excitement, or over stimulation of a 'good' emotion. These spatial features, designed incorrectly, will take occupants' state from Comfort to levels below health. And the action of drawing upon resilience to re-balance the mind, emotions and body, to get back into Comfort, will affect each person's performance. This also aligns with the work of Bluyssen[5] where over stimulation was found confusing and developed hectic signals that increase stress whereas too little stimulation was found boring.

White concludes that the level of discomfort at which anxiety kicks in and performance drops is not clear-cut and immediate. He states that a (slight) discomfort can at first have a stimulating result before it veers into significant discomfort and thus reduced performance. This balance between the states of Comfort and anxiety is where we find 'high performance' and is exactly where we are aiming for; to be the best we can in every given moment.

FIGURE 1: 07
Comfort Zone Model

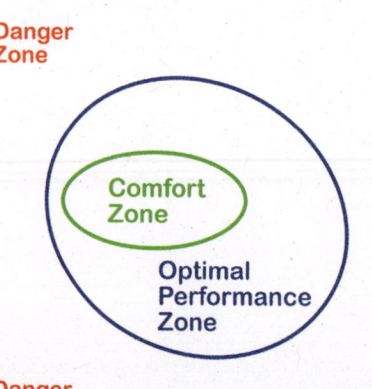

Occupant performance affected by interiors

From all of this it is proposed that:

1 Amongst all interior design features in a space, each will have an initial bandwidth of effect beyond an occupant's Comfort levels that will temporarily support performance.

2 It is expected that there will be a minimum number of design issues (layout, lighting, colour, temperature etc) that when designed outside of the occupant's comfort and performance zone, they will generate excitement initially before they create anxiety. The more issues pushing at an occupant's comfort and performance threshold, the more they will use up resilience. If resilience is not kept up through an overall state of Comfort and wellbeing then an occupant will veer into a state of discomfort. This is where productivity and health is impacted.

3 A design's performance levels, set to generate excitement and high performance for a time, can't do this permanently as it will veer into the occupant's anxiety zone. This does not mean the settings themselves need to change, if the occupant is given the choice to vary the location they are in for the task they are doing. If not, then the controllability and change of the physical features is necessary to support ongoing productivity.

As a sector we are getting close to understanding the design performance of all issues, and starting to define the level each feature needs to be designed at and correlate that with the occupants' anxiety zone. Parts 3 and 4 of this book tackle what the design parameters are for each. There will be changes within each design issue based on tasks undertaken, the nature of

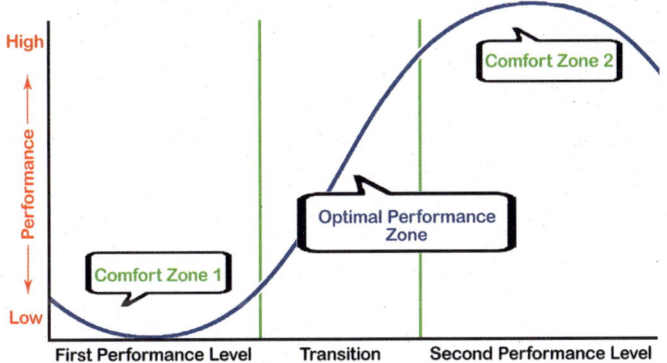

FIGURE 1: 08
Transition between comfort zones showing the expected peformance curve

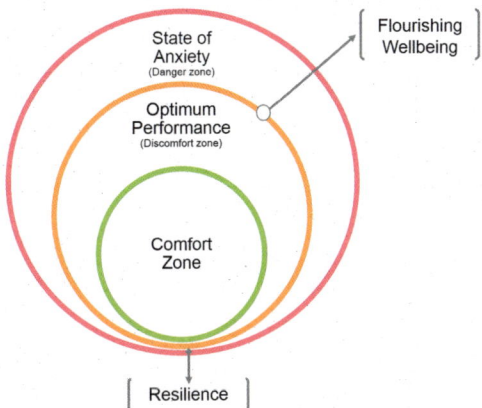

FIGURE 1: 09
Grigoriou Interiors 'Point of Flourishing/ wellbeing' diagram, evolving White's concept

FIGURE 1: 10
In retail environments, changing rooms are often lacking in comfort, impacting user's wellbeing and thus the whole experience in a store and its revenue performance

humans and the evolving awareness of the issues by occupants themselves. The more knowledge we obtain and share within our industry and society, the better users of spaces we will ourselves become. Following Alastair White's diagram (Figure 1: 09) which takes into account the change process reactions of human nature, we can see where methodologies such as BSRIA's Soft Landings[6] framework, which goes through the design process and early occupancy stages, can play a key role in the achievement of user comfort, and user experience, as a whole. Real life scenarios are full of many moments of 'anxiety' so the definition of comfort within each design issue needs to be generous to enable a real and achievable delivery in practice, and especially when we are aiming at satisfying such a high number of occupant profiles in the cases of commercial, education, leisure and the range of public interiors.

Wellbeing and productivity link

When a space can support high performance then occupant productivity will result. Recalling that wellbeing will be achieved only after a user is in comfort and high-performance zones, it is deduced that productivity from a person doing a task will ensue only from them being in a state of wellbeing. It is wise to recall at this point the other issues required in the puzzle of achieving human happiness and that although space is to be recognised as one of the important contributors, it is not the only one. Being in a state of high performance is also a reflection of human development according to Maslow's hierarchy of needs. When we are able to integrate and engage with life and work we are closer to self-actualisation. More on this in Chapter 5 of this book.

Harmony

Individual levels of wellbeing vary and are in many cases defined by harmonising personal preferences (beauty and culture) with a task at hand (sleeping or reading) and the design's performance (from comfort to danger zone).

As most interior spaces are used by more than one person and, in the case of most commercial and public spaces by thousands or millions of people throughout a year, it can seem close to impossible to deliver personal levels of wellbeing. But by generating one or more User Profiles and working to these, the harmonisation will be closer and more effective than if they did not exist. Part 2 details what User Profiles are, but for this instance, they can be understood as a profile detailing the average needs of a specific group of users of a space. Details included will inform the project team of the design issues that will affect these users' wellbeing. (We refer to these documents as

'User Profiles' instead of 'occupant profiles' as we are retaining a common term already existing in user centred/experience design. In the built environment we refer to occupants of spaces when we refer to users.)

By referring to harmony we are avoiding the absolutes of 'good' or 'bad' design, though we have of course defined 'good' interior design for the purposes of this book, i.e. the design of spaces that have the aim of supporting and enabling occupant wellbeing, using User Profiles to achieve this. There are certain features of design that are objectively 'bad' – that cause emotional depression, cause negative long-term effects on a physical level to the extents that can poison occupants. Harmony between a design feature and user requirements, is actually what makes a design effective and successful. One interior's design could be deemed successful but placed in another building with different User Profile requirements and it can introduce both functional and emotional problems; driving individuals into the 'anxiety zone'.

Examples of harmony between occupant and design features can be found in practice between the following examples:
- the colour palettes of a scheme with the psychological profile of the User Profile;
- between activities that require privacy that are not supported by the layout of the space; and
- between fresh air supply levels that are not adequate and in line with cognitive brain requirements for the number of occupants in the space.

These separate examples would need to all be considered as part of a full design scheme and be harmonised to project specific requirements.

Within the design's aesthetic 'look and feel' approach, feelings aroused by the concept design must reflect those important to occupants it is looking to support. This brings the issue of realistic and abstract into focus. Is the space looking to excite or reassure; to generate a feeling of domesticity or industry; to represent values of modernity or futuristic technology? How will the approach and focus of the design be decided to support beauty and wellbeing?

As Alain de Botton states on Le Corbusier's design aim with his central staircase in Villa Savoye '… [he] was trying to do something other than simply carry people to an upper floor. He was trying to prompt a state of the soul.' And he elaborates further… 'Spaces talk to occupants about the type of behaviour that is seen as acceptable or desirable; about the type of values held important, the age it celebrates and general ideas that are held true about the lifestyle that is to unfold within its walls. Spaces don't deliver a monologue though, as it's a dialogue between the spaces and user that enables the most harmonious life to unfold.'[7]

It is important to understand what drives and is of value to a user group, and include it in a User Profile) so we can understand which design style will reflect and harmonise with the journey they are on. Interior Designers and all the design team members must question what it is about the life of the users they are serving, that they are aspiring to, to acknowledge that there is a constant dialogue between the interior space and the people interacting with it.

Defining the values that occupants wish to live by, is fundamental to the design's success as it provides a constant daily reminder to all within, and allows the occupants to feel in harmony with the space. Defining these values is what brings an organisation's brand and culture to life. The culture and values contribute directly to the 'stickability' of an organisation's employees, the attraction of partners, clients and customers, and allows everyone to speak the same language. It is important what you – whatever organisation – hold as your core values and to know that the space advertises them to the world, whether visitor, client or friend. It allows them to be known but also empathise and support a more fluid and harmonious communication. How much faster will trust be introduced and a deal sealed when people on all sides are understood?

We achieve wellbeing through our experience of beauty in the physical, emotional and spiritual realms. Our experience will be fully enabled only if we are comfortable. We are comfortable if there is harmony between

FIGURE 1: 11
Derwent London's workplace on Savile Row, London

FIGURE 1: 12 AND 1: 13 Communicating clearly the aspirations of a space to its users, in this case by a shared workspace, Huckletree, to its members

the parts that make up the physical and emotional aspects of the space and ourselves. So the design, and all the decisions taken to define it, need to be in harmony with the User Profiles which contain occupant needs.

Once harmony is present, then the expected and required results are enabled. Whatever is defined as a space's output, whether that is to sleep, eat, sell, meet, fix, create or write, a harmonious design will ensure the output is supported in such a way so it is done to the best of the ability of that individual or group. Productivity will be enabled.

FIGURE 1: 14 Derwent London's workplace on Savile Row, London

CHAPTER 2 • OUTPUTS OF WELLBEING

15

PART 2

Design in Practice: Delivering a Design for Wellbeing

Chapter 3: Knowing the users 18 • Chapter 4: Existing buildings and priorities 39 • Chapter 5: Designing user experience 43 • Chapter 6: Design characteristics and issues affecting wellbeing 50

CHAPTER 3
Knowing the users

The User Profile 19 • Empathy 28 • Environmental psychologists 30
A specialist explaining things in their own words... 32
CASE STUDY: Huckletree co-working workplace 36

The User Profile

Developing an understanding of *who* the design is catering for is half of the equation towards achieving a design that supports wellbeing. To ensure harmony exists between the space and the occupants, all project members need to know in detail the measurements and preferences of the occupants, so that they will knowingly deliver all the features that will meet comfort and then allow them to flourish. As mentioned in a previous chapter, there are no good or bad design features, but there is a good or bad *design fit*. One space's good interior design approach is another one's problem.

In theory, one design could be delivered throughout all the interiors of buildings around each country, but for the users. The human element of the equation means that we require the number and variety of interior design proposals, as many as the personalities of the people living in spaces around the world. Of course, such an à la carte' design approach would not be effective or manageable currently – there is potential for the future due to technology-based tools and further knowledge depth from ongoing research – so all interiors must reflect the *majority preferences and needs* of *each project's* occupant *average* user. Project teams must define the details of one or more User Profiles, wherever distinctly different; such as staff and customers, customer service and marketing department or sales staff and warehouse staff; teachers and students, front of house manager and kitchen manager, and so on. In each case there will be different stresses,

FIGURE 2: 01 AND 2: 02
Retail or residential spaces need to reflect the users they serve

19

motivations and solutions and it is important to harmonise all with their space to deliver a smooth system.

Through occupant interviews and the main client briefing stages, designers and other team members need to create User Profiles that reflect the typical needs, preferences and overall use of interior spaces. Sometimes there may be more than one profile for more than one area of the project. The principle is the same as developed successfully in the web based and other service facilities where user experience consultants are employed. Ideally, but depending on the size of project, the same role and sequence of questions, investigations and understandings must be adopted for the built environment. Designers have over the years adopted various briefing methods but User Profiles need to become an industry standard and expand to include more aspects of occupants, and understand the cognitive and emotional needs to ensure wellbeing is supported. The profiles can also be defined or informed to a deeper level, by appointing environmental psychologists as part of the project team. For more on the occupancy interviews, approaches and suggestions of questions, refer to chapters 4 and 5 and further on in this part on environmental psychologists.

FIGURE 2: 03
Wall messaging by Elliott Quince at Quinky Art

Example from user-centred design personas

Understanding the impacts on occupants' wellbeing is important and part of the clarity sought on what works and what does not in an existing or proposed space. The weight attribution that impacts users' experience is important, but it also needs to be corrected in some cases following informed one-to-one interviews and conflicting insights derived from these.

There are more and more tools and survey methodologies available, in order to obtain user feedback and insights which can then inform User Profiles and occupant surveys following completion. The ones that work most effectively are:
- Observing users within spaces
- One-to-one interviews
- Group workshops
- Questionnaires – paper or digital
- Wearable technology
- Mobile phones and tailored software applications
- Seating and room sensors
- Purchasing pattern analysis
- Social media sound-bites

One-to-one interviews are the most impactful for nuanced insights on issues arising for key individuals, within relationships of individuals or team/user dynamics. Selecting the right individuals is key for this. Depending upon users, time and budget available, the interviews should accommodate those known to be the most vocal and sensitive to the space's performance, as they will give you exactly that: an extreme insight on what does not work in the space. Then, the users who think the space has least effect on them, as they tend to realise through the meeting how much effect the space actually does have on their performance of whatever task it is they are trying to do. Lastly, a proportion of the user group itself, to ensure there are enough views to clarify individual preferences and enable an average but relevant insight to be established.

There are some really good general questions to use, such as:

Q1 'Can you walk us through a typical day, from the moment you leave your home / wake up / leave work / etc?'

FIGURE 2:04 AND 2:05
Wall messaging reflecting key behaviours for an organisation, clarified following user interviews

Q2 'Are there any events that happen just once a year and that may need special preparations or space requirements?'

Q3 'What one room from the current spaces you use / work in / come to / etc. would you take to a desert island and why?'

Q4 'What one room would you put in a box and never want to see again, and why?'

For question 1 there will very likely be such a dialogue in response, between the user and interviewee:

User: 'Well, I walked out and it was raining, so took the tube. When I got to work I just switched on my machine and got working.'

Interviewee: 'Okay, that's good. Now, could we go back when you left home/work/etc., where you said you took the tube as it was raining; do you not always take the tube?'

User: 'No. Sometimes I cycle or run in. It's great to run along the river, especially in the summer.'

Interviewee: 'Great, it must be beautiful! So, when you get to work do you usually shower on these occasions, or is it pretty relaxed at the office?'

User: 'Yeah. I shower at the gym as there are none in the office/Sometimes, but usually I pat dry in the toilets/I try to but there are long queues for the showers in the morning so I go a bit later on in the morning.'

User: 'So, you have showered and what do you do with your cycling/running clothes?'

Interviewee: 'I just hang them at the back of my chair or hang them in the shower room, and then they are a bit better to wear on my way home.'

Interviewee: 'Is there space to hang things in the shower room?/Do others use their chairs to hang their wet towels?'

User: 'Managers keep telling us to keep the space tidy, but my run is important to me starting the day well and there is nowhere else to put my towel. I don't want to stay in my running kit all day but it's too important for me. My manager keeps hinting at it but I just ignore it for now.'

Interviewee: 'So, once you shower what happens then?'

User: 'Well, I make a coffee and then have a chat with Jenny from accounts, as we are

FIGURE 2: 06
Meeting room glazed partition graphics, reflecting the values of a company

trying to get a sports day organised for all the departments.'

Interviewee: 'So, where do you make the coffee?'

User: 'In the tea making area, on the side. There's usually a bunch of us in the morning, which is good, but we have to break it up when the others get working.'

Interviewee: 'What do you chat about?'

User: 'General stuff. You know, kids, holidays and stuff. We chat about problems with clients sometimes, problems with new products we've just developed, as things can get pretty heated at times.'

Listening with a set of 'designer's ears', what we can extract from this dialogue are the needs and issues that would support an individual's comfort and wellbeing within the workspace:

- Is there an umbrella stand and a coat rack for rainy days? Somewhere in addition to chairbacks, where wet things can be hung and stored? In fact, is there any space at all for larger baggage? An appropriate space to avoid cases being stacked in open areas.

- Is there space to add a drying room, or a well ventilated space for cycling and outdoor clothing? Can we design this in? If so, how many people would benefit and how does it add to one's emotional wellbeing, as much as their physical health?

- Are showers provided? If so, how many and what can be improved?

- Morning coffee forms part of their routine and the tea area provides a shared space for engagement between staff; somewhere to build relationships and share knowledge while discussing work issues, too.

- If there is no communal area, would staff benefit from one? Or would it keep them away from their desks, or affect productivity? Is the ability to take a step out and talk more valuable from a problem solving perspective, than them doing a sales call, perhaps?

- The tea point where it is at present seems to cause noise and distraction to other members of staff.

- There is also tension between staff and their management over spatial behaviour, which is likely an undercurrent to the use of social space. Is this something that is being dealt with through a change in management style or / and will the removal of the problem support their relationship, to enable them to focus on other, more productive, issues?

- Are they engaged within the company and do they feel a part of the team.

- Relationships are a big part of working life, both for direct personal engagement and to feel part of the team; also to support direct productivity in the job role.

- Situations get tense within the workspace. Management should consider how frequently this occurs, and if the design features, textures and patterns need to include features to calm the stimulation, assist in rational thinking, and clear emotional states.

- Introduce art that reflects common values. Add art reflecting personal situations of similar emotions in the common areas for staff to reflect on what may be going on internally within themselves, assisting them to recognise and deal with it, either through time in reflection in a quiet room or through conversation.

- Space or quiet rooms for reflection will be needed.

- Space for private or semi-private conversations will be needed.

The question to keep asking is 'why'. *Why* did you place the box on the floor? (Maybe not enough storage). *Why* did you get upset with the administrator? (They were not at their desk). And so on. Really understanding the pain and pleasure points and the personas of users can inform designers on what exactly is needed and how design can be approached to support a very positive user experience.

There are some good sources of advice, these days more widely available in the UX

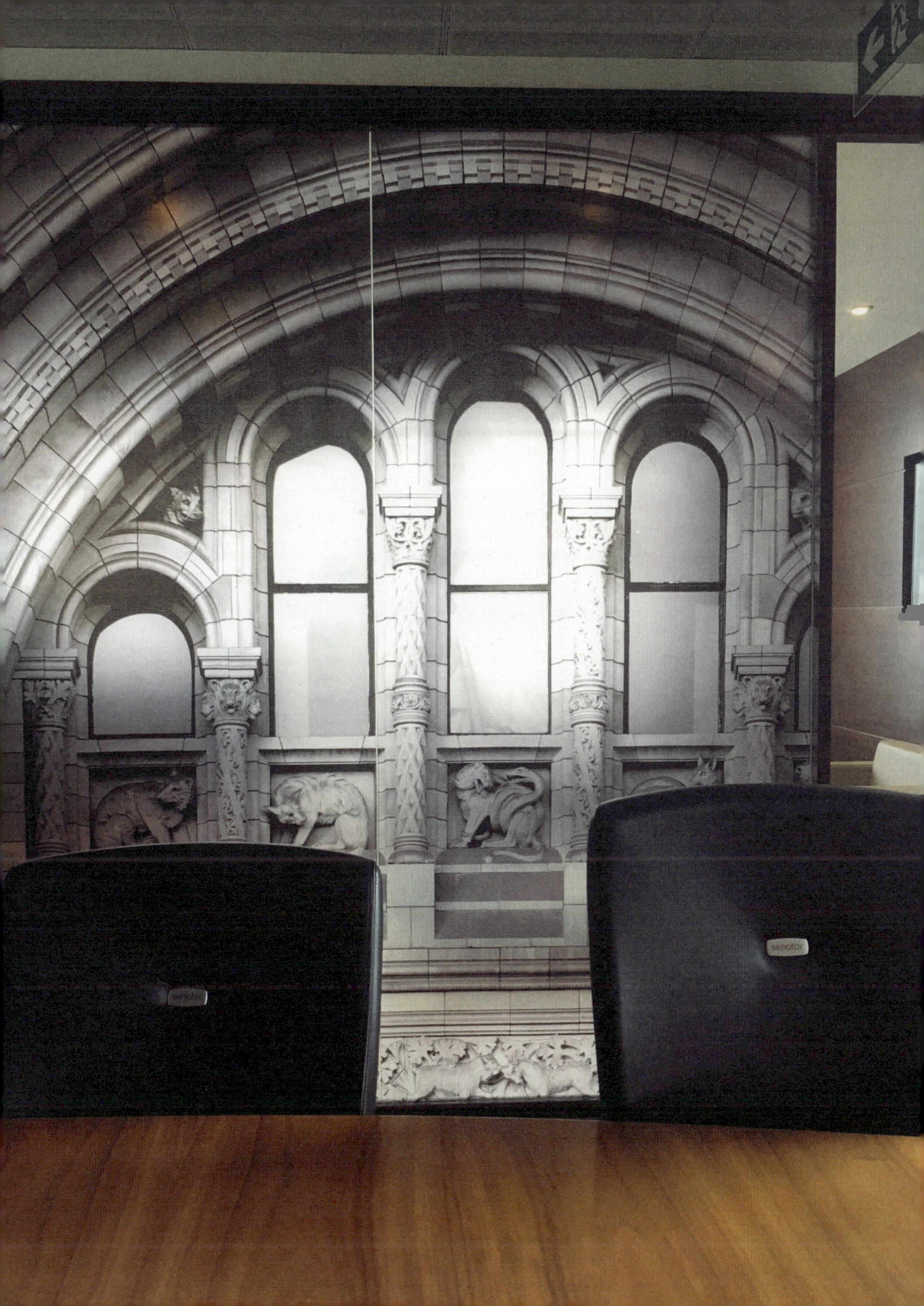
senator
senator

(user experience) arena and around good design companies. Drawing together from project experience and the advice of two highly experienced and informed sources,[1] the following guidance is provided for undertaking good and effective user interviews:

• Make sure you and the team are clear on your goal for the user interview.

• Meet them in, or close to, their own setting or that which you are working on.

• Ideally, there are two of you so one person can take notes in turn as the other asks another question or continues a natural conversation.

Make sure it is more a conversation and less an interview. Add some of your own experiences, as these will help them understand how best to respond, and also trust that you are being open with them.

• Give them an idea of the time this will take and why. Allow them to understand how they are contributing to the project and your brief is to support them and their colleagues/family/customers' wellbeing and happiness. Ask them to help you find out as part of this conversation.

• Allow the conversation to drift at times to issues beyond space, as this can give you more psychological and personality insights, but be aware you don't waste too much time. Judge in the moment and be tactful on how you bring back the conversation to the space.

• Keep asking why?

• Seek to understand drivers through the emotions they feel and use words that will draw these out in your own questions and phrasing.

• Use the same set of questions for all interviews, but allow additional ones as required and presented to you, based on the insights you are provided with. If you knew the answers already you would not be talking to them!

• Thank them for their time and the insights they have provided you with!

FIGURE 2: 07
Body language and seating positions are very important in allowing people to feel more relaxed and understand the honest and positive objective of the interview sessions

Also, be aware that:

- Users will tell you only what they remember, and not the complete story. Identifying opposing viewpoints is important, as is observing in the space during use.

- They may have an idea of what they should say or what they think you want to hear. Their tone and mannerism can give this away and it does need you to be in tune with them as a person. Active listening and listening with the eyes are two strong tools to use during the interviews.

- Users are not the designers. This does not mean 'designer knows best'. Although there is a tendency to ask users what they want or need, this is not ideal asked so directly. They are not designers (usually) so can't understand the limitations or opportunities you can from design knowledge. It may be useful to know some of the historical iterations, though, from this space or from your own previous projects around such issues. These can give you insight into what may have worked or not, as well as some preferences or dislikes.

How do we as designers align ourselves with the users and occupants who we are designing for? Empathy helps us understand their feelings and alignment starts it all off by making us stand where they do to enable us to empathise and see what they see. Can we see how and what supports their comfort and will allow them to achieve wellbeing?

Observing how people use a space is extremely insightful, as experts can observe behaviours that most users are not conscious of. Starting by putting them at ease and explaining why you are there is very important to allow them to behave as normally as possible. Additionally, they may have not created the links between an action they comment about and another specific behaviour they have, which is the reason behind their observation. For example, retail staff that have very little exposure to natural daylight in an enclosed shopping centre may not be aware that sleeping patterns and other health issues they may be experiencing are related to their circadian rhythms. Parents of an asthmatic child having repeated attacks may not be aware that the new carpet fitted is the link to the increase. Two people trying to negotiate across a table may not be aware how the conversation may be improved by sitting at a round table, and so on. Activities observed in their totality can highlight areas and become the really valuable insights, which explain cause and effect links.

A thorough overview of wearable technology for the commercial sector has been undertaken for the BCO by Lockhart, Clements-Croome and Taub.[2] It also outlines the physical aspects of the human body they can monitor to observe response to stimuli, current approaches to monitor relationship connections, etc.

The most important element of User Profiles is that they recognise the triple aspect of human beings and reference the physical, emotional and cognitive needs. What method is chosen to understand and elaborate within each is very much down to the team's ability and specialist approach for the time being. As a minimum, the contents of a User Profile should cover and designers need to:

- Define what tasks users are undertaking in the interiors and what high performance for each looks like. Define the behaviours or skills they need to be able to do.
- Define the gender they relate to, average age, cultural influences.
- What is their ability in language and reading skills, technology and any other behavioural issues relevant to the use of the space?
- Define which colour psychology group they mostly reflect.
- Define their need for biophilia, as a high or low need.
- Define their perception of beauty as Realistic or Abstract.
- Define their need for stimulation or calm
- Define their need for balance, symmetry or asymmetry.
- Define level of needs, which are mostly currently met through using Maslow's hierarchy, both through space and in engagement.
- Define the spaces most impacting them and specific features.
- Any other details core to the type of space being designed.

ANDREA IONESCU

"Be the reason someone smiles today"

Gender: Female
Age: 32
Ethnicity: Romanian
Job Role: Cleaner (UP3)

Profile summary:

I am a friendly and energetic person with a 'can do' attitude. I work effectively both within a team and individually using my own initiative. I pay great attention to detail, can follow instructions well and work flexibly. I believe in helping other people and creating a nice and clean environment for customers. The most important thing for me is my family.

ACTIVITIES

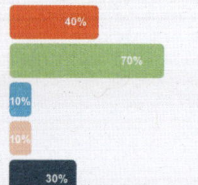

- Communication — 40%
- Collaboration — 70%
- Concentration — 10%
- Creativity — 10%
- Relaxation — 30%

HIGH JOB PERFORMANCE

UPA 3 Alertness, clarity and attention to detail
UPA 6 Emotionally supported (high and supported resilience)
UPA 9 Listening and execution of all tasks
UPA 10 Physically relaxed/well, energetic, looking smart

*UPA - User Profile Activity

PRIMARY SPACES

- Breakout space
- Kitchen
- Locker room

COLOUR

Personality type 1: Morninglight/Spring mixed with type 3: Firelight///Autumn
- Light on their feet, youthful
- Don't like to get involved in heavy subjects and too much paperwork
- Very sensitive, emotional
- Can have a hard time focusing on one specific task, known for attending to many things simultaneously
- Glass is always half full, optimistic

BEAUTY

Realistic
To allow for clear thoughts (thinking process), to relax, less busy, no confusion, support collaboration
- close to nature

RELATIONSHIPS / ATTITUDES & DRIVERS

- Maslow: 4. Not engaged / Security
- Emotional needs supported by relationship with colleagues
- "If managers take care of you then you know you can trust them"
- Show care and support, like helping people, being happy

DESIGN

Elegance 1 — 4 — 10
Not high-end, but to feel comfortable, open & trusting, home-like feel.

Balance 1 — 6 — 10
To allow for organising & following specific tasks, to also make them feel safer.

Symmetry 1 — 5 — 10

Biophilia

Harmony 1 — 6 — 10
To offer security, to feel safe.

Stimulation 1 — 7 — 10
To keep them buzzing, to reflect personality type, but not in breakout space as need to relax.

IMPORTANT SPATIAL FEATURES AND TOOLS

- Seating & ergonomics (long hours on their feet so need to relax as much as possible during breaks)
- Adequate lighting – to perform job better (e.g. restrooms looking dirty due to poor lighting)
- Dedicated changing rooms for males and females
- More kitchen utensils -- kettle, microwave
- Views out, access to green space, artwork

grigoriou interiors
design wellbeing sustainability

PAUL, RECORD HUNTER

"I'm researching about WW1 and I want to check some Civil Defence papers. I use ERO services every month and pre-order docs from home"

MY GOAL

Finding interesting information from the archives that contributes to my research goal, building a story around my research topic.

BARRIERS

- records not digitised yet
- not being able to pre-order docs I might need
- inaccuracy of records online

TECH SAVVY — **TECH RESISTANT**

ONLY ERO — **ERO AND BEYOND**

PROFESSIONAL — **PERSONAL**

KEY SERVICES FOR ME

A. PAID SEARCHES
B. SEAX SUBSCRIPTION
C. CAMERA LICENCE
D. REPROGRAPHY
E. HIGH QUALITY IMAGES
F. COPY OF CERTIFICATES

GOOD SERVICE FOR ME IS

- efficient
- good online system
- able to pre-order online
- accuracy
- check docs if needed
- access online of docs

ERO FOR ME IS ABOUT:

EFFICIENCY / PHYSICAL SPACE / ONLINE EXPERIENCE / 1:1 INTERACTION

FUTUREGOV

FIGURE 2: 08
User Profile example from a Grigoriou Interiors project for a member of staff

FIGURE 2: 09
Persona example by FutureGov for a member of staff

PART 2 • DESIGN IN PRACTICE: DELIVERING A DESIGN FOR WELLBEING

26

FIGURE 2: 10
Persona example by FutureGov for a member of staff

DEMENTIA CARE SERVICE STAFF

Dementia
Memory Clinic, NHS

William | Admiral Nurse

William is an Admiral Nurse within memory clinics service. His involvement starts from the point a patient gets diagnosed with dementia. William usually works in a 1-2-1 basis, with a primary focus on supporting carers to get practical and emotional support to cope with dementia as well as the change of lifestyle. (e.g. health advise, emotional and behaviour management, information sign-posting on supports available locally, run Tom's club to give carer the network opportunities)

He works closely with social worker sometimes to make sure the patient get the most appropriate social support they need.

"People simply want to find out how could they cope with the situation after their loved one diagnosed with dementia. Sometime contacting the social workers could be painful."

FUTUREGOV

FIGURE 2: 11
Persona example by FutureGov for a service user

DEMENTIA CARE SERVICE USER

Dementia
Memory & cognition

Existing Day Service User

Mary | 96 | The Grange

Mary is loved by her daughter and all the staff members from the day centre. She is witty and sociable. She spends her Monday and Thursday at the Grange. The rest of the days, Betty is looked after by her daughter Kate.

Mary broke her arms 3 years ago and since then she has 2 regular carers who would come for an hour every morning to help Mary to bath and get ready for the day. Occasionally, there is a sitter around if Kate can't be home. Mary always wants to go somewhere she used to grow up

Carer | Daughter

Kate | 56 | West Green

"I am just coping. A lot of things is not worth for me to worry about."

Kate is the only child of Mary's. Since her Mum has been diagnosed with dementia, she has been adapting and trying her best to look after Mary. Kate goes to Tom's club once a month and finds it very useful to speak to other carers sharing the same experience. Most importantly, she could take mum with her and not worry about leaving her alone or with temporary sitter.

Kate is not a great fan of internet. She has an old laptop. If she needs to get things done online, she does it in the library. Kate hopes getting support from the council could be simpler so that she doesn't get the extra stress of finding out what's going on.

Good service for us is ...
- Accessible (transport & parking)
- Know me as a person
- Knowledgable in dementia care
- Safe and reliable
- Come to me
- Continuity and consistence
- Something worth looking forward to

Betty needs ...
- Get out of the house
- Personal care (in the morning)
- Being looked after when Diane is busy
- Transport to the service (essential)
- Mentally stimulated
- Assisted walking (minor)
- Support to being independent

FUTUREGOV

27

Empathy

Humans can practise empathy **as a tool** to understand one another. Empathy is an ability we have to adopt – for just a few moments – the situation of another human being, bringing us closer to understanding their full experience.. It involves us taking onboard what their thinking, feeling and physical state is. Empathy needs to be applied as a design tool by all involved in a project, including all project consultants and client team staff.

Dr Brené Brown is a research professor at the University of Houston, and has spent the past decade studying themes on vulnerability, courage, worthiness, and shame. Within her insightful work, she emphasises the differences between empathy and sympathy, and the link that applying empathy has in unlocking creativity and innovation for companies and organisations, as much as for individuals and within families.

Ideas that support problem solving, that inform new product or service design, knowledge that supports good customer service and so on, are all based on the use of the cognitive and emotional capacity of a human being. Allowing a supportive and safe environment for these to be used is the way to personal, family, commercial, operational and cultural growth.

Empathy needs to be practised by a designer or client when in the briefing stages of a project, where discussions are taking place between staff or space users. For example, in a hospital when a nurse is describing the lack of storage to allow for a safe working environment, empathy will help the designer to understand exactly where in the nurse's daily life this issue impacts and what the core problem is, as opposed to looking at the plan and trying to find where there is an empty corner that can work as a store room, even if it is the opposite direction of where the nurses' station is based. Once the core problem and 'hardship' is identified, the solution will be the best possible for the users. It may not be about just adding another storage cupboard; it may be a logistics issue or about providing the storage ability in more than one location throughout the interior that will then also deliver the best operational results. Without 'getting into the nurses shoes' and mentally walking through the tasks, management expectations of them, and challenges the nurses experience, we can't provide the best design solution.

FIGURE 2: 12
Knowing who uses what can ensure we understand and meet their needs

FIGURE 2: 13
Hotel rooms are great examples of User Profiles being successfully understood or not by the level of comfort and details 'pre-thought'

'The term 'einfuhlung', which literally means 'in feeling', was coined in 1873 by the German aesthetician Robert Vischer. The English translation of the term, empathy, generally refers to the attribution of one's own feelings towards an object. However, in German the term denotes a more complex transference of one's ego into the object, whereby the object and the observer become united. The ego is believed to actually penetrate the object so that its form is filled out by the observer's emotions. Whereas sympathy recognises a parallel is between subject and object and acknowledges a distinction between them, empathy is a fusion of subject and object. And unlike sympathy, where one's own identity is still maintained whilst feeling for the other, in empathy one tends to lose oneself in the other. Empathy, therefore, presupposes an initial emptiness of the object in order that the observer can invest it with his own vitality. Accordingly, the effect of an object, such as a work of art or architecture, is felt differently by different individuals, depending upon the extent to which their ego penetrates the work.'
Fiona Gray, Deakin University, Geelong, Australia 2008 'The Synthesis of Empathy, Abstraction and Nature in the Work of Kandinsky, Steiner and Mendelsohn'.

Empathy will be able to be applied by strong designers and professionals. The bravest are those that try to apply it first and foremost. It requires an awareness of who they are themselvesan ability to set aside their own likes, dislikes, and opinions of what the users 'should do' or is 'right' and to temporarily adopt another's life scenes and open their minds.

FIGURE 2: 14
The pull detail on the chair's back indicates that the designers have understood how a user will interact with a heavy lounge chair and seeks to make a comfortable experience

Environmental psychologists

The artist Vasily Kandinsky said *'This eternally exquisite matter, or as it is more commonly called, spirituality, does not give itself up to firm expression and cannot be expressed by overtly material forms. The need for new forms has arisen.'* He focused heavily on the relationship between beauty and humans and his ideas are summarised by Fiona Gray of Deakin University as *'Kandinsky propounded the Goethean (and Platonic) notion of inner necessity, whereby form is driven from within. He saw true art as a manifestation of natural internal laws and his concept of beauty was founded on this premise. Kandinsky rejected the conventional materialistic concept of beauty, defining it instead as a spiritual quality that shone through the physical. By acknowledging the reality of an objective spirituality, the subjective reactions of like and dislike became redundant.'*[3]

FIGURE 2:15 'Free Curve to the Point – Accompanying Sound of Geometric Curves' by Vasily Kandinsky

As mentioned in earlier chapters, if we are to achieve spaces that support wellbeing, we need to be talking in project meetings about the workings of people's mental and emotional needs as much as those of the return air system and fire alarm testing which are supporting physical wellbeing. The profession of Environmental Psychologist (EP) is fast becoming known, but their integration into design teams is still to be fully adopted. They can either be appointed by the client as all other consultants on the project or integrated into the interior designer's team. If we are to harmonise the quantities with the qualities of life, we need to understand both values to ensure we are making informed decisions in the design of interiors – people and space. EPs allow clients and designers to better meet the needs of occupants on a cognitive, emotional and spiritual level and not just on the physical. We consider fire and slip safety the important issues that they are, and we ensure these issues are discussed, but no meeting agenda has so far included sections on emotional and cognitive safety and this needs to start happening.

There are, of course, various ways EPs work and interact with the design team, but inviting them to review proposed plans and contribute to the interior layout, sign and graphic language and style, or feature details that meet certain psychological needs are just a few ways.

Other professionals that can also be integrated with, or instead of an EP if appropriate, are user experience consultants; it will depend on the professional and the project as to which speciality and fit will best support the project's needs.

Putting design for wellbeing into practice

User Profiles will direct the way a project is briefed and how a design is informed, placing the users and the operation at the centre. Putting this information into our day-to-day practice can improve the way occupiers are understood, how the design team obtains the information they need, and the design details will all support user wellbeing. Below are some thoughts, actions and applications for clients, designers and wider project teams to consider:

1. Meet one or two EPs and find out more about how they can support the work you are doing and the style of the project or business. They can complement your team, so it makes sense you have great synergy.

2. Start creating templates, or first drafts of UPs on current projects. Make a start and refine as you test things out on different projects to find a content that works for your team, their creative approach and type of projects you work on.

3. Practise empathy with your colleagues or family and friends. (Also view the RSA digital animation that is based on Brene Brown's talk and titled Sympathy v Empathy.)

4. Add the use of UPs on project meeting agendas. Observe the wider team's response and build on the first steps. Help other design consultants on the project to use them within their own remit of the design and delivery.

5. Appoint an EP on a project to support you creating UPs for all the space occupants. Present your insights to the client and agree how your design will support occupant needs.

FIGURE 2: 16 Informal and varied settings can support more open conversations and participants, increased contribution. Interiors like that found at London's Museum of Happiness' open green area are a great example and can be adapted to required settings

A specialist explaining things in their own words...

The team from Space Works Consulting, Environmental Psychologists, were invited to expand what their service entailed, delve into some design principles and share an example of how their role plays out in a live project.

A user-centred guide to workspace wellbeing by Sarah Hewitt and Lily Bernheimer, of Space Works Consulting

An understanding of the interaction between our environments and our psychology and behaviour is key to designing workplaces that will support job satisfaction, high performance and productivity, and wellbeing. This chapter offers a way of doing just this through an introduction to the discipline of environmental psychology and its application to workplace design. We will first analyse contemporary workplace trends and challenges through three different fields of environmental psychology research: refuge and prospect, territory and personalisation, and sociopetal space. Secondly, we will discuss how these factors play out in real workplace design through a case study of a co-working space called Huckletree.

What is environmental psychology?

Environmental psychology is a branch of psychology that explores the relationship between people and space. Drawing from urban design, architecture, sociology and psychology, this interdisciplinary field looks at interactions between a space and its users.

Our work is usually directed by three main questions: *What*, *When* and *How*. Starting with the *what*, we look at a range of spaces in terms of scale, from an individual workstation or home-office to a whole city. Each space has its own related type of social use, from individual to population-wide use. There is also an associated level of control in any space, ranging from private to public.

So, once we've determined *what* we're looking at, we can then turn our attention to *when*. Environmental psychology can be understood as 'evidence-based design' – essentially basing a design on a solid research base. This evidence can be gathered at various different stages of a project, from pre-build or retrofit, to post-build or post-occupancy stages, or even as part of a longer-term strategy.

Finally, the *how* part of the process. As with many disciplines, there are a variety of theoretical approaches within the field. As a consultancy, we take an interactionist approach, believing that behaviour is not simply determined by architecture and design but by an interaction between a space and its occupants. Our approach underpins how we understand what's going on in the space, as well as how we collect our data. We use research methods from the wider social sciences as well as more design-specific methods to build up a rich picture of what is happening in a space. While it is important to ask people what they think and feel about a space with questionnaires and interviews, we know that sometimes people's perceptions of their own behaviour are often different from the reality. That's why we often use additional methods such as behaviour mapping, in order to provide a more reliable picture of a situation.

And crucially, as you will see through the following examples, we consider not just how well a space meets our physical needs, but how it meets our functional and psychological needs as well.[4]

Refuge and prospect: why you want your back to the wall

Imagine two scenarios of walking into a new workspace for the first time:

Worker No. 1 – *you've just joined a new firm and are shown your desk on your first day. It is in the middle of a row of seven desks, with similar rows in front of you and behind you, stretching all the way to the kitchen at the end of the office. Your heart sinks.*

Worker No. 2 – *you walk into a co-working space and find your perfect table – the one in the corner. You are now sitting with your back* *to the wall in a cosy corner looking out over the office. You get to work.*

Environmental psychologists believe that our modern-day preferences for different environments reflect inherent biological end evolutionary needs. The geographer Jay Appleton[5] argues that our ancestors favoured environments that offered a good balance of both **prospect** (hills, mountains, open settings) and **refuge** (caves, dense vegetation, climbable trees) as these elements enhanced their chances of survival.

But what does this mean for our office workers? Translating Appleton's hypothesis into a modern-day office environment is not as tricky as it sounds.

Offices that work well from a wellbeing and psychological point of view are those that offer a good balance of prospect and refuge. Except in this case we wouldn't be looking for trees and caves in the middle of the office floor, but for elements such as alcoves, low ceilings and external barriers (built forms of refuge) and windows, doors and terraces (built forms of prospect).

So, worker No. 1 sitting in the middle of a bank of desks is likely to feel overlooked by their colleagues and missing a sense of privacy. This imbalance can cause problems, such as stress and the perception of a lack of control on behalf of the worker, but layouts like this also tend to be detrimental to the way new information is absorbed and processed. In contrast, worker No. 2 can survey the office while feeling protected by the walls behind and next to them. The balance their working environment offers them means they can focus on the work they need to complete, without feeling uneasy in their environment.

So, how can we help ensure that more offices and co-working spaces are designed with this balance in mind? We should create multiple vantage points within the setting, while also ensuring sight lines are clear and unobstructed.[6] Offices should also have a range of environments within one setting, so workers can move to a different zone depending on their mood or the task at hand.[7] And you could even introduce adjustable enclosures and overhead canopies to help give the office a cosy sense of shelter.[8]

FIGURE 2:17
London's Barbican Centre external seating layout is using the refuge and prospect principles

Territory and personalisation: user control in the workplace

The archetypal open-plan office, filled with rows and rows of cubicles and clear desk policies is undeniably cost-effective – ten employees can now be typically served with only seven workspaces.[9] However, this cost-cutting comes at the expense of staff wellbeing and productivity. Offices with an open-plan or hot-desking culture tend not to have user control at the heart of the design, so workers will often experience a low level of control in these environments.

Modern workspaces do not tend to facilitate territoriality: an instinctive behaviour where we control access to a space and mediate behaviour within it. There are different forms of territory, each with an associated level of control and different cues. Leaving your paper and coffee mug on your desk in a co-working space is an example of territorial marking at a very temporary level. If you have very little ownership over your workspace, and cannot control when colleagues interrupt you, this can be detrimental to your productivity and have adverse effects on your wellbeing.

Similarly, the ability to personalise your working environment is linked to high job satisfaction, productivity, and low levels of distraction. So not being able to adjust your workstation to your specific needs or put up photographs or organisational charts is likely to negatively impact on your productivity and job satisfaction.

Finally, open-plan offices, co-working spaces and cafe working tend to be high in environmental stressors. Stressors can be noise- or smell-related, or based on sensitivity to over-crowding, lighting, and ventilation conditions. Some people may find noise levels in a cafe too high to focus on their work, and staff in an open-plan office may not be able to heat their space enough to concentrate.

However, it is worth noting that people have individual levels of tolerance to these elements. Some people may be more sensitive to being interrupted, or feel the need to personalise their space more, while others may feel the cold more and need higher levels of heating.

How do we design a workspace that suits all of these different needs? Having a range of working environments within one office is always a good start, so that there are dynamic areas suited to people who want a bit of buzz around them, but also calm retreats for people who need some peace and quiet to get on with their work. Enabling a high degree of user control over lighting and ventilation is also key to providing workspaces that work for everyone.

Sociopetal space: designing for collaboration

Many believe that designing for collaboration is key for any organisation trying to maintain a competitive edge in today's knowledge economy. Fostering face-to-face communication is particularly important for certain types of work, such as high-tech research and development, and certain personality types, such as extroverts. In environmental psychology, sociopetal space describes areas that facilitate communication, whereas sociofugal spaces discourage interaction. Spaces that are large and undefined, feel 'cold', and physically orient occupants away from each other can dramatically decrease human interaction. When people feel alienated from their environment they also tend to feel alienated from each other.

So what does this mean practically? Providing common spaces and breakout areas is the first step, but designing for truly productive collaboration is more complex. Seating

FIGURE 2: 18
Loose 'refuges' create ideal settings for commercial, public or private interiors

orientation and proximity are key to fostering communication. While we tend to think that sofas are a good place to get together for a chat, side-by-side or 180-degree orientation is actually detrimental to conversation. Sitting directly across the table from someone is more conducive as eye contact is easier, but this is an oppositional position, which people tend to take in competitive situations. The optimal furniture arrangement for cooperative interaction is at a 90-degree angle, 1.4m apart.[10] So whether using chairs, tables, or soft-seating in breakout areas, allowing for corner-to-corner seating will be most sociopetal. That said, it should be noted that while furniture arrangement can encourage or discourage interaction between sociable pairs, it has little impact on less sociable pairs.[11]

Next, how do we apply these lessons to the layout of entire space? Are open-plan offices more sociopetal, and is this beneficial to workers? Open plans are often promoted by the promise of more common space and better communication, but research has shown that it takes more than simply moving to an open office to increase face-to-face communication.[12] Common areas not placed along natural circulation routes, for instance, may have very little impact on productivity. The problem many open-plan workspaces face is that they increase environmental stressors and decrease user control, so people tend to close off just as the opportunity for productive communication has been opened.

This is why it is crucial to have a behavioural or social component to workspace design strategy and especially for co-working spaces where new members and companies move through frequently. New groups rapidly develop status systems that have a great effect on members' behaviour.[13] These initial group behaviour patterns often solidify into social norms, which can also be set by the surrounding social and physical environment.[14] Research has also shown that people are more strongly influenced by those they see as their peers, and that appealing to communal goals is more effective at promoting psychological and ecological wellbeing than appealing to self-serving goals.[15] Therefore, building a strong sense of community and appealing to a 'common cause'[16] is the best way to encouraging people to be respectful of each other's shared physical and auditory space. Finally, it is important to remember that a strongly sociopetal design is not right for every workforce. For highly sensitive or focused work such as accounting, it may be particularly detrimental to productivity.

FIGURE 2: 19
Clearly designating floor uses and expected behaviours

FIGURE 2: 20
Loose seating, views out and seating relationships allowing non-confrontational relationships

FIGURE 2: 21
Clearly designating floor uses and expected behaviours

Case Study: Huckletree co-working workplace

Commissioned to provide a design strategy for a new co-working space in Clerkenwell, London in the UK called Huckletree, the designers sought our human factors expertise. They were looking to craft a workspace that would encourage collaboration, innovation, and sustainable behaviour, and support occupants' wellbeing.

We contributed to the project in two ways. The first task was to help create a space 'etiquette' that would encourage equitable management of shared resources within the workspace and motivate specific sustainable behaviours. Co-working spaces are unique in that there is no one company policy for workers to adhere to, so management policies must be carefully communicated to foster community. We applied recent psychological research on social norms, behaviour change, and small group ecology to guide the Huckletree etiquette, and subtly integrate it into the design. The core strategy was that a common cause approach must be adopted to encourage occupants to be respectful of the resources shared within the space, as well as those they use in the world at large. We made specific recommendations to implement this through signage and visual imagery throughout the space.

The second part of our role was to help integrate some key environmental psychology principles into the design for the space. We worked with Grigoriou Interiors to produce a stunning design with great sustainability credentials, which crucially also worked for a variety of users. Once the initial designs were drawn up, we then made suggestions on the elements that worked well, and areas for improvement. For example, in the main work area, we suggested providing partial screens between workstations to give workers a sense of refuge and screening off informal meeting areas and breakout spaces to introduce a sense of privacy in an otherwise open environment. We also suggested ways of integrating the messages from the etiquette into the wayfinding and graphic design within the space. The plans were finalised and the space opened for business in May 2014.

FIGURE 2: 22
Refuge and prospect in communal informal meeting spaces

Returning to the space, we found strong examples of where our psychological strategy had been implemented throughout the design. The screens at the end of a row of workstations were constructed from glass with graphic messages on them, allowing light to filter through at the same time as providing refuge and privacy. Messaging we had phrased to engender a sense of community and guide usage of different areas were nicely written and drawn into the graphic code of the space. Most members rated their overall sense of community highly, as well as the management of shared resources. Members reported that the combination of phone booth 'time machines' for private calls, breakout spaces, and the first-floor reception/meeting area supported varied work activities and needs. These design and graphic elements were successful in creating a culture of respect around space and noise. As one member described, *'people tiptoe around it a little bit – I don't think anyone's been disturbed.'*

The survey additionally found that 80% members felt working at Huckletree supported their wellbeing and productivity, and this was supported by the qualitative feedback. One member who works at Huckletree four days a week said, *'my productivity is definitely better here than at home, any more days at home and my productivity definitely goes down the pan!'* Our survey also revealed that members felt they had a high level of control over different environmental characteristics of the space, including noise levels, which is an important finding as we know workspace control is directly related to wellbeing and productivity. Overall, we were happy to find a sound evidence base for the impact of our design strategy work on worker wellbeing and communal culture in Huckletree.

Summary

The principles discussed here provide general guidance for incorporating human factors in design, but what makes a better space will be different for each organisation, so situation-specific evaluation is needed to inform successful change. However, in this climate of such great transformation in the workplace, companies should first and foremost adopt a person-centric approach to organisational change.

FIGURE 2: 23
Refuge and prospect in open-plan areas without screens to allow for easier collaborative working

Putting design for wellbeing into practice

From having created basic User Profiles, you can work with EPs to expand, detail and inform how occupiers are going to be supported in a space and through its use to support occupant wellbeing. Understanding the drivers behind occupant behaviour can correctly inform which features, shapes, colours, everything really you choose to be part in an interior design. Below are some thoughts, actions or applications for clients, designers and wider project teams to consider:

1. Find an EP who will complement the project and discuss the scope of their contribution to the design process. What are the gaps you would like them to fill in to gain an understanding of the space users?

2. Work with the EP to define what is important in the project's key performance indicators (KPIs) and how these get affected through the occupant behaviour and personalities. (Project KPIs are discussed further in chapter 5.)

3. Share the User Profiles in progress and discuss what information is required and they can contribute on.

4. As appropriate to each project, you could ask them to be involved in any number of activities; invite them to meet users as you undertake interviews, discuss design principles, set the KPIs for the project itself as far as the occupant wellbeing and productivity issues are concerned and so on.

5. Share proposed plans, design concepts and full proposals with the EP and invite feedback on how they see the design supporting or not the emotional and cognitive needs of users as the design evolves.

6. From the design approach options the project can choose from, decisions should be made on: Is it a need, and if so in which spaces, does the project need to adopt a sociopetal or sociofugal layout, introduce refuge and prospect and provide alternative territory marking approaches.

CHAPTER 4
Existing buildings and priorities

Selecting and working with existing buildings 40 • Prioritising issues 41

Selecting and working with existing buildings

Adopting new design approaches is challenging enough in itself as a learning curve, but putting them into practice on existing buildings always puts design teams through their paces.

Case studies with suggested approaches, and research studies that are conducted within framed situations, are reassuring and provide a strong reference of evidence for us to work from, but none of them can really tell us **exactly** how to adapt the design principles in a building interior that is as unique as the next. There are no two buildings the same and even more so, no interior space that is set up and performs as the next. No matter how extensive one's experience is and how strong a talent we may have in understanding interior spaces, there are always variations from one project to the next, even if you are applying an age old principle. Delivering nationwide and global hospitality and retail branded design concepts is a very good example of this.

This is true for other sectors too as with interiors, where designers are usually working on a space they have never worked with before, with requirements that are tailored in their combination, in market and social expectations that are constantly changing, and knowledge that is ever developing and improving. You may wonder why a point is being made about this. There is an expectation by professional designers, with the ability to create proposed sketches and walkthrough virtual interiors, that clients can be completely sure of the final effect of the design. Recognising that until a design is fully delivered and lived in, the client will not be sure if it is what supports their wellbeing and purpose of use, can help manage expectations and the process of adapting the interior following occupancy. This is again the reason why the BSRIA Soft Landings Framework process is championed as a method of creating buildings and interiors that meet more closely occupier needs. It is helpful also in the process of working with existing buildings and dealing with their legacy issues.

Existing buildings come with many limitations as well as opportunities which are unique in each instance. Every feature of the interior will be inherited in such a way that it will either support or hinder occupant wellbeing. So how do we adapt the 'ideal' design approach when existing buildings can restrict it?

There are a few issues to deal with here: first, is the building and space in itself a good fit for the wellbeing of the intended occupant? When purchasing a house, other than price, school locations, commute and general character, there are few questions and surveys on the way it will impact the occupants' wellbeing. Similarly when

FIGURE 2: 24
How much capacity is designed into existing buildings?

FIGURE 2: 25
Retail store with deep plan, maximising the use of daylight

renting workplaces or retail premises, are the characteristics of a space going to support the wellbeing of occupants and if yes/no, to what degree? There is, as with every decision a point where a change will not make investment sense, where the changes or limitations of a space will be counterproductive to the lifestyle and performance of the occupants. So the User Profiles and KPIs come into play here in the selection and assessment of moving into an interior, and the search criteria themselves. Making sure the building you are taking on has limitations on the least impacting issues of wellbeing, is a good starting point.

For example, if a creative company is looking to lease a workspace, it should be looking at buildings that can have ceilings installed at 3m, to enable a number of spaces with large volumes. (More on spatial volumes, and their impact on people in following chapters.) If all other features are supporting wellbeing then the decision needs to evaluate this one de-valuing feature and ensure productivity from the impact of height still makes business sense.

Adapting or not existing buildings will depend on whether the impacts on wellbeing are so many that it should be recommended to look elsewhere. Knowing to look at the issues affecting wellbeing and not just the cost, location and overall character, is something surveyors and agents must start introducing in discussions of leasing or purchasing transactions of property. Understanding wellbeing and how features impact on the selection process will make adaptation of existing buildings less restrictive and achievement of the harmony between people and space more successful.

It is an opportunity for developers and self-build individuals to create briefs responding to specific User Profiles. For residential and workplace design it comes into its own as the business types attracted in certain areas of a city are typically known or part of an evolving planning strategy, and designing buildings to attract them will create win–win situations.

Prioritising issues

If a building has very little natural light coming into it, it's hard to adapt as a tenant, so understanding some issues such as daylight, fresh air supply and views out, similarly dictated by the existing architecture from the start, is very important. What tenants can do though is ensure they are from the start of the concept design process not unknowingly reducing further the amount of daylight travelling through and into the interior's depth. For example, the way internal walls are set out and the materials selected for these can support or hinder the way, and the amount, of daylight made available to occupiers. Placing solid walls parallel to external windows or installing tall furniture and solid screens in the same way, will reduce the light and access to views out. If the space is also naturally ventilated, the layout of tall or full height items will also be impacted.

FIGURE 2: 26
Prioritising issues during interior renovations

There are occasions in every project, where some issues can seem to conflict and negate each other; for example this happens frequently on issues relating to fire evacuation and security – doors need to have an easy opening method but not one that can leave the building vulnerable and unsecure. The same can be found with issues relating to energy efficiency and wellbeing; increasing the amount of fresh air into a building by mechanical means can increase in cases the amount of energy consumed. Another example is the manual opening of windows which is a great example of user control and adjustability to changing needs but can create a noise problem if the building is located in a city centre. This can also cause a problem if the city has poor air quality; here a mechanical air supply could be selected where fine particle filters can be added to reduce the interior's air pollution from outside. Occupants are going to be outside of these buildings of course at some point in the course of the day but the amount of impact from pollutants can be reduced.

Some of the key design considerations occupiers and project teams need to look out for and make a clear priority on each project to meet the need in the User Profiles are described below:

Key design considerations
- Controllability of the environment v limiting performance of building systems to support the reduction of energy and water for reduced environmental impact. Increased controllability reduces occupier stress.

- Natural v artificial provision:
- Openable windows v mechanical air supply. Openable windows can provide a sense of user control and generally occupants are known to prefer the feel of fresh air to mechanically supplied ventilation systems.
- Natural light and occupant connection with its daily cycle supports circadian rhythms. Large glazed building sections can have a lower thermal performance and increase energy consumption trying to support thermal comfort. (Increased daylight use will reduce the operation of artificial lights.)

- Natural air movement when external air quality is poor can be less beneficial than a mechanical system, which can have double air filtration at the point of entry. If there is a high number of occupants with respiratory elements or very young/elderly, it may be preferable to filter the air to reduce aggravating conditions.

- Visibility and sound v human connection: the whole discussion around open-plan offices not working is usually because concentration provision has not been provided. Connecting people through placing them all in one space, can provide the advantages of proximity, but are negated from lack of care through the impact increased occupation has on the senses. Avoiding sensory overload is critical to success. For example making the kitchen or servery open to seating areas in cafes provides a sense of fun and theatre but can also add noise and make conversation across a table, or concentration for reading, difficult.

- How much of a space will be designed exclusively for one or multiple activities and occupants. Look at the User Profile task/time allocations and group sizes to support the balance of design approach.

In instances as these above, it is not advisable for a solution to be provided from past projects without knowing all the other parameters of the space and its location, and most importantly, its users. The solution should be a compromise that's looking at the stated needs of the project and prioritise based on the impacts to wellbeing. It is a type of risk assessment approach, but adding the wellbeing and occupant impacts to the thinking, allows for a holistic approach that will ensure more sustainable results.

More details on the impact and valuation approach in Part 5.

CHAPTER 5
Designing user experience

User experience through spaces 44 • Entering into a building 46
Multi-sensory design 47 • Biophilia 48

User experience through spaces

The user and visitor experience is coloured through the way we enter into a building and how room-by-room movement around the interior spaces occurs to complete tasks. This could be a child entering their home after school with homework, playtime, dinner time, bath time and sleep; it could be an elderly lady at a bank branch needing to speak with the manager about her savings account, or it could be a young executive joining the departmental team on a workshop day in the head office. Whatever we are doing in our life, we are entering and exiting a building with around 80% of that time inside the interior of a building undertaking a number of tasks. *How* we move around these spaces is in the end making a difference to the quality of those tasks, and our life.

The cultural approach of creating a division between front of house and back of house areas must be mentioned and discussed in relation to its appropriateness in our aim of supporting wellbeing. Whichever instance is looked at where this occurs – whether that be in a retail store, an office or a home – it indicates value of one user higher than the other, which will not support emotional wellbeing. This also translates into physical impacts through the quality of air, lighting and aesthetic impacts to the senses. Eventually, if one party's wellbeing is not supported, both parties will eventually experience it as they form part of a system. To ensure interior spaces support wellbeing, such inequality of perceived value difference needs to be recognised and addressed, or rebalanced in other ways.

Design fluidity is experienced also through the harmony of design approach through all spaces, and the harmony between user ability and design approach. Designing spaces which are not speaking the usability language of the users, where the way they will interact and use the space does not meet social norms familiar to them, will create difficulty in use.

FIGURE 2: 27 AND 2: 28
The different materials and overall experience through an interior will affect how a person feels and behaves.

FIGURE 2: 29 AND 2: 30
Designing communal areas with intent and beauty is vital in the overall user experience of an interior. Above is a commercial workplace circulation space and to the left is a public train station circulation space whose features do not support wellbeing

CHAPTER 5 • DESIGNING USER EXPERIENCE

45

Entering into a building

The design of a building's entrance has historically been the first 'signal' of whether we are welcomed or not into it, or looking further back in history and in the case of castles, what relationships occupants have with others. Observe the design of high-end jewellery shops as opposed to high street clothing shops; a collection of store design features, from the visibility into the shop or the perceived 'accessibility' of the product. In either case it will attract or not the relevant audience. These design characteristics prove the inferred way, through design, in which we draw in or repel people by the way we communicate behaviour, values and culture.

Where buildings have a canopied entrance, the canopy initially makes an impact on supporting wellbeing or not by its height from the ground and relative size. Lower canopies can have a tendency to create unwelcoming looking spaces. Low light levels and sound quality also have a large part to play in this experience, but it is the space and volume itself that is created that influences people to feel one way over another upon entry.

Another approach in entrance design is the defensive or inclusive recesses. By creating a recess into the space, users are provided a respite under cover before entering and it acts as a conversation space on arrival or departure, supporting emotional wellbeing.

Entering through a space that allows small or few views into the building, or a small and cramped volume without much light, can make people feel uneasy which in turn will show in behaviour movements and tone when greeted. Different people will feel the effects more or less depending on their confidence and experience, but in all cases the

FIGURE 2:31
The recessed entrance into the retail store is practical, supports users by allowing them to use it away from a busy high street and is visually welcoming

entry experience can absorb attention and require users to 'deal' with features to process their safety or 'messaging' when entering a building. If the entrance lobby and reception spaces are in harmony with the culture of an organisation or the lifestyle of individuals then whoever is entering will receive this impression, develop clarity and trust through the consistency of messaging and communication. If there was already a cultural or communication alignment, it will only be re-enforced and results supported.

Multi-sensory design

Walking outside a bakery is a memory that most can recall from early childhood. This is unlikely to be due to the visual features of the bakery store design.

In addition to the more attention grabbing tactile and visual elements of interior spaces, a human sensory experience of a space will also include the sense of smell, hearing and taste. As outlined by Turner et al (2018),[17] in their case for a multi-sensory design approach, the current approach to the design process and the way spaces engage with occupants falls short of their full potential. The main point being that designing spaces that fully recognise and cater for all the senses acknowledges the opportunity to purposely set an intent for the interaction of the space with all senses. Acoustics and the experience of sound is also an area that needs a proactive and sensual approach as a design process rather than seeing it as an engineering problem to try and resolve. Turner et al propose a Sensory Toolkit that is a very useful starting point for all designers during the briefing stage and exploration of the user experience as they design an interior and discuss the process with clients.

FIGURE 2: 32
Different textures

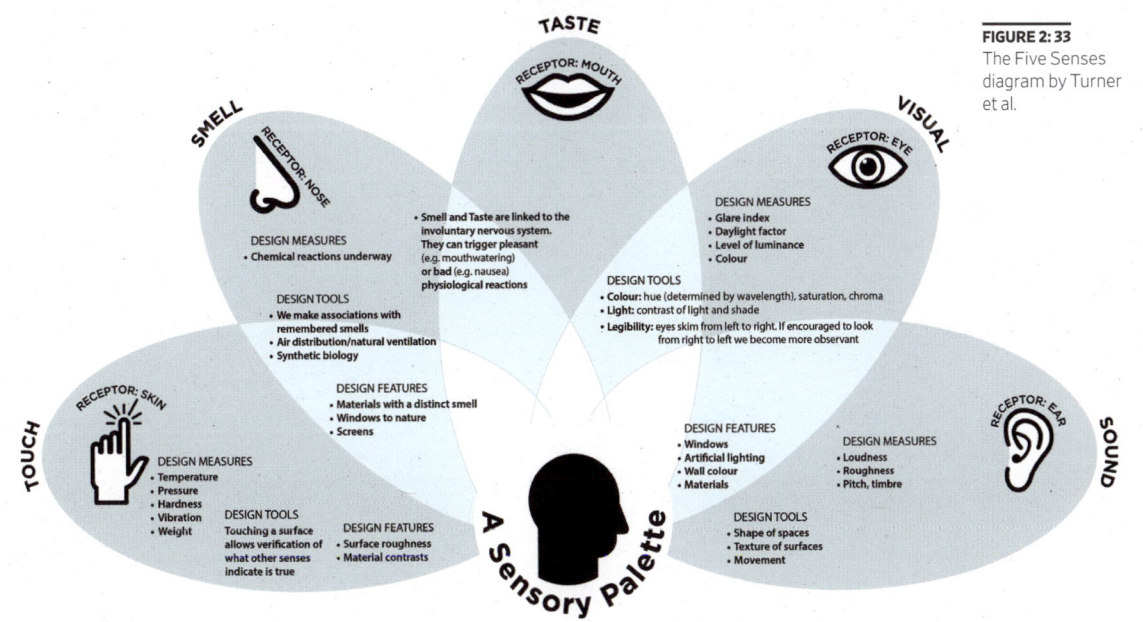

FIGURE 2: 33
The Five Senses diagram by Turner et al.

Biophilia

Biophilia will not be tackled in one specific chapter, as it is a central issue that carries through in all design features. The term is used to describe the effect of humans' connection with nature. We are part of nature and have developed as a being, within it for the most part, over the millennia and so respond to it positively when in contact. Living within manmade and urban environments, increasing the break with nature, is seen to cause impacts to our wellbeing. It is ironic that the reasons we have developed our living world the way we have was for our wellbeing itself, but it seems that we have gone too far and need to rebalance. Trying to put a dry and safe roof over our heads, to streamline the servicing of spaces and comfort have gone so far that we feel alienated from our origins. biophilia can explain, and be the solution to, many issues affecting our physical and emotional response to space, but it will not explain more than that. We have developed as a species beyond where we were while living in caves, huts, draughty cottages and developed societies and lifestyles very different to those we evolved in the earlier centuries. So the aim of a good design that supports wellbeing is to understand how much, and in what way, it is to introduce biophilic features but not try to emulate an exact green forest.

'The most successful interior design is that which most closely echoes the natural environment.' HRH the Prince of Wales

When people hear the term biophilia they usually immediately think of plants. Nature is not composed of just organic parts but also inorganic such as stone and systems of patterns in river and lightning formations. When we refer to biophilia, we will be including the link to all that makes up earth and its ecosystem from textures, features, patterns and systems. The detail of how this occurs is weaved within detailed chapters further on.

FIGURE 2: 34 AND 2: 35
Biophilic features in food retail interiors

When developing a User Profile and assessing the desired characteristics for a scheme, consideration of the overall inclination for the design to be on the scale between biophilic or manufactured is recommended. For example, tech start-ups may find a softer and less 'managed look' in a design approach with a strong biophilic effect does not express their determination and streamlined work ethic. So although they will require the design to provide them with ways to relax, humidify and filter the air etc, they may still be provided these in mechanical ways. For material considerations they may feel in harmony with formed concrete instead of slate, high contrast hues instead of softer tone-on-tone and harmonising colours, highly processed materials instead of organic and looser shapes. The design will be successful when it is, as a coordinated package, harmonising with the needs of the users.

FIGURE 2: 36
Biophilic-themed ornate metal building grill

CHAPTER 6
Design characteristics and issues affecting wellbeing

General design theory books and online sources provide long lists of design principles that can be, or should be, considered in the process or that exist as features within it. We can adopt a view which states that these are *all* important, as they are all in the end aiming to deliver an aesthetically and functionally beautiful design, and as discussed earlier, if done correctly, this supports wellbeing. But there are some principles that have a more direct and perhaps critical link with the process of designing to support occupants. As the principles are always applied in different contexts, sizes and combinations, this is an initial list which is expected over time to develop and refine further.

Design characteristics

Based on the premise outlined so far that the perception of beauty, and thus wellbeing, can be found in the detailed design characteristics and interior components present, the following **design characteristics** must be considered:

1 Elegance
Features look as if less physical effort is required for the task undertaken. Examples can include something hanging that is designed in such a way that viewers wonder how it is supported, or the use of space is experienced so that minimal and effective number of movements is needed to complete a task. The opposite effect would be to allow *improvisation*, assuming no one wishes to show *neglect* intentionally.

2 Harmony or stimulation in composition
Parts are more or less harmonious in style and components amongst themselves. The less harmony there is, the more stimulation and 'noise' there will be.

3 Balance or imbalance and symmetry or asymmetry
The design approach and composition responds to one or both to a higher or lower degree. Is a Realistic or Abstract approach needed and how will a high or lower scale of balance or symmetry in the design features work to achieve this?

4 Proportion
The shapes and products of the interior and the space are proportionate between themselves or not, or follow specific relationships. Are they biophilic, balanced asymmetrical or elegant?

5 Biophilia
The design will be more towards reflecting biophilia or a manmade approach.

6 Repetition
The patterns, shapes or arrangements contain aspects of Repetition. Repetition creates trust.

7 Fluency
Spaces are designed so they are fluently understood by their users. Details and their usability are based on social norms for expert or inexperienced users as required in each situation.

FIGURE 2: 37 AND 2: 38 Examples of asymmetry and fluency

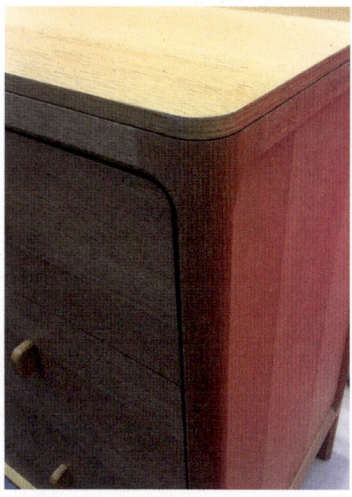

8 Authentic
The interiors authentically reflect the personality and needs of their occupants or a 'created' culture.

9 Realistic or Abstract
Is the design aiming to meet a perception of beauty that responds to users' perception of being Abstract or Realistic?

All the above characteristics can be present along a scale from 1 to 10 or indicate their presence as a percentage of contents or surfaces. Each designer, design company or client should find the way and tools to help them communicate, and manage these issues during the project. It is really important to be clear on the overall position of each characteristic and as to 'why', so the whole team can keep referring back to it during the design process, creating a common language and baseline reference for design decisions.

If upon application it is found that some characteristics need to move up or down on a scale then that needs to be fed back, discussed with the wider team and client and adapted in the design's linked aspects.

If all characteristics and components are present and harmonised, they will support a design's fluency, which in turn can support a person's physical, emotional and spiritual wellbeing. The higher the fluency and harmony of an interior to its users, the more support for their wellbeing there will be.

Design issues
To enable occupant wellbeing to be considered in all three ways that it is affected – body, mind and emotions – designs need to apply the design characteristics mentioned above onto the following built environment features and their finer details. The performance of every interior needs

FIGURE 2: 39 AND 2: 40
Examples of biophilia and design fluency

to consider the following design issues in relation to their support of occupant wellbeing:
- Elegance, balance, symmetry and patterns
- Acoustics
- Colour and its psychology
- Materials and textures
- Shapes and volumes
- Art and symbolism
- Layout, furniture and space planning
- Indoor atmosphere
- Views and controllability

Additionally, other issues which form part of a project's process and are core to delivering harmony and extracting wellbeing's true value in a project, include:
- User Profiles
- Environmental psychology
- Occupant evaluations
- Value returns and measuring wellbeing

We have so far covered in detail the integration of User Profiles and EPs. Occupancy assessments and measuring wellbeing is dealt with in the later chapters. Many of the characteristics and issues are discussed next, focusing on specific issues that target clients, designers and wider consultant team interests and needs. The chapters aim to demystify, provide some knowledge and understanding of how to put into practice and how to adjust each issue for a variety of commercial or residential designs.

'Do not fear to be eccentric in opinion, for every opinion now accepted was once eccentric.' Bertrand Russell (1872–1970) philosopher, historian and social critic

Putting design for wellbeing into practice

This chapter outlined the Design Characteristics, issues and process tools which require consideration and inclusion in each project if it is aiming to support occupant wellbeing. Integrating actions into the day-to-day practice of the design and process could include some of these following suggestions:

1 Define how many User Profiles are required for the occupants of the spaces being designed. As part of the creation of the personas define what is deemed as beauty for these users that will reflect their values and inspire them.

2 Question and define the culture or lifestyle the occupants are currently experiencing. Find out if this is going through a period of change and upheaval or stability for the foreseeable life cycle of the interior.

3 Decide how the levels set for the Design Characteristics will aim for comfort or stimulation and thus productivity/effectiveness of tasks, and whether an Abstract or Realistic aesthetic will support the desired culture.

4 Define the Design Characteristics for the project so that they harmonise with the needs identified in the User Profiles. Relate levels to support the achievement of the project KPIs, including occupant wellbeing.

5 Discuss how the Design Characteristics are achieved through the various design issues with the client and project consultants to support understanding and how it will be achieved in practice.

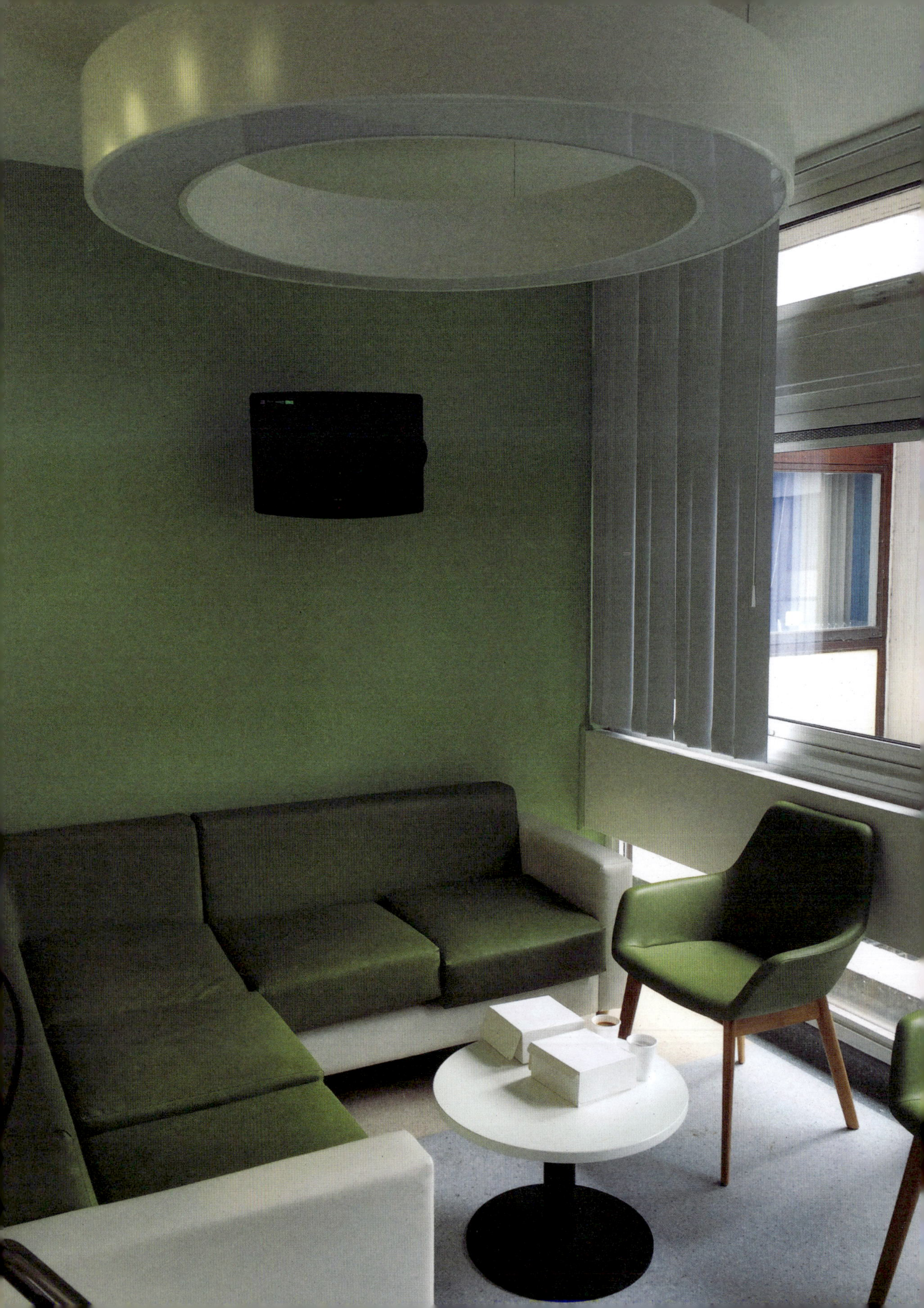

PART 3

Design in Practice: Aesthetic Issues Affecting Wellbeing

Chapter 7: Elegance/Elegant 57 • Chapter 8: Balanced or symmetrical 60 Chapter 9: Colour and the psychology behind it 67 • Chapter 10: Repetition and patterns 77 • Chapter 11: Shapes, volumes and proportions 80 Chapter 12: Symbolism 94 • Chapter 13: The use of artwork in interiors 97 Chapter 14. Materials and Textures 108

The following chapters are grouped into aesthetic, Physical and Process related design issues, but it is acknowledged that all issues overlap, either directly or as a series of linked effects. So if one issue is included in this section as an 'aesthetic' it must also be recognised that there will be indirect or consequential physical impacts to interior users. For example, the effect of symmetry will be experienced as much in a pattern of repetition as much as with the array of light fittings.

Alexander Baumgarten, the German philosopher and educator, in 1739 defined aesthetics as the 'science of perception' or 'science of sensitive knowing'.

In Baumgarten's theory, with its characteristic emphasis on the importance of feeling, much attention was concentrated on the creative act. For him it was necessary to modify the traditional claim that 'art imitates nature' by asserting that artists must deliberately alter nature by adding elements of feeling to perceived reality. In this way, the creative process of the world is mirrored in their own activity.
Source: Encyclopaedia Britannica 2016

The artist Mark Rothko, in *The Artist's Reality*, expands on the 'plasticity' of the work of an artist to communicate reality and truth accurately through either representing it exactly and applying some 'colour wash technique' for example to express atmosphere, or interpreting and abstracting what reality is understood to be by the artist and reproduced/reformed to be understood by others in turn within a different context.[1] Emotional and cognitive types of communication are core for both approaches aiming to create an aesthetic experience whose aim is to communicate real beauty. In Rothko's case specifically it was very clearly aiming for the ultimate achievement of life, that of self-knowledge and happiness.

FIGURE 3: 01
Preconditions of research on aesthetic experience of colour by Ulf Klarén, SYN-TES – Nordic Interdisciplinary Network on Colour and Light

CHAPTER 7

Elegance/elegant

It's often found that elegance is considered as part of opulent and luxurious spaces. The definition of 'elegant' is found to describe things that are well-thought through yet simple, or that have refinement or grace, and perhaps also have scientific exactness and precision. The definitions are marrying a process that achieves the need for 'just enough' and a non-aesthetic platform of thought, all this to create something that is aesthetically and operationally attractive.

What we can deduce from this is that the elements of an interior will have been composed in such a way that we feel an adequate amount of thought and technique has been applied in its composition, and we know the result will suit the users. But using the word 'simple' only as a design characteristic could be too minimal for certain users; thinking something through does not necessarily signify a removal of excess; an exclusively engineered approach can be clunky as it may not consider a rounded experience. So it is the combination of all these features that allow a design to be elegant, and by consequence considered the best it can be.

When we see something that is elegant, we immediately either know it or clearly respond to it in an obvious fashion. Alain de Botton provides his rather poetic approach of what elegance is, and why it is found by people to be so, in his book *The Architecture of Happiness* with the following statements *'...exceptionally nimble, apparently effortless way in which it carries out its duty. ...a subcategory of beauty we can refer to as elegance, a quality present whenever a work of architecture succeeds in carrying out an act of resistance – holding, spanning, sheltering – with grace and economy as well as strength; when it has the modesty not to draw attention to the difficulties it has surmounted.'*[2] This is a very emotive and lyrical description of design characteristics we can request to be present in every act of interior design. Imagine the change it would have in supporting wellbeing if the spaces currently delivered for homes, workplaces, and especially spaces such as schools and hospitals, were always part of a client's design brief.

More poignantly, de Botton also suggests that we abhor the opposite of what elegance stands for: neglect. Something that is not elegant has had some neglect in the way it was thought about or executed.

Following the theme of these descriptions and taking a look at old and new interior products that have been popular, we can observe the way their design incorporates elegance, both in approach and execution.

FIGURE 3: 02
Elegance in the support of a handrail

FIGURE 3: 03
Even fire exit signs can be designed to be functional and elegant

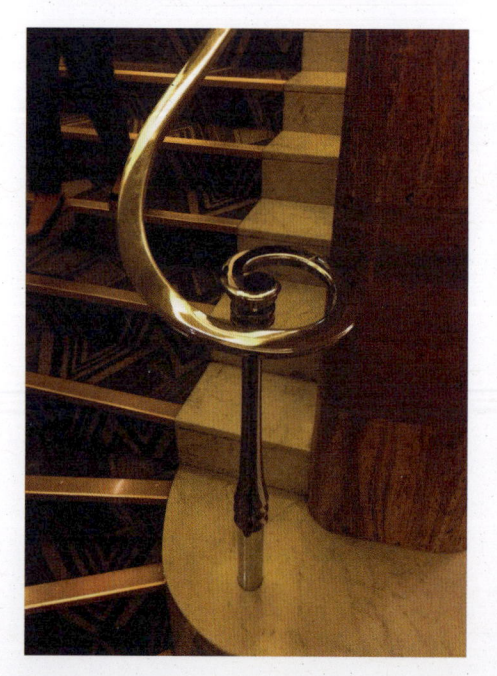

The Hat Factory by Erich Mendelsohn in Germany was designed and built in the early half of the 20th century. Although the interior has been in a variety of conditions from run down to newly refurbished, the design's elegance shines through it all. Its features are deemed 'elegant' through the thin visible building structure flowing across the bays and through the delicate meeting points seen in the centre. The curved corner of the beam and column connection is also refined, as design attention has clearly been given through the application of a curve as opposed to an angular 'clunky' connection. It allows the eye to run along the structure and creates visual fluidity. The eyes are drawn up into the central meeting point also hinting at the cathedral effect. The fact that the middle section allows the eyes to relax and conceive of more space beyond, adds to the overall comfort and feelings of lightness and beauty.

FIGURE 3: 04 AND 3: 05
The Hat Factory, by Erich Mendelsohn, Germany

CHAPTER 8

Balanced or symmetrical

The relationship of nature, proportion and symmetry 65

The effect of the presence, or exclusion, of balance in the interior design or architecture of a space, can reduce distraction and allow features to coexist, to harmonise, making us feel less unsettled in our effort to assimilate what we are seeing.

Within the context of design and buildings, an image referring to 'balance' can bring to mind a more traditional, perhaps Palladian style of design. This inclination to its definition can be limited. 'Balanced' does not exclusively indicate the same objects on both sides. Balance can be achieved through a higher number of smaller objects on one side of a room when a single strong coloured wall is on the other. A 'busy' textured wall finish will balance the effect of an equally eye-catching floor finish of deeper colour in the space. As opposed to balance, the symmetry of objects is the repetition of the same exact object and colour on two or more communicating sides or surfaces.

In the context of a private residence or an organisation wishing to represent 'change', 'progress', and express an approach which encourages questioning the status quo and that want to be known and encourage a constant evolution of ideas and actions, then a level of *asymmetry* amongst balanced objects will introduce stimulation, disruption and increase alertness. This will communicate a message that will harmonise with the experience of people interacting with the owners or organisation, and support the activities and values experienced.

It is important to note that 'alertness' can't be experienced if not seen as a contrast to its surroundings of 'calmness', so introducing features that contrast in an overall balanced

FIGURE 3: 06, 3: 07, 3: 08, 3: 09, 3: 10 AND 3: 11
Balance can be introduced through circularity and artwork or through the layout of the interior itself and the relationship of furniture to the architecture and views out

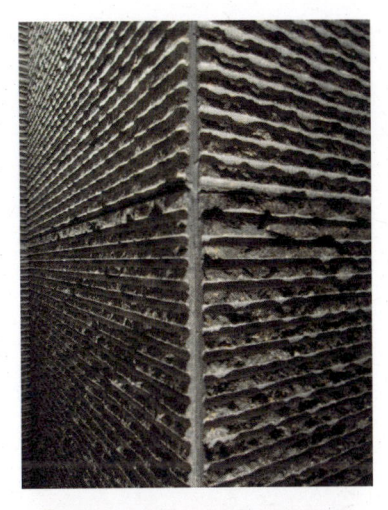

CHAPTER 8 • BALANCED OR SYMMETRICAL

61

FIGURE 3: 12
Introducing balance through a busy wall

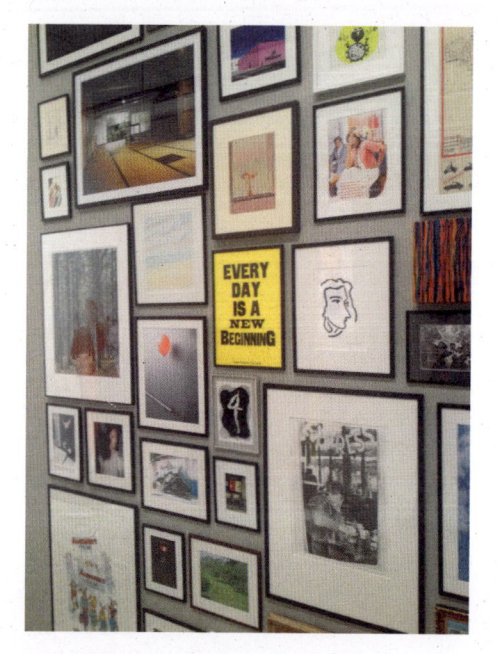

surrounding is required for this to take effect. A balanced surrounding will also support a more long-term result. Too much stimulation can actually, by its nature, seem harmonious thus missing its objective.

In the context of retail or other public spaces such as travel terminals, and the issue of wayfinding, asymmetry can be used to direct users effectively through peak or busy times and improve customer and operation experience.

Within workplace or public spaces, asymmetry in circulation spaces can support areas where there is a wish for people to congregate and exchange ideas, or briefly interact, which will increase their happiness through improving relationships and making friends.

Symmetry is in fact an extremely wide and well-applied quality; it spans from physics all the way to art. The Oxford English Dictionary describes it as *'The quality of being made up of exactly similar parts facing each other or around an axis: this series has a line of symmetry through its centre crystal structure with hexagonal symmetry.'* Within an aesthetic context it is described as *'Correct or pleasing proportion of the parts of a thing: the overall symmetry makes the poem pleasant to the ear.'* And in the context of physics and mathematics *'A law or operation where a physical property or process has an equivalence in two or more directions.'*

We can find symmetry in the experience of moving through the spaces of an interior, as much as within a single room or a single elevation within it.

FIGURE 3: 13
Example of asymmetry in a building entrance feature wall – through its directionality it guides arrivals to it

FIGURE 3: 14
Example of complete lack of balance or symmetry in a university auditorium where concentration on the screen needs to be supported

FIGURE 3: 15
An asymmetrical layout in a corridor creates direction that supports wayfinding

Discoveries of symmetry by Plato, Galileo and Kepler, epitomised the way in which a broader understanding of the symmetry principles inherent in mathematics began to uncover the hidden unity of nature. They extended into modern laws of physics by Einstein and Noether.[3]

So it would seem that by following the principle of symmetry, humans as natural beings, bound by our own state, feel in harmony with nature's principles and structure. This is a strong demonstration of an aspect of what we refer to as biophilia.

As mentioned in the Introduction of this book, the question that needs to be asked by designers and clients during the early stages of design, and reverted back to throughout development stages, is how can

FIGURE 3: 16 AND 3: 17
Examples of symmetry in The Wallace Collection, London

CHAPTER 8 • BALANCED OR SYMMETRICAL

63

FIGURE 3: 18
Internal atrium of the Reina Sophia Museum, Madrid

interior design enhance wellbeing in user experience. What will this look like, in form and in experience for each and every space?

Symmetry, on a symbolic level, is used to express constancy and longevity through its presence. Through its use to achieve contrast, it can express individualism. And through the natural patterns symmetry follows, it is generally perceived as a descriptor of beauty. To demonstrate how engrained it is in our nature, scientists developing robotic technology have been working towards understanding how human cognitive functions operate and knowledge is generated, and have been referring to the principles of symmetry in the knowledge process to progress their research.[4]

We can have a symmetrical composition but because of other aspects of it, such as colour, features or textures, we can find it ugly. Where emotive or social norm aspects exist, the typical design principle effects will be overridden. For example, this is seen in the research conducted studying the shapes between curved familiar and unfamiliar objects. The studies show a distinct preference for curved objects, known as the human's curved bias effect.

Designing rooms independently of each other does not take into account another issue, that of experiential symmetry, which is the way we actually experience spaces as users. Decisions on the way the ceilings may start lower but increase as people move into the interior may support the functions and desired feelings of exclusivity/openness, or a constant ceiling and room size may re-enforce modularity and organisation. Experiential symmetry is a result of the full effect of our senses engaged so needs to be acknowledged, considered and reflected through the design process by all project teams.

The relationship of nature, proportion and symmetry

Proportion and symmetry support occupant wellbeing when designed into the features of a space; both architecturally in the fabric of the rooms and their spatial layout, as much as in the selection of furniture design, accessories and finishes.
Though studies looking at the variations in nature where phyllotaxy is not accurately represented is considered nature's way of adapting to local conditions, Douardy and Couder state specifically *'In particular the fact that the divergence angle tends towards an irrational value is often thought of as being useful for the plant: the leaves along the stem are never exactly superposed so that their exposure to the sun is optimal.'*[5] This hypothesis translated onto the way we apply and see the Fibonacci and golden ratio proportions allows for harmonisation to local conditions but retaining a general principle. This consideration does go to some extent towards rationalising the 'exactness' or not in which we deal with the proximity of proportions to the golden ratio; just because they don't fall exactly on the proportion does not mean that, because they are close, the theory can still stand that we prefer these proportions – or ones close to them. The question raised then is how close is 'close' and when do we say definitively that the proportion it not applied?

If the golden ratio proportions are to be thought as with the human face, to have one 'ideal' measurement and proportion, then how can we accept the worldly variations of beauty that contradict these? We could construe that it is perhaps more *likely*, and that by following natural laws, there are local proportions of beauty to be studied in the world's main geographic locations.

The fact that the golden ratio has been repeated at such frequency and associated with positive values of human behaviour and an ideal life can be one explanation of why the Classic design approach is seen as widely attractive. It could be the result of a social norm.

In Miranda Lundy's book titled *Sacred Geometry*, she discusses the similarity and attraction to music that follows certain rhythms similar to geometry and proportion.

She states, *'Geometry is "number in space", music is number in time. The basic set of musical intervals is the elementary set of simple ratios, 1:1 (unison), 2:1 (the fifth), 4:3 (the fourth) and so on. ...Musical intervals, like geometrical proportions, always involve two elements in a certain ratio...'.*[6] This principle speaks about certain fixed proportions, but mostly to the fact that there is a known and coordinated harmony between every composition itself. This is what is being proposed for interior spaces, a creation of harmony. What type of music each interior designer, as creator, wishes to produce is down to skill and current need, the main point is a harmony must be achieved within the interior's elements to support occupant wellbeing.

FIGURE 3: 19
Furniture in the form of a blooming flower

FIGURE 3: 20
Hotel corridor with balance and symmetry

Putting design for wellbeing into practice

This chapter outlines the principles of elegance, balance and symmetry, and expands on the core importance these play to human existence and daily perception. By including these design principles in the brief, overall design 'look and feel' or on selected features, designs will be supporting wellbeing and user activities. The important decision to make at the briefing stage is to decide:

1 How much elegance, balance or symmetry needs to be targeted for the design to support occupant wellbeing? Based on the User Profiles and overall culture, define the amount required to be integrated in the overall design language and layout.

2 If time and cost can't be allocated to the whole project address issues uniformly, find areas for elegance by applying some focused attention..

3 In the design team's service and fee agreements, clients to support and allow designers to apply elegance by acknowledging the proportionate time this process can take.

4 Consider and seek out through the user experience the points where balance, symmetry or asymmetry need to be present. Consider ways and locations they can support design fluidity and wayfinding.

FIGURE 3: 21
Main staircase art installation ZOBOP by Jim Lambie, celebrating shapes and colour during the Royal Academy's 2015 Summer Exhibition

CHAPTER 9

Colour and the psychology behind it

Introduction to colour psychology 68 • The impact of colour 69
Use of colour in interiors 70 • The psychological properties of the main hues 70 • Process of colour selection 73 • The four colour groups 74
The interdependence of shape, size and colour 75

The issue associated mostly with the role of an interior designer, according to society's sound-bites, is colour. Although colour is very important to the role of a designer and integral to creating spaces, few designs show an informed approach to its selection.

It is worth clarifying at this early stage that choosing white or black is also understood as working with colour. The psychology of why one would only work with these two and none others should become apparent as we progress.

In this section we are going to delve into colour psychology, and how when used correctly, colour affects and supports our emotional and mental wellbeing. The physical effects of colour are also discussed but it must be recognised that these are in the majority indirect effects of our mental processing of seeing colour. The chapter on light and its effects with our circadian rhythms explains how the reception of light through eyes and its travels within our body have a physical effect. Light is in fact colour, as colour is parts of light affected by the physical makeup of an object. Light and colour are in fact the same thing.

Introduction to colour psychology

How we select colours as part of an interior's design 'look and feel' must be harmonised both with nature's principles and with the personality profile the majority of occupants fall within, to ensure it is supporting their wellbeing. A personality profile must not be confused with a User Profile, as a User Profile may have a dominant colour personality profile but be a mix of two. The most thoughtful and demonstrated work behind the research on effects of colour on human psychology is by Angela Wright. Wright is a highly experienced colour professional with her own practice Colour Affects. Most importantly she has an excellent book under her belt titled *The Beginner's Guide to Colour Psychology* which provides access to knowledge of the field. While she defines the four colour psychological personalities and their characteristics, she has also studied over her career, the way specific colour combinations evoke natural behavioural reactions from people, demonstrating visual languages to be adopted or avoided, depending on how we seek to make occupants feel inside an interior.

Wright, describing the link with nature and providing a direct link and example of biophilia, is quoted as saying on colour psychology that it is a universal non-verbal language that everyone speaks and understands. That we are all born with an innate instinct for colour, needed historically for our survival through evolution as nature's signal for danger or change. Wright uses the example of a fly and a wasp with the typical reaction humans have to these two, stating colour as the signal to the difference between an irritated or agitated behavioural response. Within food colour psychology is at work when we see a green steak or green apple, a pink grapefruit or pink cheese.

Colour is mentioned on occasion as the first and strongest influence in our response to a design. And although its importance is accepted, we must also acknowledge the undistinguishable link between colour, shape and texture. To believe that colour alone is the most important trigger is ignoring the other primal triggers we have of shape and texture. Consider the texture of an alligator or snake's skin and the shape of a sharp tooth, cave stalactite or a floating cloud. Colour a cloud pink or red and it will be disquieting, but colour a sharp tooth red and our alarm goes up another level.

FIGURE 3: 22
Colour psychology is always at work, especially when specifying interior finishes

The impact of colour

Within research of UK hospitals, Hilary Dalke, a colour expert, has observed the following on the use of colour and patient recovery *'Colour and lighting can have an impact on people's perceptions and responses to the environment and also affect patient recovery rates, improving the quality and overall experience of patients, staff and visitors. Colour and appropriate lighting are also powerful tools for coding, navigation and wayfinding. Colour can also promote a sense of wellbeing and independence...'*

There are many examples of interiors that have shown good use of colour to the benefit of an improved function of the occupant's life. The impact of colour on occupants is through the harmonisation of the colour's wavelength with the users, with the absorption of colour through the eyes and the eventual effect specific colours have in the brain during processing. When light touches people's skin, objects and textures, they will absorb all the rays of light apart from the ones whose colours have the same wavelength as their own mass, their own atomic structure. Wright explains, *'When light strikes the human eye, the wavelengths do so in different ways, influencing our perceptions. In the retina, they are converted into electrical impulses that pass to the hypothalamus, the part of the brain governing our hormones and our endocrine system. When light strikes any coloured object, the object will absorb only the wavelengths that exactly match its own atomic structure and reflect the rest – which is what we see.'*

The hypothalamus (with the pituitary) governs:
- Water regulation
- Sleeping and behavioural patterns
- The balance of the autonomic nervous system
- Sexual and reproductive functions
- Metabolism
- Appetite
- Body temperature

The hypothalamus also houses the body's biological clock that regulates our circadian rhythms. This phenomenon is also expanded in the lighting section in more detail.

In experiments looking to evidence the impact different colours have on brain activity, emotional response and physical response, a team from Chiba University summarised their findings in the *Journal of Physiological Anthropology*[7] and noted the following on feelings *'the various psychological influences of color on human beings have been a focus of attention. Regarding the emotional effect of the object color, it has been reported that warm colors in the red color system arouse genial, positive, active feelings, and neutral colors such as green promote moderate, calm, ordinary feelings, while the cool colors in the blue color system produce cold, passive, quiet feelings.'* The monitored brain activity, due to the stimulation of viewing red, green and blue colours showed a significant difference in brain activity for each. The activity was in a specific part and types of movement of the brain, and further mining of this information and research field is required. It was clear though that initial results demonstrated areas of the brain which focus on concentration and alertness were stimulated significantly more when viewing red colour than when viewing green and blue.

FIGURE 3: 23
Warm colours generate warm feelings

Use of colour in interiors

If you are not blind or colour-blind, you have already an understanding of colour and colour preferences assuming you choose a direction to move to in a retail shop, you choose objects to pick up or choose food to eat on a daily basis. We choose all these based on our innate response to colour, cultural biases and social norms. For example, placing a glossy red wall surface ahead of a walkway is going to divert anyone walking towards it to a passage coming off it if they can choose alternative routes; a black and yellow striped floor pattern will warn us and symbolically tell us to pay attention to danger; and a deep green or brown background will make red apples look more inviting and entice us away from cake. Applications are literally endless, but colour can be used with intent in interior design to:
- Provide emotional comfort and support
- Act as a signalling tool for safety
- Function as a layout tool and support wayfinding
- Symbolically to represent an idea, re-enforce culture, lifestyle and brand
- Support activities being undertaken in a space.

Wright's theory is based on harmonising the wavelengths of colour with the objects and users. Each colour profile is aligned with the colour group due to its wavelength which is understood through each colour's temperature. She also integrates the placement of colours and their combinations with direction from nature's use.

It has been evidenced through her work that each individual will be more or less aligned with one of four colour psychology groups, and may also have some behavioural characteristics of a secondary group. The four groups include behavioural descriptors associated with each which also reflect on other choices of life, preferences and dislikes. So if you observe occupants' behaviour, discover their preferences in lifestyle choices and expressions of manner, you should be able to harmonise them with one of the main colour groups. Wright found that by aligning people with their colour groups, they felt and behaved better; they were less tired or agitated and felt in harmony with their external expression of character.

In application on interiors we may find on occasions that some colour choices are directed by the activities being undertaken in these. For example, hospital lighting and wall colours need to support the activity of diagnoses of patients through healthcare professionals observing the skin's colour[8]. If the lighting and colours of the space affect how accurately this is observed it will impede the diagnoses.

The psychological properties of the main hues

The following sections are adapted extracts from Wright's work on the issue.

Colour works in the same way as music does: every note has its own properties, just as every colour does. However, they do not evoke much emotional response until they are combined with other notes, or colours. They can be harmoniously combined, producing warm, pleasant feelings, or they can clash and create tensions.

The four psychological primary colours are Red, Blue, Yellow and Green:

Red – Affects us physically, evoking what might be termed 'lower order' psychological activity. The universal physical stimulus of bright red can be perceived as exhilarating and exciting, or aggressive and demanding.

Blue – Affects the intellect, promoting thought and 'higher order' activity. It always influences thought, but can do so in a number of ways. It is the value and intensity of the blue and its relationship to other colours near it that control how it affects thought. Is your blue going to encourage reason and calm or logical thought expressing cold bureaucracy?

Yellow – Affects the emotions, self confidence and the ego. Too strong a yellow, or a badly combined colour scheme, can turn the optimism and self-confidence positively invoked by yellow into fear and anxiety.

Green – Affects the essential balance between mind, body and emotions – a more important consideration than is often realised. It is very reassuring, because green in the natural environment indicates healthy vegetation and therefore little danger of famine. It is also the most restful colour to contemplate, since it is in the middle of the spectrum and therefore requires no adjustment to look at it. A walk amongst the greenery outdoors can be relied upon to improve your mood every time – your balance is restored. Negatively, all that stillness and peace can feel stagnant and any action-oriented person can find green a bit stultifying.

The psychological effects of the remaining hues are combinations of the psychological effects of these primaries.

Orange – A mixture of red and yellow, it combines physical with emotional response – activating awareness of secondary survival issues of food, warmth, shelter and sensuality. It can be carefree and thrilling – but with no element of thought balancing the pure orange, it can be hedonistic, mindless and irresponsible.

Indigo – A mixture of blue and violet, and invariably a dark colour – evokes deep introspection and thought. It can be too introverting, bordering on depression.

FIGURE 3: 24
Red can be exhilarating

FIGURE 3: 25
Blue encourages reason

FIGURE 3: 26
Confident or fearful yellow

FIGURE 3: 27
Green supports contemplation

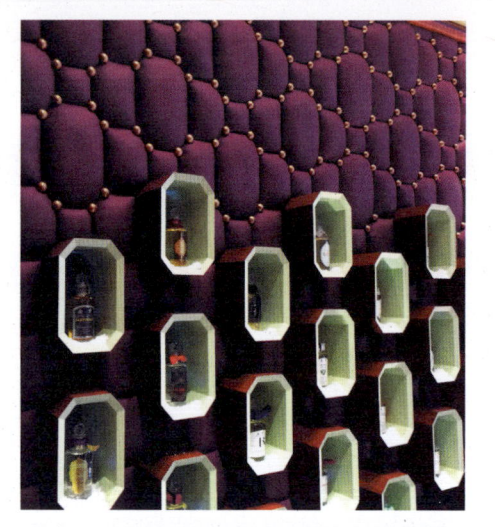

FIGURE 3:28
Taking awareness to a higher plane of thought

FIGURE 3:29 AND 3:30
Colour psychology is always at work, especially when specifying interior finishes

Violet – A mixture of red and blue, physical and mental – appears to take awareness to a higher plane of thought, stimulating imagination and consideration of wider philosophical ideas; it can be described as the colour of the 'spirit'. The wrong purple can have the opposite effect, indicating poor quality and creating a strain.

Traditionally it has been thought that long wavelength colours – reds, oranges, and yellows – are stimulating and shorter wavelength colours – greens, blues, and purples – are soothing. Also, long wavelength colours are deemed warm and short wavelength colours cool. According to Wright's experience this is not accurate. There are soothing long wavelength colours and stimulating short wavelength ones. The important factor in a colour's stimulating or sedating influence is chromatic intensity; a very soft, light red – i.e. pink – is physically soothing. Equally, a very strong, saturated blue is mentally stimulating. However, whether stimulating or sedating, the red wavelength always evokes a physical reaction, the blue a mental reaction and so on.

Process of colour selection

At the early stages of creating the design brief, the occupant colour profile(s) and activities to be undertaken in a space, need to be defined. The users are to be allocated one of the colour psychology categories whose properties they reflect the closest. Following that, working with the colours in each group, consider the colours and combination of colours and materials supporting the activities occurring in the interior spaces of the project, i.e. communicating, sleeping, eating, reading etc. Once the allocation of a colour group has been made to each User Profile, and the activities clarified in the various spaces, we are ensuring there is harmony between the colour palettes and meeting occupants' psychological (mental and emotional) wellbeing.

It must be acknowledged that in the colour selection processes, personal influences from past or current impacts, will create a bias and must be accounted for. As with any emotional and mental process, the more self-awareness a designer has of their own inclinations of like and dislike, the more they can fairly service their clients' own preferences and support their wellbeing.

Once we have the characteristics of each colour, the following step is knowing where and how to use all of them. Wright provides these broad guidelines when the aim is to support occupant wellbeing, in addition to instinctively taking our cue from nature:

1 Relate the predominant hue to the predominant activity of the space. Walls tend to have the biggest impact but in cases where large expanses of floor or ceiling are dominant these could be considered as the predominant locations. If there is a desire to balance the effect then introducing secondary colours or other materials with a texture and complementing finish can work.

2 Grey is understood to be psychologically neutral and provide a dampening effect on the mood of a space. If introversion is sought and efforts to tone down the energy of a particular lively group of people on a constant basis, then it will be appropriate.

3 Combinations found in nature can provide strong clues on the combinations perceived natural and which will support occupant wellbeing. When using the term 'natural colours' we are referring to bright pinks, deep purples and similar intense or deeply rich colours and not just beige or taupe which tend to come to mind. Using the palettes of a year's seasons can be a helpful start. Each palette reflects the relevant characteristics recognised such as fresh, bright and perky. The next warm, soft and deep, followed on by depth, impressiveness and richness, finishing off with sharp, quiet and intense characteristics.

4 Wright states, *'The colour schemes are unmistakeable and they are all very different. Nature does not mix them up.'* On occasions where the interior's design 'look and feel' language reflects a User Profile that has less balance and higher asymmetry, introducing one or two colours or textures outside of a natural palette will be appropriate and necessary to reflect a step away from the status quo.

The four colour groups

The four colour groups Wright has created she refers to as Morninglight, Dreamlight, Firelight and Starlight, following the types of light rather than seasons. They can also be referred to as Group 1, 2, 3 and 4 as in this book. She recommends that we start with the main user harmonised group and work within that to define the colour palette. It can be found in practice that there are on occasions demands for integration or alignment with current brand language and cultural norms, so the palette may evolve but needs to stay mostly within the group's characteristics if supporting the occupants' wellbeing is the primary aim. For example, a brand may use four specific colours already that are not all in the same colour Group as shown below. As interiors should use colours to support activities undertaken in them and the needs of the user, the brand colours need always to evolve.

Group 1 Morninglight
Qualities:
- warm, clear and delicate
- fairly bright but not particularly strong

Quantities:
- Warm hues (containing yellow)
- High Lightness value (little or no black)
- Relatively low chroma – also known as Saturation (delicate colours)

Group 2 Dreamlight
Qualities:
- cool, subtle and soft
- can be darker than Group 1, but never heavy

Qualities:
- cool hues (containing blue)
- lower lightness (often greyed)
- relatively low chroma

Group 3 Firelight
Qualities:
- fiery, off beat (no primaries)
- greyed and subtle

Quantities:
- warm hues (containing yellow)
- low to high lightness
- low to high chroma

Group 4 Starlight
Qualities:
- cold and dramatic
- either very light, very dark or very intense
- no mid tones

Quantities:
- cold hues (containing blue)
- very high or very low lightness
- high chroma

There is still so much to learn about how colour influences our health and wellbeing, but one thing is certain: disharmony creates a negative effect.

FIGURE 3: 31 Morninglight
FIGURE 3: 32 Dreamlight
FIGURE 3: 33 (OPPOSITE) Firelight
FIGURE 3: 34 (OPPOSITE) Starlight

The interdependence of shape, size and colour

The perception of a colour, and the shapes they embody or coat, changes from initial small samples to the final interior surface, object and context in which they are placed. There could be a relatively small spatial volume, but depending on which surfaces are illuminated and coloured for impact, the space can look larger, smaller or asymmetric, which in turn will impact the user experience differently. The question is how to know the way a colour will respond on a wall with surety, when it has never before been applied on this particular surface, in the same quantity, same illumination and same harmony with the other room features before. Science is progressing and there are some emerging studies designers and specifiers are guided towards to consider during the design process but we are some way away from knowing how to account for all the variables in every different project worked on. One way of working around the issue as a starting point when it comes to final colour adjustments, is to hold off painting walls until the interior lighting has been installed and switched on. The lighting quality and rendering can change a paint, wall or floor finish colour dramatically.

Working with contractors and decorators on site to conduct sample patches on each coloured wall can allow the final tweaking to hues and tones and make the difference between harmony and all other results. Start working from the longest lead-time materials and then the shortest lead times to adjust the harmony right near project completion.

The colour combinations and tonality in the work of Josef Albers is extremely relevant to understanding how colours could affect each other when combined in different proportions and ways.

In a study by Xiao, Luo, Li and Hong[9] looking to resolve the difference in perceived effect between the colour on a small swatch card and that which is seen when applied on an interior wall, it was found that colours appear lighter and more colourful when applied on the room walls.

The study also shared work by Monica Billger who observed how colours will appear stronger in colourfulness, higher in blackness values, and hues will alter based on lighting approach in each location. So the size and location of a coloured or textured material will affect how it will be perceived within the space.

We all instinctively respond to design harmony. Colour, shape and links to emotions are evident wherever we are and their impact is immediate and constant. How well we select and use these for a positive outcome which supports occupants is an opportunity we have.

Small patch of colour	Higher chroma	Less black
Wall of colour	Direct bright light	Lighter chroma/ High blackness levels
Wall of colour	Indirect low light	Darker chroma/ Higher blackness levels

FIGURE 3: 35
Relationship between chroma, light and perception of colour

FIGURE 3: 35
The columns in this space look a different colour from different angles due to daylight illumination and reflection of other colours surrounding them

Putting design for wellbeing into practice

This chapter shares some insights on how colour can affect occupants and why it is important. Putting this information into our day-to-day practice can improve the way colour will support occupant wellbeing through their use in interiors. Below we share some applications for clients and designers to consider:

1 Consider the personalities each group of colour has and select the one that will align most with the User Profile characteristics of the interior's occupants.

2 Define the predominant tasks occurring within each space and select a predominant colour hue, and the colour palette that will support the activities and the levels of comfort or stimulation sought.

3 Consider how the colour palette will be best applied on the most prominent or impactful surfaces of the interior.

4 Consider how the light settings and colour will influence the way colours will be perceived in place. Make sure the lighting designer, supplier or electrical engineer designing the lighting is aware of the colour palette and that you are coordinating the issues.

CHAPTER 10
Repetition and patterns

The proportions of an object, or of a surface's dimensions, and of those between two or more relating objects within a space itself, are also known to affect how we feel and what we experience in a space.

The simple act of repeating shapes within a composition is seen to improve judgements of 'liking' through improved visual fluency. The complexity or simplicity of the composition, and its positive or negative content, are known to require consideration in application. An initially displeasing shape, or theme content, can be seen after repeated exposure as attractive.

When a feature is repeated vertically and has a generally abstract composition that is repeated within it, it can have a less favourable impact on space users than a repeated composition that has favourable prototypical shapes and content. Vertical repetition is seen to have a higher ease in fluency processing, which is important considering that the human eye views mostly on the horizontal plane. What does arise from all this, is the question of whether there is an overall proportion and content relationship that supports liking through process fluency. By creating likeable interior spaces we will be supporting wellbeing through beauty and also creating harmony between the users' needs and conditioning and the spaces they occupy.

Could the fact that the golden ratio, and the sheer repeated exposure to these proportions, and where in most cases they are associated with positive values of human behaviour and the ideal life, be an explanation of why the classic design approach is broadly perceived as attractive? The golden section theorists will have a field day with such an attempt to simplify this much loved and debated subject to such a theory, but these days we will find it hard to distinguish between the two effects.

FIGURE 3: 37 AND 3: 38 (OPPOSITE)
Examples of repetition within a composition

We introduce shapes in an interior simply by creating the space or adding products, so it is inevitably an issue we must deal with on each occasion. The effect of shapes on occupants will happen on two main levels: the less dominant 'background' shapes and the feature and eye-catching ones. Both will impact how a person is feeling just by walking past them, or sitting and facing them for a length of time. Based on the science now made available, and our experiences from industry, we can understand how to best match shapes, with occupants and tasks, to harmonise with their needs.

FIGURE 3: 39
The Scarab fabric is from a hand printed linen collection that is produced by Ivo Prints in London under license to The Royal Botanic Gardens, Kew. The design was created to represent the biodiversity of nature within the collection and to serve as a conversational piece. Scarabs are very auspicious and chosen in this case to represent all beetles and the very essential work that they carry out

CHAPTER 11

Shapes, volumes and proportions

Shapes 81 • Contours and angles 81 • Symbolism of shapes 84
Proportion of shapes and patterns 86 • Fibonacci sequence and
the golden ratio 89 • Volumes of space 91 • Ceiling height 92

Shapes

The shape of an object or material finish can represent an abstract idea or speak to our basic human instinct. We are affected by the lack of shapes as much by the proliferation of them, and by the allocation of shapes in specific spaces and on specific objects that will support our wellbeing, or not. Over time certain consistent shapes have adopted wider meanings and are used to represent these rather than for the properties these shapes have of themselves. There are ways to use shapes and patterns to support wellbeing and performance and the following sections will elaborate how.

FIGURE 3: 40
Circular shapes and timber feature on the ceiling of the female WCs of the V&A Museum in London

Contours and angles

There is a natural inclination for humans to favour items that have curves (contours) than ones with sharper angular shapes or points as seen in studies by Bar and Neta (2006 and 2007). There is also research that indicates a different behaviour of brain activity between exposure to curved and angular objects.[10]

The propensity of favouring curved objects has been attributed to human nature and psychology. We are drawn to objects that are familiar to us and nothing is more so than the female human body, full of curved parts. This response is also said to be linked to our sense of security as we associate the female form of mother with safety as infants.

FIGURE 3: 41
Contours as details to furniture

FIGURE 3: 42 AND 3: 43
Angular shapes in meeting rooms can increase stimulation

CHAPTER 11 • SHAPES, VOLUMES AND PROPORTIONS

81

FIGURE 3: 44, 3: 45, 3: 46 AND 3: 47
There is some evidence for improved patient experience when exposed to 'flowing' images of nature

Humans have higher alert levels when there is a potential for danger – something sharp, dangerous or perceived aggressive. Our reaction is processed through a part of our brains called the 'amygdala' and is the area where fear is processed. The processing does not factor in preferences but reacts purely based on perceived potential threat. As curves generally do not pose a threat they do not raise internal alarms and are, by immediate reaction, liked more. The principle does not apply on its own for objects to which we have an existing emotional attachment or association with – this is seen to override the amygdala's reaction, but to what extent this occurs needs to be studied further. The overall study results indicate that by adding curved shapes in, for example, a dentist's waiting and treatment rooms, may be less influential than when entering a new hotel

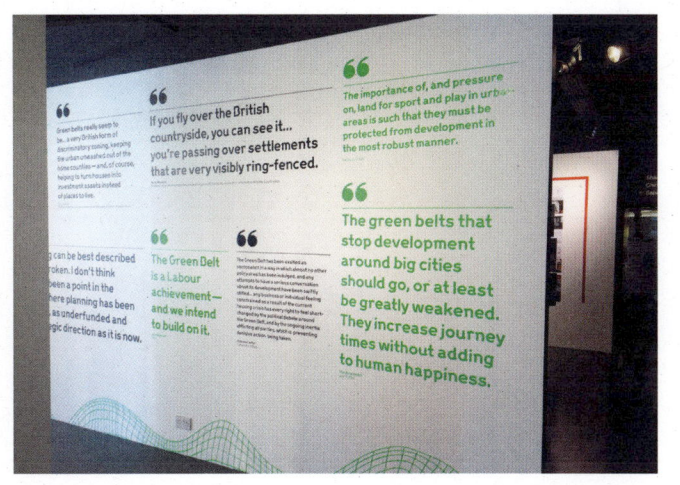

FIGURE 3: 48, 3: 49 AND 3: 50
Angular shapes in meeting rooms can increase stimulation

lobby full of soft lines as there are more likely some existing emotional attachment at the dentist's, but not with the newly visited hotel. The question is whether the curved shapes in the dentist's interiors will reduce to a noticeable degree the stressful state some patients experience, rather than aggravating it through a predominant use of sharp lines and angles. Healthcare environments have shown a propensity for improved patient experience and healing when exposed to features or images of nature – these are typically 'flowing' and have many soft shapes.

The combination of contours and angles therefore in objects, to which we don't have an existing emotional connection to, will appeal. The decision of how much of a shape, product or interior space's features must be made up of contours or angles must be based on the expected activities intended to take place and the amount of comfort or stimulation desired. If for example, an interior space is intended as a working environment where focused analytical work is to be performed, then an increase of angles is likely to support the required occupant state of alertness that is supporting the cognitive activity, hence the person's performance and wellbeing. If the interior is intended as a welcoming room or relaxation space, a higher degree of contours and soft lines is expected to lower alert levels and allow body and mind to be at ease; again supporting a state of comfort and wellbeing. In both cases note that it is a *relative* level and not a complete makeup of purely angles or contours. In a workplace for example we are still aiming for comfort as an enabler of concentration; too much alertness will conflict with the space objectives.

The shapes are very much one part of what will impact an occupant; shape colour, the combination between them and illumination on and of them, are also impacting and work dependently with each other.

The decision of how much of a shape, product or interior space's features must be made up of contours or angles must be based on the expected activities intended to take place and the amount of comfort or stimulation desired.

FIGURE 3: 51, 3: 52, 3: 53 AND 3: 54
Shapes acquire different properties with different colours making them evolve from soft fluid to hard stimulating influencers

CHAPTER 11 • SHAPES, VOLUMES AND PROPORTIONS

83

Symbolism of shapes

There are associations with contoured and angled shapes that are symbolic, reflecting national and traditional cultures. The historic, and in many cases religious, propensity to represent earthly and heavenly physical representations through the use of a square and circle can be seen in many instances in the built environment. This could be attributed to early instances of 'social norms' i.e. one person after another started using it in a specific context and then as a symbol, and through repetition it simply became a normal way to communicate such a message or context, or it could be attributed to other lines of thought which look at the links between energy and other earthly phenomena related with life on earth and human existence. Such examples can be found from Swiss psychoanalyst Carl Jung's psychological interpretation of the archetypes and their link to the cosmos, to the Chinese culture's fervent belief of the links between the square, circle and triangle, to man's existence on earth. Whether one believes in spirituality or not, the explanation to these links or not, the fact these associations exist in many cultures requires designs to respect and consider them carefully in application.

Carl Jung's approach during his later years suggested links between patterns of psychology to those found physically. He suggested this by visually representing them in parallels using the electromagnetic spectrum alongside biological and non-biological organisms, a comparison that NASA has also used in their work. To further question his perceived links between human psyche and the physical environment is of keen importance when considering avenues of further research. This work could respond to questions looking at the deepest levels of our being, going beyond ideas of social norms, emotional attachment and physical comfort. Jung wrote in his book *The Structure and Dynamics of the Psyche* the following:

FIGURE 3: 55 AND 3: 56
Shapes acquire different properties with different colours, evolving from soft fluid to hard stimulating influencers

'All the most powerful ideas in history go back to archetypes... This is particularly true of religious ideas, but the central concepts of science, philosophy, and ethics are no exception to this rule. In their present form they are variants of archetypal ideas created by consciously applying and adapting these ideas to reality. For it is the function of consciousness, not only to recognize and assimilate the external world through the gateway of the senses, but to translate into visible reality the world within us.'

So how does the external physical world reflect the 'world within' (ideas, emotions, creativity, etc) and, could it support all our aspects of wellbeing? This book is aiming to touch upon the path of where this opportunity lies.

Old philosophical traditions suggest that the physical environment reflects our true selves, our own consciousness. For example, according to oriental symbolism, the circle, triangle, and square forms represent all things in the universe. This can be seen by many historical forms within the environments of Ancient Greece, Chinese and Egyptian empires, through basic structures such as monuments, pyramids or other burial forms, plus ruling and religious objects such as the United Kingdom Queen's sceptre (a globe) and the yin and yang form (two halves of a complete entity that form a circle), and art. A very exact representation of the concept is created in the Kennin-ji temple in Kyoto,

FIGURE 3: 57
Sunrise by Jeffery Courtney

FIGURE 3: 58 AND 3: 59
Shapes acquire different properties with different colours, evolving from soft fluid to hard stimulating influencers

CHAPTER 11 • SHAPES, VOLUMES AND PROPORTIONS

85

where there is a garden called the *'Circle Triangle Square Garden'*. The shape of the circularly arrayed gravel, the triangular tree and square water well, all tie in to manifest the cultural belief that they are the fundamental shapes of the universe. We have seen a copy of similar settings in the west, in areas wishing to imply calmness, relaxation and spiritual balance, but without the harmonised cultural belief these can only serve their purpose so far. The question arises of whether a space with such *imitations* can develop a relationship with its audience, considering the potential for disharmony with other features of the interior such as colours and air quality.

In fact the bias for curved objects and the combination of contoured and angled shapes, can suggest a much stronger link with humans' natural setting and innate sense of existence rather than symbolic representations of earth and heaven. Associating a higher feeling of comfort which can allow us to support a heightened levels of wellbeing could explain its long-standing use in such contexts. This suggests that our wellbeing is primarily affected through the impact of the physical environment.

FIGURE 3: 60
Dome in cathedral, Rome

Proportion of shapes and patterns

The current systematic research on explaining the links between shapes, patterns and their proportion in application is in its infancy. There are some indicators to direct our selection more or less towards an informed direction, but more insights from the sales practices and approaches is also, from our own experiences as customers, a good indicator of response.

What we are after is to know how the use of specific proportions in design can support occupant wellbeing. We know there are preferences humans have shown to some, but when and how are these occurring for us to understand when and how to repeat?

First, let's look into some basic thoughts around the issue of proportions. The ancient Greek development of mathematical ideas was a source of influence on the Islamic approach to geometry. Found in the extensive library and online database of Islamic art and geometry by David Wade, there are records that historic Islamic brethren built on the Pythagorean principles of religion and philosophy, to communicate a united view of humans and the world we live in. Ancient Greek philosopher and mathematician Pythagoras expanded on Platonic views of 'the self' and its context within nature through the use of numbers, shapes and proportion. This was pursued as Platonists believed that fundamental beauty and morality of beings, and thus wellbeing, are intrinsically linked to specific shapes and proportions. Islamic art has become an expression of the philosophic principles of the 'ideal or true self' and seeks to express this philosophy through symmetry, proportion, geometric patterning and eternal qualities in artistic compositions.

A circle was considered by philosophers as a symbol of the 'perfect self' and thus complete, perfect and beautiful. All other triangles, squares and polyhedra are concepts of the physical world, temporal and based on the time they exist, so incomplete and imperfect. As Platonic ideas are the basis of thought and law in Western culture, we should perhaps consider further the links between Islamic patterns and notions of wellbeing, and also reflect on the things the world's cultures have in common rather than differences.[11]

Following this trail of thought and reflecting on patterns of nature itself, we will be able to reflect our integral human physical links within it. By introducing proportions of shapes and patterns like those found in a field, a landscape or the sea, we are introducing Biophilic metaphors and reminders, which by consequence provide a relaxing and grounding effect. If proportions in nature look strange, we tend to pay attention as something is disrupting them. This approach is also used in design: create disproportion in the array of proportions which seem un-natural and you attract the attention of people. How much disruption though is enough to attract attention but not scare? This

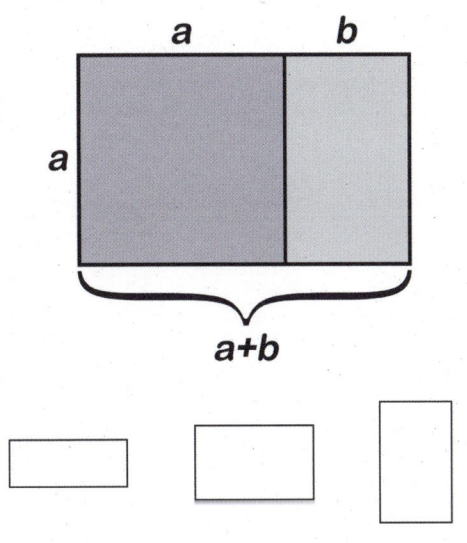

FIGURE 3: 61 AND 3: 62
The golden proportions

FIGURE 3: 63
Islamic patterns at the Grand Mosque of Paris, France

CHAPTER 11 • SHAPES, VOLUMES AND PROPORTIONS

87

will be different for each audience and user group the design is being created for.

In practice, when we are in the design process and selecting floor and wall finishes and considering the proportions and patterns these will be installed with, our selection approach could consider supporting the wellbeing of occupants, and if so how that may be done. Hopefully the project has created User Profiles during the briefing process and the design team knows if the creative process needs to embrace biophilic patterns more or less, and if there is a need to reflect ideas of balance and symmetry, either because it reflects brand attributes or supports the tasks being undertaken in a space, the patterns can follow the natural proportions to a lesser or greater extent as required.

For example, if the design process is being undertaken for a school's classroom where concentration, stability and comfort are required, then working with proportions of the golden section for shapes, and using patterns found in nature, will support the teacher's and students' comfort needs. In another example, if a design is being undertaken for a start-up tech company which is defined by innovation and wants to create at the same time a sense of trust to investors and the market, patterns and proportions in their workplace need to support wellbeing and cultural brand symbiosis, which will be interpreted in the design by using general volumes and shapes along the biophilic, balance and symmetry lines, but within them and on them, also apply asymmetry and rectangular patterns to stimulate and reflect movement and disruption.

FIGURE 3: 64, 3: 65, 3: 66, 3: 37, 3: 68 AND 3: 69
Pattern and proportion in nature

Fibonacci sequence and the golden ratio

The fact that many proportions and patterns found in nature follow the Fibonacci sequence and golden ratio or angle, supports the use of these as guides for creating patterns that are evolutions and separate creations by the human hand.

The relationship between these proportions is close to those found with the golden ratio, where ϕ (phi)[12] is approximately 1.618. The Parthenon is frequently used as an example of having an elevation, and various sculptured elements on it, which come close to the proportions of the golden ratio. Another equally well-known but more contemporary application of the proportion is seen on Villa Savoye by Le Corbusier and The Homewood by Patrick Gwynne (a home designed and built by Patrick Gwynne for his family and lived in by himself). The homes reflect in a perfect way the use of proportion and repetition, in addition to connection with nature and other varying details of good design. The result is to experience a very comfortable and elating journey through the main living areas, especially in The Homewood; the proportions of the living room's length, depth and height follow the golden proportion and create a well-balanced and comfortable feel when in it. If one assumes the dining room wall was removed, it can be easily imagined how the proportions and effect would be more 'stressed' and create a very different feeling for occupiers.

The Fibonacci sequence, and proportions that derive from it, have a link with the golden ratio as found by renaissance astronomer Johannes Kepler (1571–1630).

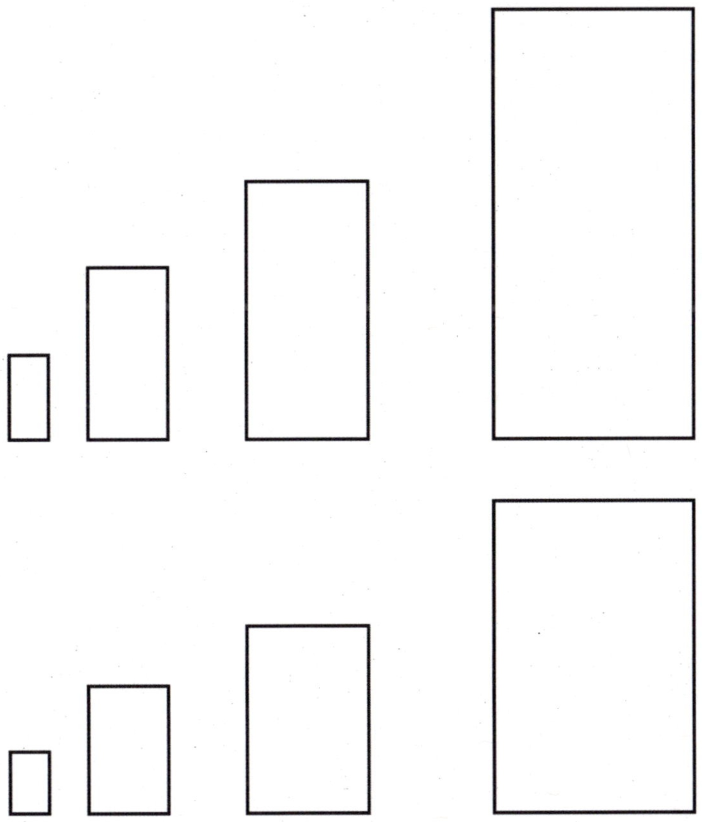

FIGURE 3: 70 AND 3: 71 Rectangles on the top line have extreme proportions and the shapes on the bottom line follow the golden proportions

FIGURE 3: 72, 3: 73, 3: 74 AND 3: 75
Shapes and patterns depicting the golden proportion or Fibonacci sequence

He proved that the golden ratio is the limit of the ratio of consecutive Fibonacci numbers.[13]

Fibonacci is also found in phyllotaxy: the arrangement of leaves on a stem and branches on a tree. The patterns of distribution for branching systems of rivers, lightning and trees are identical in so much as they rollout their shape and system in the most efficient way. David Wade in his book *Symmetry: The Ordering Principle* (2006) states that *'[systems] are the simplest way to connect every part of a given area using the shortest overall distance (or least work).'*

All this would suggest that if we are looking to design an interior that supports wellbeing through a high Biophilic and nature-linked way, then selecting furniture and features whose dimensions and proportions emulate these would be right. Also, fabrics and any other patterned surface could adopt these patterns and be selected for supporting innate links to nature.

Volumes of space

Spatial volumes and their effect on occupant behaviour are dependent on the shapes and proportions with which they are created, as much as the flow from one space to another and the user experience created from the relative difference between them. One is a static experience and the other a dynamic one as a user moves from space to space, or even within areas of one space which has varying features.

Below we look into studies showing the effect different sizes of space have on the improved performance results of specific tasks, and which, in addition to the refuge and prospect environmental psychology effect, come into play when setting the size and sequence of volumes in the design process of interiors.

Experiential symmetry is one of the effects that designers could choose to follow or contrast when planning an interior. This approach requires Harmony. This does not mean that all things are the same but that there is a common thread of connection, which will be a thread running through the spaces. It is quite poetically described, through the Principle of Similitude in Similitude by D'Arcy Wentworth Thompson in 1917.

'...The waves of the sea, the little ripples on the shore, the sweeping curve of the sandy bay between the headlands, the outline of the hills, the shape of the clouds, all these are so many riddles of form, so many problems of morphology, and all of them the physicist can more or less easily read and adequately solve: solving them by reference to their antecedent phenomena, in the material system mechanical significance; but it is on another plane of thought from the physicist's that we contemplate their intrinsic harmony and perfection, and "see that they are good"'. Nor is it otherwise with the material forms of living things. Cell tissue, shell and bone, leaf and flower, are so many portions of matter, and it is in obedience to the laws of physics that their articles have been moved, moulded and conformed. Scales which include light-years, parsecs, Angstrom units, or atomic and sub-atomic magnitudes, belong to other orders of things and other principles of cognition.'

'The scale of human observation and experience lies within the narrow bounds of inches, feet or miles, all measured in terms drawn from our own selves or our own doings.'

All features relating to 'shapes' come into play when they are mixed and combined to create a three-dimensional interior space: the room, a chair, fitted shelving, a round pendant, square rugs etc. Shapes are never experienced on their own but rather as a combination, against other things, and as a *dynamic experience* rather than a *static* event.

FIGURE 3: 76
Hallway in the National Portrait Gallery, London

Ceiling height

A study by Meyers-Levy and Zhu[14] on a retail setting with real consumers, showed that low or high ceilings influenced respondents in a different way, and in different types of thought processes. The types of human processes observed are also relevant to many other instances in day-to-day life, so the response to the ceilings and effect in behaviour could be considered more universal. For example, if we are designing a school study area or workplace quiet rooms, where in both cases occupants are undertaking concentration tasks, both space types will be appropriate with lower ceilings. Higher ceiling and space volumes support creative thinking and wider conceptual cognitive tasks.

Nikravan Mofrad[15] studied the effect various ceiling height norms had on residential occupants' perceived comfort. The feedback was about heights ranging from 2100–4000mm and observed that the majority found most comfortable the 2700–2800mm level. Too high or too low was not liked. This would be relating to the spatial volume created in each instance, which would have given a feeling of 'squeezing' in or out the side walls and creating a high stimulating effect taking occupants into the discomfort danger zone as discussed in Part 1.

In spaces such as reception areas, event spaces and lounges in hotels or residential spaces, there may be a desire to provide a specific experience to those entering. Part of these experiences typically is to impress, welcome or direct behaviour such as visual attention or walking path. Working with the size of spatial volume leads us in two directions, these are referred to as the cathedral or chapel effect. If you would like to make people feel small and that there is a larger machine managing everything for you, then working with tall ceilings will support this intent. If you want to support focused activity thinking and separation between parties then lower ceilings and spatial volumes should be considered. Wellbeing is supported when the combination of a spatial volume is aligned with the type of

FIGURE 3: 77 AND 3: 78
Entrance spaces for a university and theatre utilise high ceilings implying high aspirations and creative spirit

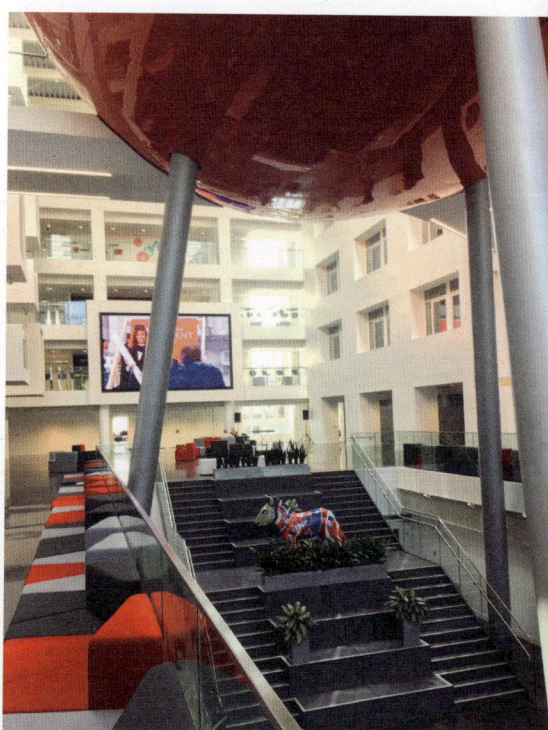

people and their activities when using it, acknowledging what is likely to be their frame of mind and feelings upon entry and working to support their wellbeing from that point.

Considering the shapes and proportions that would support occupant wellbeing, designers must start by deciding on what part of the scale is the desired effect on occupants between the following:
- comfort – discomfort
- tradition/static – contemporary/evolving
- safe/calm – challenging/stimulating.

In summary, the golden proportions are found attractive when occupants of a space are looking for certain reassuring messages to be expressed: safety, calm, tradition, non-stressed relationships and clarity of process. Opposite to this, if the design is located in a place where the occupants wish to change how things are flowing and evolve what is seen as a 'social norm', then designs implying a break from calm should be used more appropriately.

The presence of symmetry and balance seem to be much more viewed as aesthetically pleasing than the presence of an exact proportion. A consistent proportion unfolded throughout a design scheme gives rise to consistency and order, and makes a design coherent and thus increases its attraction.

Putting design for wellbeing into practice

This chapter shares some insights on how shapes, proportions and volumes can affect occupants and why it is important to consider them when designing spaces to support wellbeing. Putting this information into day-to-day practice can improve the way designs will support occupant wellbeing through interiors. Below we share some applications for clients and designers to consider:

1 Consider the character and cultural objectives of the occupants and organisation occupying the spaces and select the degree to which they seek to express tradition or evolution.

2 Define the predominant tasks occurring within each space and select the predominant shapes that will support the activities and the levels of comfort or stimulation sought. Are creative or logical thinking tasks being undertaken and where in the interior?

3 Consider how the light settings and colours of the shapes will influence the way shapes will be perceived in place.

4 Consider the symbolic importance of the local culture or that of visitors.

5 Consider the need to reflect nature either obviously or metaphorically throughout the shapes of the interior.

6 Consider the user experience intended from space to space and how the spatial volumes and space plans support comfort of users. When specifying the amount of shapes and angles within a concept, designers need to establish where the point of 'wellbeing' sits between comfort and discomfort. Ask if occupants are going to be very active or require a more sedate surrounding.

CHAPTER 12
Symbolism

Shapes can be symbolic in their use; whether that is to nudge occupants to 'walk on' instead of stand still, or nudge a specific behaviour to happen in a certain way or to symbolise and express themes such as constancy, movement or a sense of adventure. The effect of a shape will be symbolic due to resemblance of a natural or manmade item or because it has emotional weighting due to our association with it personally or historically.

Certain shapes and colours have different cultural links and symbolism, and further studies need to be conducted to record social norms around them that can assist designers working internationally to follow, or evolve within context, a culture specific design. For example, using dark green in an interior where occupants follow a Muslim way of life should be carefully placed as the colour is sacred, or using purple in the UK which is associated with royalty, or black in Greece which is mourning and so on.

The use of certain shapes as symbols or signs can be seen over time in historic cultures and present countries. Like dialects, shapes can 'suit' people in a specific area inside a country more than another and knowing which to use is based on harmonising and using them effectively and with an informed objective.

Mark Riddle in his paper 'Circle and Square: Explorations in Symbology' (2010), which focuses mainly on the symbolism of the circle and square, notes *'A symbol is commonly defined as an arbitrary sign that has acquired a conventional significance, something visible that by association and convention represents something else that is invisible.'* We will find millions of religious physical representations of the earthly and heavenly/spiritual relationship shown as a square (earthly) and a circle (heavenly). These are present in every religion or long surviving culture but also are found to have been used in similar opposing but complementing relationships, for other applications. Riddle suggests as examples the graduation gown and square black hat to symbolise earthly knowledge and a white gown and round hat to symbolise heavenly, which leads one to consider the Catholic Pope's dress code for the latter. If we refer to the interior design

FIGURE 3:79
Image of Gyro table by Brodie Neill

of the respective spaces the principles tend to follow in a similar approach.

We will not list the full definition of symbols that have existed and are used currently as that is an extremely well referenced area and others more specialist in interpreting them can be referenced, but what is of particular interest is the acknowledgement of the effect these have on individuals and wider communities on their behaviour and way of life.

As we become a more connected world with blended cultures, we need to pay attention to the assumed symbolic meanings of historic cultures as they evolve based on current beliefs and meanings. This brings us back to the fundamental meanings found within nature, where we see many links between nature-reflecting interiors and objects and those found within cultures. Something sharp can be natural as much as something curvy; proportions and context though will be specific to a location and culture.

In his book *Symbol, Pattern and Symmetry: The Cultural Significance of Structure*[16] Michael Hann shares the views of J. L. Fischer in *'examining the relationship between social stratification in societies and variations in art style and, on examining the distribution of design elements in works of art proposed positive associations between visual repetition, empty space and symmetry in design and egalitarian societies, and between enclosed figures and hierarchical society.'* He shares the views of anthropologist Levi Strauss who drew relationships between structural characteristics of artwork and structural aspects of societies.

In each case, the context of a symbol is core to the way it will affect people; he notes that symbols have substantially different meanings in different cultures, but also within the same ones if used under different contexts. And tying this up with Harry R. Silver's observation on the subject of considering symbolism in the visual arts, he explained that *'context often clarifies a symbol's significance where several meanings are possible.'* However obvious it may seem to make this acknowledgement, it is important to pause and highlight this fact:

> *'...the use of shapes and meanings can drive the behaviour of people. Knowing when and how to use them to ensure they are in harmony and in context is key to support occupant wellbeing.'*

> *'Examining the relationship between social stratification in societies and variations in art style and, on examining the distribution of design elements in works of art proposed positive associations between visual repetition, empty space and symmetry in design and egalitarian societies, and between enclosed figures and hierarchical society.'* Fisher

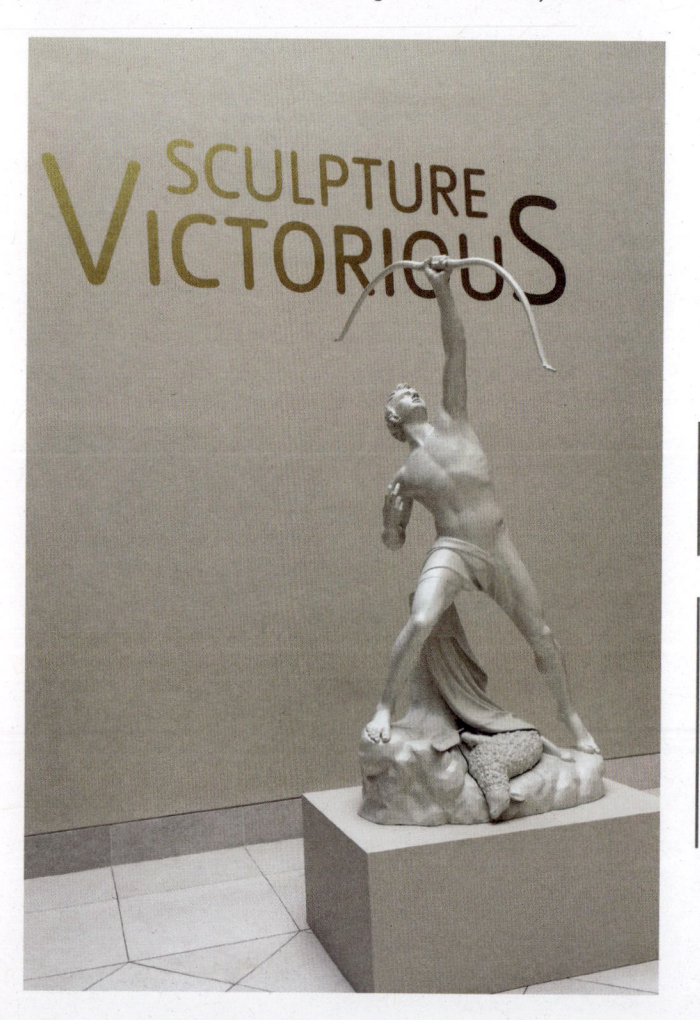

FIGURE 3: 80
Sculpture Victorious exhibit at Tate Britain, London

CHAPTER 13
The use of artwork in interiors

A specialist explaining things in their own words... 100

As quoted by many a wise person, there is no survival value to friendship but the reason to survive. And so with art. You can survive and do reasonably well in living a life in an interior with no art, but at some point there is no purpose to it, and that's where the purpose of art comes in, so to speak, for the interior. It is the point at which an interior space is not just being less mean but actually adding value to people's life for the sake of flourishing.

Mark Rothko, in *The Artist's Reality*[17], summarised the purpose of an artist's job and the objective of the artwork once it is completed. It is his theory that each artist is seeking to express the truth of their time. With 'truth' he refers to existential issues and what is understood to make up a person's life, to understand who they are and the world they live in. How do people find purpose in life who may be hardworking goal setters? For what purpose? Why are we creating all these interiors for example? Isn't architecture enough to put a roof over our heads and keep the weather out? Why do we live the life that we live and for whom, why and what, are some of the issues that art can deal with.

FIGURE 3: 81
Circular artworks can help people reflect on existential questions...

Placing interpretations of similar ideas into spaces that we live in provides a supportive and guiding platform to deal with day-to-day challenges as they arise. Whether it is a work crisis/success, a family issue or a situation in a leisure setting, there is always scope to reflect on our thoughts and behaviour with the aim of bettering it and living a happier life.

Our wellbeing is first and foremost dependent on our emotional and mental state. Introducing artwork which reflects issues occupants can relate to and need support on will be fundamental to creating an interior which supports their wellbeing.

> *'Art holds out the promise of inner wholeness.'*[18] Alain de Botton, philosopher and modern day thinker.

Alain de Botton and John Armstrong propose the purpose of art within therapy itself, to serve specific functions[19]. I summarise these within the following functions:

- Help with remembering, seeing more of what actually is rather than silos of information
- Gives hope, generates optimism
- Deals with sorrow and feelings of sadness
- Establishes a balance within ourselves, provides perspective
- Helps to understand our selves, the way we behave, think and feel about the world around us
- Helps us grow as beings following its assistance in self-knowledge and guides us on esoteric intangible issues that help us be better beings
- Allows us to appreciate situations and life, what we actually already have, increases our feeling of happiness.

From a practical point and looking at the process of the art issue, the first step to take is making sure this item is actually on the design meeting's agenda and is included in the project's budget. Practical issues that need to be considered in advance also include structural modifications to support a piece if it happens to be large and weighty, lighting design to support illumination of the pieces, the floor plan to ensure the required physical space is provided – especially if it involves live performances such as choir singing, musical bands, theatre or dancing. In such

FIGURE 3: 82
Art can be considered as an application for every surface of an interior, including ceilings

instances the acoustics of the space and the floor finishes must also be considered to support these activities happening successfully. There are a few instances that such efforts are introduced with good faith only to be part implemented which causes a lukewarm result and are then as a whole seen ineffective and not repeated.

Budgeting for artwork is closely linked to defining its return value. As stated, it has no survival value but makes life worth living, happily. Putting a price tag on 'a life that is worth living' can be rather challenging but very relevant to designing for wellbeing. But, not as challenging as working with a team that don't comprehend this issue to start with, which is for the most part a designer's biggest challenge. The market value of artwork is surrounded in the slightly murky waters of commercially-driven collectors and buyers who purchase art as investments rather than the 'truth' that the piece is trying to reflect. Acknowledging this but still looking for some value metrics, one can refer to painting sales at auctions which in the last decade alone have exceeded $US100 million for single paintings by artists such as Rothko, Basquiat, Klimt, Picasso and others. Looking at the opposite end of the spectrum, pieces in a local town market or side street gallery go for as little as £200 for a small canvas painting or sculpture. Monetary value is not the place to look for a definition of arts' real value to a person or a society. As with the argument on using a country's annual GDP metric as a mark of progress (a natural disaster increases GDP, but we are worse off as a society), so with art; its value measure must be sought in evidence of the betterment of life rather than on considering only cost.

A specialist explaining things in their own words...

Bridging the gap between the art world, which understands its value, and the world of spaces are a few art specialists such as Victoria Hume. Victoria, an artist herself, worked for a number of years within the healthcare sector. She outlines the approach and effect of art in a hospital and generously shares her insights.

Art in hospitals, by Victoria Hume

In terms of public buildings, the hospital perhaps has a unique relationship with wellbeing. Cleanly separating wellbeing from health is an almost impossible task. While a person living with chronic disease may be said to have poor health, however, their wellbeing may fluctuate (as with anyone) between dreadful and excellent. The environment's capacity to 'heal' may be questionable, but its impact on wellbeing – something also closely aligned with the capacity and desire for recovery[20] – is unassailable.

Over the centuries, hospital design has been subject to an astonishing variation in quality. Far from the aspirational architecture of philanthropically funded Victorian sanitaria, or even earlier buildings like the Royal Hospital in Greenwich, co-designed (for free) by Wren and Hawksmoor, much late 20th-century hospital design suggested the creation of warehouses for sickness of one kind or another. Hospitals were built (cheaply) in a way which reinforced the need to avoid them. Nor is this problem confined to the UK. In a spot test at a presentation in Johannesburg recently, 50% of my audience raised their hands when asked: 'Who doesn't like going into hospitals?' We agreed that the places have a reputation for contagion – both literal and in some way existential, as if one could 'catch' physical or psychological vulnerability, could pick up a nasty strain of mortality by lingering in the hallways too long.

Years of underinvestment in health infrastructure had led to a pretty degraded environment in the average late 1990s UK hospital. In the years since then, however, things have largely changed for the better. Thanks to the interventions of organisations

FIGURE 3: 83
Common area glass window artwork at Charing Cross Hospital in Hammersmith, London

like the Commission for Architecture in the Built Environment (CABE)[21] (sadly one of the first government quangos to bite the dust in 2011), and many others, the aspired-to hospital (if not always the real thing) is no longer a breeze-block affair on a ring road, but a place that might be an architect's masterpiece. Maggie's Centres, for example, have done much to elevate the status of healthcare buildings, through creating spaces which consider wellbeing in all its subtleties. And huge projects like the Evelina London Children's Hospital have shored up the notion of the hospital building as an architectural showpiece. But behind these inspiring examples is a huge swathe of work being undertaken within existing, often compromised buildings, often on shoestring budgets, to change the environment of care through the use of the arts.

This itself is part of a wider movement to bring the arts and health together – supported by organisations such as the National Alliance for Arts, Health & Wellbeing (England)[22] – which embraces a wide range of disciplines: the arts therapies, participatory work of all kinds in communities and institutions alike, the medical humanities and art/science collaborations.

A significant part of this movement is the growing acceptance of the concept of arts in healthcare buildings – from hospices to GP surgeries. This chapter is intended to give a few examples of what hospital art can be, and why.

In 2005, John Tusa (then the managing director of the Barbican Centre) said that

> *Art is about searching and sometimes finding; it defines pain and sorrow and sometimes softens them; it is about exploring confusion and defining disorder; ... it is universal though it may be attacked as exclusive; it is diverse and not homogenised; it resists categories and makes connections across them.*[23]

There is much in here that makes sense of art in healthcare buildings.

The concept of softening pain and sorrow, for example, is central to considering certain areas of the hospital. Visual art has a real value in spaces where families are told of a loved one's death, in viewing rooms, or in the anterooms next to them. Imagine a box-like space with magnolia walls, plastic chairs and no pictures, and then imagine somewhere with decent furniture and an original work of art of some kind. It is all about indicating care.

But hospitals are not all about endings – and as in all of life the arts have different roles to play at different times, and in different places: 'Just to say how much I enjoyed the art on display. It was cheering and stimulating and especially appreciated at a fraught time as my daughter was in ... for an operation. Seeing the beautiful exhibition on the way in sent me up to the ward in an optimistic mood each day.'[24]

Returning to Tusa, art 'is diverse and not homogenised.' What palpably does not work in hospitals is the careless reproduction: the endless fade-to-blue Monet posters which were for some time the art of choice in hospital (cheap, safe, filling) seem now almost worse than nothing. Rather than breaking up space, giving us landmarks and points of interest, the Impressionists (ironically enough) have been forced actively to contribute to institutionalisation.

And the institution is a place we are conditioned to fear: a 1984 place, where our identity is steamrollered by the machine. In hospitals, we lose many of the trappings of this identity: control over our own bodies, for one, but also the stuff we collect about us that reinforces our sense of self: clothes, linen, books, music, watches... And what's more, the buildings themselves seem designed to lose us. People ask directions at reception and have disappeared again within ten yards. Often each floor repeats each other floor in shape, colour, and size. Often the signage is out of date – departments move more quickly than the 'wayfinding' budget allows. Staff rush around emitting complicated urgency while patients and families stand still in front of panels, dazed by vocabulary: nuclear medicine, echo testing, pacing, histopathology, immunology... The building seems designed for everyone except the person who most needs to be there.

The arts resist this loss of self, in many ways.

Part of this is practical, providing something recognisable (turn left at the sculpture, the picture of a cow, the piano). Another part is in providing something upon which it is safe to have an opinion: for many, some of the discomfort of hospital is the fear of rocking the boat, of putting your overworked doctor off you and compromising your treatment. Medicine has not yet evolved to the point where the default is a relationship of co-learning between physician and patient. We go in, feeling bad, and intimate stuff is done to us by strangers. And so perhaps to be able to say 'my child could do that' about a piece of abstract art in your ward goes some way to restoring a sense of control, dignity, capacity to judge.

A third part is best explained by a participant in a recent workshop at Royal Brompton Hospital:

My illness only existed when I went through the double-doors of the hospital, because that's when they started describing it ...

And then I met this doctor, and he came in – I had my phone with me ... he started scrolling though looking at my paintings, and we started talking about painting, and we didn't talk about clinical stuff at all ... and I thought, there we go! That's successful. And I didn't feel as ill – you know you just don't feel as ill when people are talking about something you're interested in rather than talking about what you're suffering from.

Occasionally, research has attempted to assess exactly which kinds of art work in medical settings. Thus in a study assessing the impact of music on changes in heart rate and heart rate variability, Trappe (2010) concludes that:

The greatest benefit on health is visible with classical music and meditation music, whereas heavy metal music or techno are not only ineffective but possibly dangerous and can lead to stress and/or life-threatening arrhythmias. The music of many composers most effectively improves quality of life, will increase health and probably prolong life, particularly music by Bach, Mozart or Italian composers.[25]

Trappe's study is based around an assessment of rhythms in the body mimicking those in music. But his conclusion goes further, implying that only a certain kind of western classical music will 'increase health' in patients vulnerable to arrhythmias. While the study did include heavy metal and techno, without testing every kind of music (including perhaps music from outside the Western canon), drawing such a conclusion seems a leap of judgement which might be less acceptable in, for example, a drugs trial.

This is not to criticise the researcher, who doubtless intends his work to be part of a much wider consideration of the subject; the trouble is that in a relatively empty field these things have sometimes been seized upon as absolutes: in the highly specific, risk-averse world of the UK hospital it can be tempting to accept such judgements as guidance for practice, and to default to Mozart and landscape painting. This is partly because any advice is better than upsetting someone who is unwell. And partly because arts programmes are generally small, fragile projects, at the mercy of the hospital system; the risk of generating a nasty opinion on twitter – or worse, in a newspaper – has very real potential impact on the programme itself.

For me, art in hospitals is there to start a conversation rather than anaesthetise it. Thus, when new work was commissioned from Quentin Blake in 2006 by The Nightingale Project, a charitable organisation based in the Central and North West London NHS Foundation Trust, *The Times* noted that:

A third [patient] observes: 'There's a lot of conversation in them if somebody takes the trouble to make any.' There are plans to use Blake's work as a starting point for therapeutic discussion.[26]

More important perhaps than an idea of 'suitable' art are four key points: the preceding relationship between the listener/viewer and the work, the care with which the 'art' is delivered, the context, and the degree of control exercised by the 'audience'.

I heard an anecdote recently about a young man in a coma whose mother played him opera repeatedly through headphones, to no avail. But when she played him one of his favourite 'alternative' musicians, he woke up. And asked her why she'd insisted on playing him all that opera.

Too much reliance on what might be called populist classicism (in all art forms) runs the risk of reducing the arts to a kind of sedative – designed to be unobtrusive, but to subtly manipulate mood. At its most unnerving, this is the canned music in One Flew Over the Cuckoo's Nest, or the music used to soothe crowds at the entrances to edgy underground stations.

There may be a place for this kind of intervention, but it is important to remember that 'soothed' is not the only thing people in hospitals want to feel. The success – amongst other hospital-based dance programmes – of both Akademi and the Dance Art Foundation's Breathing Space project[27] testifies to people's desire for activity.

The arts are not there primarily to inoculate us against feeling – but perhaps to support us in our feeling, and sometimes to help us rediscover our sense of self, always at risk of running adrift at times of crisis. In 2012 rb&hArts received this letter in appreciation of Paige Bradley's Vertigo sculpture:

> *As a recent patient I was enchanted by your sculptures in the foyer. In the anxious 'other' world of hospital life your art and also the lovely words which accompanied the art were a breath of fresh air and a much appreciated 'remembrance' of what is truly real – if we allow it to happen. I had escaped from the madness of my ward for a while ... and I sat beside the free falling figures and read your words and felt uplifted and 'connected' again ...*

The arts can even directly address health conditions treated in the building. One current project-in-progress, Stream, for example, looks at blood flow in the heart – as well as the relationships between medical imaging, clinicians and patients. It is based around a collaboration between artist Emma Hunter and Philip Kilner, Consultant and Reader in Cardiovascular Magnetic Resonance (and also an artist himself).[28] The process has included a number of workshops with medical students, with practising clinicians and with people living with chronic conditions affecting the heart.

The work will eventually be installed in the hospital from which it derives – something to stimulate discussion around the interior of the body and how it is depicted, and around medical imaging and the power invested in it. Perhaps a 'healthy' thing to have in a medical imaging department.

Often, though, the best art is the stuff made by, or with, the people who spend time in the space. Ownership is an extremely important part of making sure that work doesn't end up behind someone's filing cabinet, replaced by an academic poster. But more importantly, feeling part of its creation is part of why people enjoy the finished work.[29]

This can happen in a number of ways. Like a number of hospital-based arts programmes, rb&hArts holds an annual exhibition of work by staff, patients, and their immediate families at the hospital. It is consistently the

FIGURE 3: 84
Solve et Coagula, by Emma Hunter

year's most popular show, and has yielded a number of artists who have gone on to undertake solo shows or commissions. There is a democratising effect in realising you are a better watercolourist than your cardiac surgeon, but showing your work also establishes a different kind of relationship with your hospital – one in which you are represented not by your diagnosis but by something you choose to represent you.

Another method is to use professional artists to guide the process of making new work. In 2012, artists Emily Allchurch and Sue Snell collaborated with rb&hArts and the family of a young man called Andrew James to create a series of new work for Royal Brompton's congenital heart unit. Called One Step at a Time, the work was created from collages made by people who regularly attend the unit. It was a way to honour Andrew's memory – he had been attending the hospital regularly since his birth, and his own sketches were included alongside those of people who came to weekend workshops with their families. It was also a way for Andrew's family – some of whom had not been back since Andrew's death – to reconcile themselves with the hospital, and in their words, 'give enjoyment to patients and visitors to the ward and help to make their stay as pleasant as possible in what can often be trying circumstances.'

The arts can be a powerful means of binding a building to its community. Thus, further afield, the Chickasaw Nation Medical Center in rural Oklahoma (opened in 2011) was designed to be *more than just a healthcare facility for the Chickasaw Nation; it was to be a civic venue for their people and other American Indians in that region of Oklahoma. The design team focused on creating a facility that would provoke a sense of ownership and pride and was derived from and conceptually based on their culture, history and future aspirations.*

The buildings' appearance and layout is based on Chickasaw culture – in one example, 'the diamond pattern of a culturally significant beaded collar is reflected in the lobby flooring, ceilings, exterior canopy and landscaping;' and, crucially, 'artwork by Chickasaw artists is displayed throughout the building.'[30]

In this case, art both inspires the architecture, and sits within it – overtly acknowledging that culture is central to our sense of self, of belonging, of status – all things which are threatened immeasurably by ill-health.

Art cannot prevent this threat, but it can help us work through it, and find a way of reconciling ourselves with physical and mental vulnerability. As the former editor of the *BMJ,* Richard Smith, has said, 'If health is about adaptation, understanding, and acceptance, then the arts may be more potent than anything that medicine has to offer.'[31]

And although when it comes to clinical trials the arts struggle with being a square peg in a pharmacologically shaped hole, there is a growing body of evidence, from the social sciences and elsewhere, that

FIGURE 3: 85, 3: 86 3: 87 AND 3: 88
One step at a time

indicates the arts' impact on health and wellbeing – both in hospital settings and outside them. Staricoff and Clift's 2011 review of medical literature from 2004–2011 contains many notable examples of direct impact: ten journal articles reviewed by Newman (2010), for example, suggest that the intervention of music in the operating theatre is highly beneficial, significantly reducing the amount of sedation required and recovery time[32] (with all the concomitant cost implications). And Staricoff's own 2003 study demonstrated – amongst many other significant findings – that 'chemotherapy patients who were able to view rotating art exhibitions during recovery showed reductions of 20% in anxiety levels and 34% in depression, compared with control groups.'[33]

There is research from outside the hospital space, too: Tommaso and colleagues' 2008 study, for example, found that a 'view of paintings previously appreciated as beautiful produced lower pain scores,' leading to the conclusion that 'pain may be modulated at cortical level by the aesthetic content of the distracting stimuli.'[34]

More recently, an international literature review from Manchester Metropolitan University Arts for Health (2014) has sought 'to evaluate the long-term relationship between arts participation and physical/psychological health'. One cited study, for example, of over 8,000 young people (Cuypers et al., 2012) notes that 'highly culturally active adolescents seemed to be better protected against the effect of obesity-susceptibility genes when measured in young adulthood.'[35]

Some of what arts programmes in hospitals are trying to achieve is to change our feelings about the building itself. Our impressions of the environment prejudice us towards or against the care we will receive – something which may in turn have an impact on the success of that care. Exhibitions and live music, for example, have two roles to play: to make us feel comfortable as we come into the space ('this doesn't feel like a hospital'), and to reinstate the hospital as a building central to its community – to make it somewhere you might consider going for pleasure. Then, when you have to go there, perhaps, the building is your friend, not your enemy.

And just as important as making hospitals accessible is making art accessible. Thanks to many factors, from the outreach work conducted over the past decades by major arts institutions to undergraduate programmes teaching artists how to work in community settings, to artists like Jeremy Deller who make it their business to be as socially engaged as possible, much has changed in our sense in the UK of what constitutes quality in art, and the mutual suspicion which for years characterised the relationship between 'high art' and 'community art' has to a certain extent dissipated.

FIGURE 3: 89 AND 3: 90
Whether art is silently hanging behind a lunch table or spread out over a hotel's corridor floor, it is affecting occupants

But people – especially those who do not consider themselves 'arty' – remain, sometimes justifiably, suspicious of being left out of the joke. And in hospitals, perhaps more than anywhere, this is something to be avoided at all costs. Arts interventions should attempt to communicate with the widest possible audience all the time – but it is vital to note that this is not the same as dumbing down. In fact it is the opposite: artists and arts managers must think more carefully than ever about their craft, and how it reaches people. It is only then that, as Tusa put it, art 'resists categories and finds connections across them.'

In the end, art in hospitals can be superficial, political, bright, abstract, representational, messy, textile, sculpture, oil, fast, slow, music, books, cinema, theatre, dance… in short it can be whatever art can be, as long as it's not careless. Artists must work around complex buildings, acknowledge that in that space they are one of many, many people contributing to wellbeing in diverse ways – and find their place in the maelstrom. That – the imagination to open up that space, and to offer it to others – is the unique value of the arts concludes Victoria Hume..

Artwork involves materials and shapes, which as mentioned in an earlier chapter can impact the way a human mind responds to them; shape and curvaceous shapes combined with specific colours will change the way we perceive and respond to them. It is expected that if the artist and the selection of art is successful, then the emotional valence of the work should override these.

Art can be one of the main mediums of communicating emotions and ideas to other space users; its omission is a clear gap in efforts to meet the needs of humans.

Putting design for wellbeing into practice

The above chapter expands on the purpose and aims of art. It outlines the critical role it plays for emotional wellbeing and productivity too. There are some simple steps that clients and design teams can take easily and some that can require a wider project effort, such as some of the following:

1. Include the issue of art in the project meeting's agenda. Provide insight of the impact of art.

2. Through the User Profiles, consider the need to support emotional wellbeing through the interior design. Is it being supported more through management or relationships perhaps? How does the use of space impact emotions on a day-to-day basis?

3. Consider the type and form of art which should be adopted for each space, taking on board delivery and maintenance considerations.

4. Employ an Art Consultant or engage with a multi-media art gallery who could provide expert advice.

5. Gauge the harmony required between the user's needs from a psychological point of view and what style of art will match. Is the culture hierarchical or egalitarian? Do the audiences find beautiful a Realistic or Abstract style?

CHAPTER 14
Materials and textures

Materials 109 • Textures 110 • Measuring the effect and amount of texture 115

We could approach this issue, the impact and importance materials and textures have in interiors' impact on occupant wellbeing, by bringing up examples of spaces where they are seen to lack these, spaces such as jails. If you are a fan of London's Southbank Centre or any contemporary art gallery around the world, you may wonder why the lack of material variation or softness, is associated with ill-being. And you would be correct. What this chapter aims to inform is why material variation and the textures of materials, support wellbeing of users one way and not another. There is not one bad texture or material type but the incorrect combination of these for a specific setting and user group.

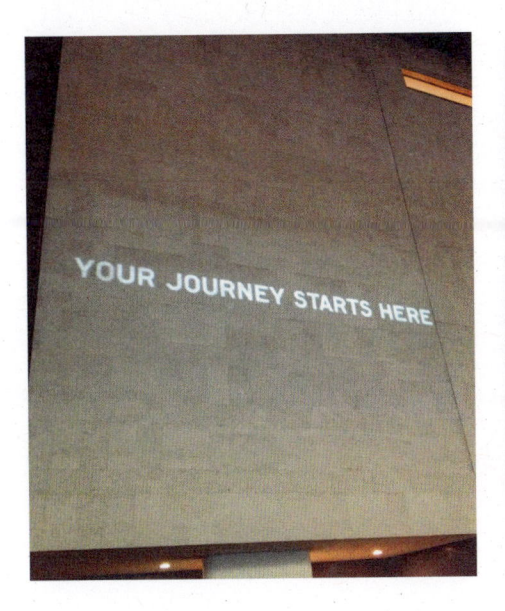

FIGURE 3: 91 AND 3: 92
Projected words and film on the lightly textured concrete walls of Festival Hall, London

Materials

Through the term 'materials' we refer to an object made from a specific atomic composition. A distinction between a natural material and a manmade one where choice goes beyond the actual texture it has on its external surfaces, for example, the difference between real wood and a laminate imitation of a wood panel. The fact a material is 'natural' can support the occupant's wellbeing if the Users Profile requires there to be natural materials in a visible and perceptible way. On the other hand, if an organisation or family culture is about change and requires beauty shown in abstractive forms, then using technologically developed materials will suit their User Profile. This choice is affecting the emotional and cognitive support of occupants.

Authentic v artificial materials is a significant decision to be made in the design approach of a project. Understanding how one and the other reflects symbolically these different sources and how it is used as a visual brand message is important in making decisions that harmonise the users' and an organisation's culture, with the selection of materials. For example, seeing an artificial composite floor finish in a retail shop that champions authentic food and honest ingredients, can sit a bit at odds with their messaging. Another example is a timber imitation floor finish, which looks visually real and solid, until you step on it and your foot does not receive the solidity in motion or hear the deep thud expected. What messages and levels of service would be expected from such a place if it was a hotel or restaurant?

109

FIGURE 3.93 AND 3.94
The importance of selecting materials

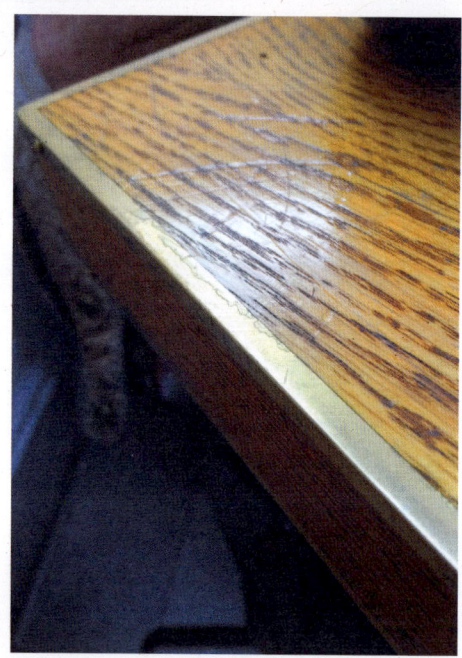

Textures

Beyond the actual material a finish or product is made from, the top finish that this material presents to the human senses will be impacting on their comfort, joy and overall sense of wellbeing. For example, a cold metal surface or a heavily textured wall finish will look very different, and in touching a cold door handle or staircase balustrade users will experience a different journey through an interior.

Mark Rothko, discussing the impact that materials have on viewers, shared the following thoughts:

'We use the word sensuality instead of sensation because we know now that sensation itself is devisable. Through our study of the apparatus of sensation we know that man's final sensation is a synthesis of atomic particles of separate sensations. But the summer is out, the final indexed to reality that is the synthesise result, can be understood only through sensuality. For sensuality applies ultimately to our sense of touch, to the tactile, which, whether we wanted it to be or not, is still the final justification of our notions of reality. Our eyes, ears – all of our senses – are simply the indications of the existence of a veritable reality that will ultimately resolve itself to a sense of touch. That the sensual is so closely interlaced with the entire mechanics of procreation is further evidence that man in his most profound biological functions is impelled by his sense of touch.'[36] Mark Rothko, *The Artist's Reality*

His presentation of the experience users have of the effects from touch is working on a fine level of understanding of the process at play, and clearly outlines the impact textures have on our stimulation and feelings linked to our innate biological makeup.

Textures are a means of communication and survival as they are used to tell us if something is hot or cold, help us orientate in space, provide signals of time such as the ripeness of a fruit, or warn us of a wet floor. They tell us if something is going to yield to pressure or not so we can decide our approach to an activity. Beyond the functional and survival based purpose they can also be used symbolically to represent values and meanings and affect people emotionally and cognitively.

It is a given that texture is always present when a material is introduced. The question is how to use textures with the aim of supporting occupant wellbeing. We look to deal with the questions: how much *variety of textures* and what *type of textures* are ideal in an interior composition that supports wellbeing.

Especially noted in commercial workplaces and residential developments over the last decades there has been a predominant introduction of hard flat surfaces with little colour variation. In the most recent years we see an inclination towards introducing designs with a wider variety of textures and colours. The look makes for a deeper sense of texture and higher sensory experience. Is this supporting wellbeing though and can there be such a thing as too much texture for a space?

Referring back to the initial chapters, and looking at *how* and *what* supports the comfort and enables wellbeing of an occupant, we need to understand how the use of texture supports design approaches such as realistic or abstract, and how specific textural combinations would be reflecting the characteristics of a colour psychology group type. If a group of users is profiled as a type 4 colour group for example, the textures that would harmonise with their style of behaviour would be highly contrasting with very hard and deep textured surfaces, distinctly cool to touch, beside deep soft textures where you can sink your fingers through.

The recommended texture approaches that harmonise with the psychology types of the User Profiles are as follows:

FIGURE 3: 95 AND 3: 96
Examples of texture in varied mediums

FIGURE 3: 97 AND 3: 98
Examples of texture in varied mediums

CHAPTER 14 • MATERIALS AND TEXTURES

Type 1: similar types, shallow, soft, cool textured surfaces

Type 2: part contrast between types, soft and deep textures, mix of warm and cold to touch

Type 3: part contrast between types, deep textured, soft and hard, warm to touch

Type 4: high contrast between finishes, deep/shallow texture, hard/soft, warm/cold

The tasks occurring in each space will also nudge the combination of textures towards a direction, as they also need to respond to a need to stimulate or calm the senses. This will be through controlling the amount of variation between the textures rather than the fact there is variation in their group characteristics. The way each material will be then used to form an object will depend on whether the users consider beautiful items that are tending towards realistic or abstract forms.

FIGURE 3: 981
Type 1

FIGURE 3: 982
Type 2

A research study on primary school environments[37] looked at textures in interiors and their effect on the performance of the children in these spaces. The study places textures within the conversation of stimulation; materials will either increase sensory arousal and stimulate or the opposite and allow boredom to set in. It describes the number of many textures as diverse and the variety of them as novel and atypical, summarising the outcomes as less or more complex. The more complex a combination is the higher the arousal and stimulation of a person, and the opposite for less complex compositions. The paper also makes a case for a specific approach to making a composition, suggesting that people find attractive compositions that have an average amount of complexity but within an orderly fashion. This is echoing the earlier sections in this book which stated that humans feel calmer with balance and symmetry overall as it states trust and safety. So this combination creates initial attraction and excitement

FIGURE 3: 983
Type 3

FIGURE 3: 984
Type 4

FIGURE 3: 985
Harmonious wall textures

and then underlines it with order and clarity. It suggests that the effect of order in a composition can be achieved through uniform texture, distinctive elements, focal points, low contrast and replication of features. These features are suggestions and not to override the properties of the group types.

The report is seeking to clarify an approach to support spaces catering for children and their responses, but rings true in a broader extent for adults also. Recall the social studies referenced in the environmental psychology section and then in the patterns and repetition section. We note that humans seeking order and clarity prefer symmetry and repetition. Another point, which the report makes, is *'People like places that make sense and offer involvement. Features that increase involvement include diversity and the promise of further information ahead.'* with *increased involvement* being what stands out here. As humans enjoy connection rather than disconnection this provides further understanding on why diversity of textures and materials is recommended in an interior that supports wellbeing through meeting some of the primary human needs.

The inquisitiveness and need for information is also an aspect to consider in the strategic placement of texture. In the context of retail spaces,[38] people will touch objects in order to fill a gap of knowledge or make a value-based judgement on it. This opens up a very different issue in the application of texture which needs designers to consider the motivations behind occupants' use of a space or specific objects within it.

Textures used as part of communication and relying on users touching them, interacting with them, can support a design seeking to introduce or support a user's emotional journey. This can be deeply emotional with joy or sadness, and serious or playful. If a material is highly textured, people will usually walk up to the finish to touch it, or brush their hand over it as they walk by – there is the sense of interplay from this activity. This can be attributed both to simple human curiosity for something that stands out in its setting and asks us to discover it, and also to the need for stimulation and connection to our physical environment, to feel a sense of belonging and safety. The emotional valence of the object can then steer towards joy or sadness; the names of the dead written on memorials being a strong example, when families can touch their loved one's name. There is a big difference between just seeing the name written on a hard wall and being able to step up to it and touch it. Touch makes a difference to our experience and is very powerful.

FIGURE 3: 986
Textures used effectively to enhance and better communicate a memorial

How textures and materials are used on objects is also important on the impact they will make as a combination. Using a material that surprises the user tends to stimulate and takes a risk in the person liking it or not. For example, creating a natural looking pattern with a composite material such as a timber patterned concrete entrance facade, or using straw to create an animal sculpture. If the User Profile needs high stimulation or a sense of abstraction in the style then being more playful and surprising in the use of textures will support the wellbeing of those users.

Measuring the effect and amount of texture

Supporting a more refined approach in the selection of textures is the research conducted by Peck and Childers with a measurable scale.[39] Further research on parallels in their approach and the right psychology theory is required and would be very positive work.

In 2006 the BRE Trust funded a research project *Measuring the wellbeing impacts of interior materials*[40] on the opinions of building occupants on the materials used inside buildings and the impact of those materials on their wellbeing.

They looked at the refurbishment of offices, schools and hospitals and surveyed building users and delivery teams on the impact of materials. They found that the choice of interior materials in working environments is important and can have a variety of impacts on the psychological and physical wellbeing of the users. They also discovered that materials, which are worn out, dirty or shabby, can cause feelings of depression for building occupants or cause embarrassment when clients, patients or the parents of pupils come to visit – in line with the subject of Elegance discussed in an earlier chapter. A particularly pertinent finding of the BRE work was that office building occupants were generally more satisfied with their doors, ceilings and walls, and less so with their floors and windows. This reflected the condition in which the floors were in due to the wear and tear and visual lack of beauty, and the fact windows were inoperable.

FIGURE 3: 987
Artist Bob Johnston's wicker corgi

Putting design for wellbeing into practice

Materials are involved in all projects, their selection sometimes being a mixture of the colour and tactility effect perceived by a designer. Understanding how users are affected by an interior's textures, what role the use of textures can play in supporting wellbeing and what decisions are available to the client and design team are all available to act on. Below are some considerations in this effort:

1. During the briefing stage and creation of the User Profiles, understand the scale required on the issues of:
    a. Authenticity v Artificial
    b. Realistic v Abstract
    c. High Stimulation v calmness

2. Define what the material selection strategy is at an early stage and ensure all selections work to this.

3. Define the level of textural variety needed to support the User Profiles.

4. Consider if increased tactility in the design and way users will interact with the space, could support connections between users.

5. Consider if there is a need to nudge occupant behaviour in certain spaces and how material selection and their tactility can be used to support this.

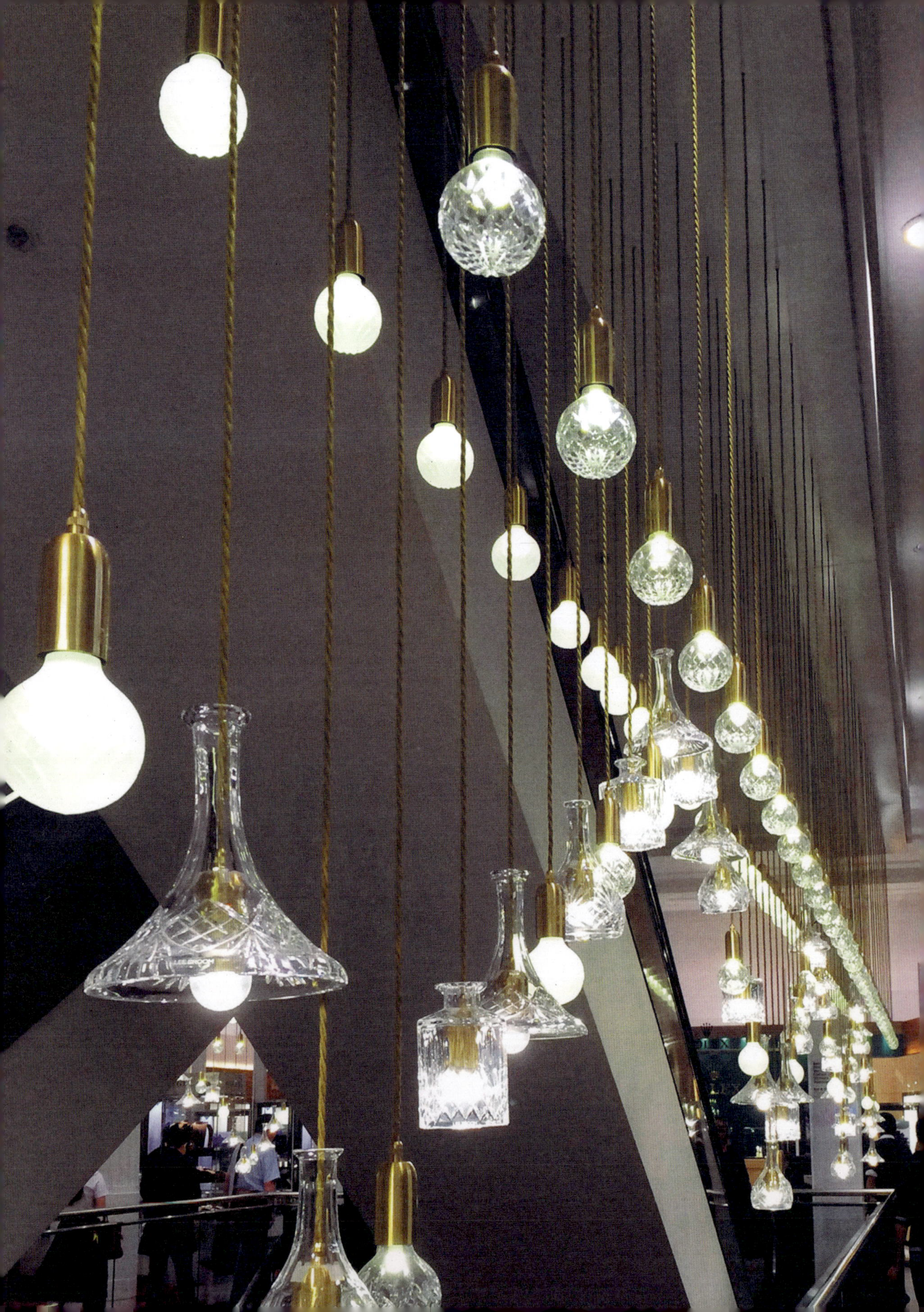

PART 4
Design in Practice: Physical Issues affecting Wellbeing

Chapter 15: Interior atmosphere 120 • Chapter 16: Illumination and light design 135 • Chapter 17: Space planning 147 • Chapter 18: Acoustic design 159 • Chapter 19: Operational issues 166

All interior environments are affected by a number of chemical and physical based features beyond the typical subjects of colour and patterns, and if you have ever felt too cold in a room or sleepy during a meeting, you will have personal experience of these. Of course one person's 'too cold' is another person 'perfect', so how do we know what good design is which supports occupant wellbeing? The tailoring of what we refer to as physical issues is to ensure these harmonise with the User Profiles, and essential to a design's success. Some issues have been considered over recent years and there are some averages that indicate good practice and only some small tailoring is required to harmonise with each project, but others perhaps due to the lack of visibility in the case of issues such as air velocity or fine air particles and material off-gassing, have less awareness by occupants and we rely purely on current research.

FIGURE 4: 01
Will a warm dish or cold dish be more pleasurable when feet are resting on a cold floor?

As with aesthetic issues affecting our emotional and cognitive health, physical issues impact our physical health. In cases, their effect is immediately perceived in removing comfort and being unsupportive in achieving wellbeing.

The main physical issues in interiors that impact occupant wellbeing are indoor air, light, acoustics qualities, and also the way that the room and the furniture itself are arranged, allowing for certain views within the space. These issues, as also seen with the aesthetic issues, all depend on each other. Daylight entry into a space is dependent on the room and furniture layouts considering the light's travel: acoustic quality can conflict with greater views through an interior or thermal comfort could conflict with the amount of fresh air being provided into the interior. The relationship of these issues between themselves is dynamic, this is important to consider and keep in mind throughout the design process as development of features occurs in an iterative manner through the design stages.

Another consideration that is very important to mention is the dependency and relationship of the aesthetic and physical issues; both areas of design must be designed with view and consideration of each other. For example, if the temperature of a large public space is set at 21°C for the summer in North Europe; the walls are painted in a cool tone of turquoise, combined with a white polished tiled floor and glossy fittings or furniture, the occupants are more likely to feel comfortable than if this combination was proposed for a workplace, home or cosy leisure location.

Will a warm dish or cold dish be more pleasurable when feet are resting on a cold floor?

The effect of colour and texture of shapes on human physiology has been expanded in previous chapters, and now we will add the physical effects into the mix. Although the immediate effects of the following issues around indoor atmosphere are physical, their effect on occupants turn very quickly into psychosomatic emotional and cognitive problems. As soon as the body is taken out of its comfort state, it experiences stimulation.

FIGURE 4: 02
How will this corridor affect how comfortable its occupants feel?

FIGURE 4: 03
'A glass of Atmosphere', part of Japan's installation at Somerset House Design Biennial, London, 2014

The more stimulation in this situation, the more the body starts experiencing stress. The more stress the body experiences the more of it turns into emotional and mental discomfort from exhaustion and eventually from lack of resilience.

There is a fair amount of available information on how to deliver 'good practice' levels of air, light and sound quality in interiors on a technical level. What is not available and flowing freely in design team meetings, is the link between this information that can be highly technical and the desired result required to support wellbeing by a designer and client. Clarifying the links and approaches to support the wellbeing of occupants based on the other design elements is missing an adaptor plug, and we aim to meet this simple but highly challenging task over the next few chapters.

There are projects where a highly capable engineer is appointed and produces in-depth reports, schedules and drawings which go over the heads of most designers and clients. Not due to any party not being capable enough, but there is insufficient time or effort required, to get their heads round such complex information. In some cases designers and clients see only costs associated with additional items needing fitting and are not enabled to view the full picture coming together or how the various aesthetic, operational and physical issues are dependant on each other. In the following sections we aim to simplify, without losing the weight of knowledge, the issues which impact on user comfort and the ability for them to achieve wellbeing.

CHAPTER 15

Interior atmosphere

Air quality overview 121 • Thermal comfort 121 • Humidity 127
Fuel for the mind 128 • Air health 129 • Specifying products and
materials 131 • Study highlights of indoor air quality testing
outcomes in occupied spaces 133

Air quality overview

Although air quality gets little airtime in interior design conversations to date, it is the most complained about issue in interior spaces based on occupant feedback audits. It usually is referred to solely as air temperature and does not include all other properties and parts of the air we breathe and live within. Based on this it can be quite hard to get clients excited about talking about it or wishing to focus and invest time and money into issues surrounding it. But evidence and personal experiences of bad design and costs due to this issue are increasingly more prominent, meaning this is starting to get increased attention. The question is: how do we engage with it when designing an interior and what does it actually mean to design good quality air as part of the interior design of a space? These are issues which an engineer on a larger design project will be brought in to inform and design for, but on many interior refurbishments and smaller fit-out projects, the 'air design' is down to the interior designer and perhaps a mechanical equipment supplier to do. In many cases small modifications of only a part of an office or retail shop floor will be undertaken by a builder or construction company without engaging any design thinking, resulting in imbalanced results, compromising the rest of the space's performance.

Although there are many research studies[1] undertaken on the effect of the indoor environment on the performance of occupants, every reader without a doubt will have experienced at least one occasion where they were too cold/hot and lost comfort, or a space was too noisy for a task they were trying to concentrate on, or found themselves slowly drifting asleep during a meeting, lesson or conversation resulting in loss of knowledge and bad communications. Using studies to demonstrate some simple truths can sometimes take much of the energy and effort available away from the area it's needed most. Projects can lose time and money trying to prove why comfort needs to be designed for, rather than actually using the time towards achieving this key performance.

More technical data and benchmarks on air quality issues can be sourced in the Philomena Bluyssen's book *The Indoor Environment Handbook* (2009).

Thermal comfort

A survey of 1100 office workers undertaken by BCO[2] shows factors which were reported as important at different levels. Highest in priority were comfort, temperature and lighting. This also aligns with the Estates Gazette survey undertaken by Jones and Grigoriou and published in a report *Wellbeing Matters* (2013) under the Feeling Good Foundation stating the top perceived impacting issues in UK office worker environments were light levels and indoor air quality.

Over the last few decades, mechanical services have been designed to supply specific air temperatures which have been set as acceptable to all occupants. These are based on a 1970s study, based on clothing and cultural behaviours of that time, and have not evolved over recent times. These parameters determine the temperature even if a specific group of occupants find it overall outside of their comfort zone.

This raises the following issues for consideration:

1 The responsibility occupants have to respond to seasonal weather through clothing and behaviour patterns – having a dynamic relationship with their environment and not a static one where the building needs to flex to the occupants' requirements no matter what.

2 That the settings are reflecting current weather patterns and the variety of these that exist around the world. British and USA thermal comfort standards have been applied in the Middle East, Africa and the Far East with little consideration of the local opportunities or conditions. The results have meant higher environmental impacts.

It has been found through studies by Oh (2005) and Clements-Croome (2014) that people can adapt to air temperature, but the impacts to productivity are proportionate. According to Clements-Croome[3] and US office market research[4] the following temperature and productivity relationship conclusions were found to exist:

- Heat exhaustion begins at about 25°C.
- 24°C is the maximum air temperature recommended by the World Health Organization (WHO) for workers' comfort (but note that in the UK there is no legislation covering maximum allowed temperatures).
- 16°C is the minimum temperature recommended by the UK Workplace (Health, Safety and Welfare) Regulations 1992 (13°C for strenuous physical work).
- 78% of workers say their working environment reduces their creativity and ability to get the job done.
- 15% of workers have arguments over how hot or how cold the temperature should be.
- 81% of workers find it difficult to concentrate if the office temperature is higher than the norm.
- 62% of workers state that, when they are too hot, they take up to 25% longer than usual to complete a task.

Through the briefing process of all projects, designers and clients will hear very differing views on what the occupants of a space consider a comfortable temperature. And although the above study and others do provide a range of temperatures to work around, they will not be able to respond fully to each day's requirements throughout the year and for all occupants.

There are a few approaches which can be adopted and a few activities that can be integrated into a project's design process and operation to support comfort and wellbeing.

During the design process, the following topics can be relevant and considered to establish what is comfortable for the occupants and how best to provide these conditions depending on the nature, size, conditions, budgets and complexity of each interior.

Openable windows: mostly relevant as a problem to commercial or public spaces and needs to be considered alongside health and safety issues around the risk of falls, but it is good practice to consider if the space can operate with openable windows. This is overall the most preferred approach for occupants in many studies undertaken around the world. This approach needs to consider other factors too relating to external air quality and noise but the ability to open a window tends to reduce stress and make users happier overall. Attention must also be given to local geographical or cultural preferences, for example, there is an anecdotal story that in certain Central and Eastern European countries commercial buildings without openable windows are seen as lower standard. Once you start viewing local letting agent adverts and the list of features of buildings on the market, openable windows feature alongside fully mechanical HVAC systems and flexible floors and ceilings. Removing a feature that may be considered a social norm can increase stress and discomfort of users.

It must be noted that with the introduction of air conditioning to spaces with openable windows, property owners and tenants must ensure that sensors switch off the systems if a number of external windows are opened to support energy efficiency.

FIGURE 4: 04
The ability to open a window tends to reduce stress and positively impact wellbeing

Mechanical air conditioning: if the space is going to have the air temperature conditioned through a mechanical means, then the system design itself will be undertaken typically by a mechanical engineer as this has now become such a specialised field. How temperatures can be locally adjusted by occupants, needs to be discussed and understood through the design process; how will the temperature be adjusted if it can be, how will the air flow speed coming out from the grills and slots be felt on the skin of occupants, and how quickly will the system respond to a change of temperature when adjusted at the controls. Sometimes users adjust the temperature gauge, unaware that the response time is slow and complain or adjust even further thinking the system is not working, causing stress and overall disruption to many occupants. Many of these issues can be considered as part of a Soft Landings handover training process or though clear information beside control panels within spaces themselves.

Engineering solutions tend to evolve every couple of years to introduce better hardware for air distribution, but for commercial spaces typically the use of round air diffusers, as opposed to square ones or long thin ones, provide a softer feel of the air flow on occupants' skin, face and hair. The use of long thin slots in retail settings and high-end residential spaces are in fact, on many occasions, a conflict between visual aesthetics and actual thermal comfort when using the space. If these types are adopted, their location needs careful placement in relation to the perpendicular or in-line surfaces to allow air to travel correctly and blend in the interiors. They also need careful sizing to suit a more subtle airflow distribution.

Central v local system: depending on the way a building or interior space will be occupied and how ownership of the day-to-day space's use will be allocated, the choice of system will make a big difference to the way users will feel they have some control, and the way the system can meet more localised needs of users.

Hot and cold spots near external glazing: in most interiors that feature external glazing more notably, the air temperature of the external air will be felt more intensely to those in the proximity. This tends to become an issue with workplace or classroom settings where users are sitting over a longer period of time without physical movement. During place allocations it is good practice to raise awareness of these conditions and to ensure users that may have a higher sensitivity to temperature change are not placed there.

Hot and cold spots under mechanical vents: as with the external glazing areas, placing occupants with higher sensitivity under grills or air diffusers will mean they feel discomfort intensely or the rest of the occupants' needs will be compromised. This is where the design of the grilles and air supply flows are not calculated properly, especially in relation to the ceilings and walls around them to use them as aids for air distribution.

Seating/working positions on plans and day-to-day information: creating visual seating or workplace area plans with expected air temperatures annotated on them can support space users in making more informed decisions about where they work or what they wear. These plans can be as simple as the fire exit route plans that currently exist in rooms so all types of users can find them easy to reference. As technological base solutions develop, introducing a live feed into a digital plan on company or school intranet sites would allow more refined information to be made, and link it with wearable technology.

Clothing and activities in space: discussing it as a *dynamic* relationship between users

FIGURE 4: 05
Restaurants and cafes where consumers are coming and going frequently find it difficult to maintain good thermal comfort without introducing lobbies

with the heating and cooling approach is very important in the successful result of any strategy. Whichever strategy is opted for, it will on peak times of the year, not fully meet all occupant comfort levels without them also taking some action. By wearing more or less clothing depending on the situation will support the regulation of body temperature. Changing the location they are using to another more suited to the temperature they find comfortable is also an approach to be considered introduced as part of the design thinking. The idea that the space has to adjust to each person's own comfort and they need to do nothing is rather unreasonable and practically unachievable. Yet users on many occasions are not advised of the limitations and they are disappointed when they finally occupy the space and find it is not responding as expected. According to Clements-Croome (2014)[5] adaptive response factors are physiological, psychological, social and behavioural.

Material finishes: thermal comfort is extremely important for building occupants, influencing them both physically and emotionally, and the perception of temperature has been shown to be influenced by interior materials. The flooring material of a building can affect thermal comfort: occupants can feel a sense of warmth or cool through their feet. Cool flooring materials such as concrete or marble can provide comfort for people in warm and humid climates whilst warmer surfaces such as carpet or linoleum are preferred in colder zones.

Smart and wearable technology: with more technology being developed by the day, in both the building systems management and the occupant wearable technologies, we can now consider more and more introducing completely interactive relationships between spaces and the average preferences of occupants. Smart technology is not found only in phones any more but is also being introduced in building systems, city systems and transport systems. The ability to tailor environmental preferences provides the ability to add and refine preferred air temperature as much as other space variables.

Local adaptive temperatures: According to the work by Clements-Croome (2014) and Nicol et al (2012), thermal comfort in an internal space needs to be adaptive and set in relation to monthly mean temperatures. This principle, in combination with the above smart technology approach, would maximise user comfort in a constantly variable and extreme climatic system.

FIGURE 4: 06
The flooring material of a building can affect thermal comfort

Climatic preferences: through the work of deDear et al (1998) it is found that people living in warmer climatic regions prefer higher air temperatures than those in colder climates. Designing for different clients or the same client in different climatic regions, it is vital that this behaviour pattern is adopted and a one-size-fits-all approach is avoided.

The state of the interior's air temperature and the supply of fresh air can be a sensitive balance to achieve. On occasion users may believe the air temperature to be too cold when air velocity from a mechanical system to be too high (fast flow of air). A natural ventilation approach tends to remove such situations, but it does not provide as much adjustability should a change from normal settings be required. A study on office facilities in various cities of India[6] demonstrated how a change in speed of fans increased thermal comfort without increasing the use of the air conditioning system. This study also correlates with the conclusions made according to Clements-Croome, by Chrenko in 1974, and where he found that users thought the air more 'fresh' dependant on the air flow and temperature, so comfort on air quality is dependent on both and not just temperature.

Ventilation

Ventilation approaches can be natural or mechanical, or a hybrid of these. For residential interiors this tends to fall under natural with openable windows and more commercial spaces will start reverting to more passive approaches again under efforts for more energy efficient buildings. This will be positive for the purposes of achieving occupant comfort as humans tend to prefer a natural flow of air on their skin and are seen to accept in naturally ventilated spaces, a wider range of air temperatures through behaviour and psychological adaptation.[7]

In a paper published by the World Health Organization,[8] analysis and solutions were made for the provision of natural ventilation in healthcare settings. The idea that natural ventilation can be applied on such acute settings when following a good design process is a strong example of design for wellbeing. This approach will support the wellbeing of both healthcare staff and patients during their treatment and recovery period. A number of case studies from around the world also demonstrate the way adjustments can be made to enable the varying climatic conditions design teams need to work with.

FIGURE 4: 07 AND 4: 08
Interiors benefitting from natural light and openable windows

Trickle window ventilation is recommended for residential interiors, especially as buildings are being sealed for thermal efficiency and very low air changes can occur on acute cold or warm days of the year. When mechanical systems have been introduced into homes there have been very poor results from studies undertaken recently in the UK. Research architects Cartwright Pickard and the Mackintosh School of Art & Design on air quality in homes[9] summarised one of the insights are follows *'We found that most residents were ill-informed about the controls and technology in their homes. The heating and ventilation controls in most of the homes were over-complex so residents had trouble understanding how to use them correctly. Most residents complained they had been given little or no face-to-face introduction to the controls and systems in their new homes, and that even the property managers had a poor understanding of them.'* The research report offers a number of recommendations on improving air quality in homes, and we list them below including a few good practice additions:

- Adopt good building handover to the residents and training on any systems related to ventilation and heating.
- Consider full life cycle costs as part of the design decision making.
- Provide simple controls and accompany with clear picture-based manuals.
- Install trickle vents in windows and full height doors. Consider the locations and handling of the vents to be accessible to the occupants, especially where elderly or users with limited abilities are residing.
- Consider introducing dedicated drying areas, and adding dedicated ventilation or/and extraction should the expected volumes of use be high.
- Consider introducing dedicated extract to specific rooms with activities or equipment that emit high levels of gases or dust such as large copier/photocopy rooms, spraying activities or chemical storage or mixing.
- Ensure installation of any duct-based systems is undertaken correctly and ducts are adequately sized and laid out in straight lines.
- Ensure central and secondary ducts are cleaned thoroughly annually and after any building works. The maintenance to include the cleaning and changing of all filters.
- Ensure that the ventilation fans selection is conscious of the noise output. Noisy fans will get disengaged by users if they are too noisy.

How much fresh air is required into an interior to ensure the best possible indoor air quality is provided also depends on the quality of the air externally. Although natural ventilation may be preferred from a haptic effect on occupants' skin, the air quality as far as the toxicity of the external air is concerned, may aggravate occupants with respiratory sensitivities. In these cases, a mechanically ventilated space will support occupants' health better. Many recognised standards around the world will these days recommend double layers of filters that catch different sizes of air particulate matter. A discussion with a knowledgeable engineer or filter manufacturer in these cases is advised but information can also be sought in industry guides.

FIGURE 4: 09
Images taken from report on duct cleaning to show their before and after condition

Humidity

On occasions one may observe that museums, galleries and zoos get better air quality detail design than some of the spaces humans actually live in. The atmospheric balance achieved in an art gallery for the protection of the artworks for example feels 'comfortable' and 'light' as an experience of air quality. These conditions and especially the humidity levels would seem as an aspiring condition to achieve in interior spaces where the air quality is specifically important to the User Profiles and when the other spatial features that impact air quality, such as the provision of views out, openable windows, the provision of live greenery and alike, are not higher in importance than the air quality.

In standards provided within the British Building Regulations, CIBSE and ASHRAE, to which engineers work in general commercial workplaces and public spaces; they require humidity levels to be designed within the very broad bracket of 30–60% relative humidity. Due to climatic and personal use of spaces, any specific target will tend to be difficult to maintain unless the interior is designed as a purely mechanically managed space. This is possible in easier ways in recent years as buildings have become air tight for energy efficiency purposes, and may be the best option if the users' needs for air quality are a higher priority to others such as a sense of control by opening windows and doors and links to the external seasonal weather. Extreme experiences of humidity levels such as too damp or too dry will create a sense of physical discomfort through the feel of the air on the skin (tight skin around face, dry eyes especially with the use of contact lenses), the experience of breathing (dry or tickly sinuses) or respiratory difficulty through lung sensitivity to bacteria in the air. The more balanced the levels of humidity are around 45–55% the more we will have feelings of lightness and physical wellbeing. People with eye sensitivities or wearers of contact lenses can experience long daily discomfort through low humidity in mechanically serviced interior spaces such as education or workplaces. The constant sensitivity and stimulation caused by the discomfort erodes levels of resilience steadily over a period of time and distracts from the activities undertaken such as concentration[10] or a productive flow of creative thought.

FIGURE 4:10
Living plants can be an important part of an interior

Inclusion of live plants can increase indoor humidity and counteract air dryness if spaces use electrical equipment and have air conditioning and mechanical ventilation.

It must be recognised that humidity as with temperature is totally relevant to local climatic conditions and seasons of the year. To achieve one perfect level is not possible unless a complete mechanical approach to a sealed building is taken. The other issue surrounding the experience of altered levels of humidity is that within a Biophilic approach it will be natural to vary throughout the year and be local to the climate. Many passive ways can remove extreme discomfort and as noted earlier under the natural ventilation issue, users are much more tolerant of natural conditions even if they are outside agreed standards of comfort.

According to Nazaroff (2013), and Mudarri and Fisk (2007), due to the presence of dampness and mould in USA based homes, the attributable number of asthma cases is estimated at 4.6 million and the associated annual cost of these at $3.5 billion.

Fuel for the mind

Just as it is said about nutrition, that you will be as healthy as the food you eat, so with the functioning of the mind; it will work as well as the food we supply it with. Depending where one is and other activities surrounding them, the basic composition of what we call 'oxygen' will be a mix of oxygen (O_2) and also carbon dioxide (CO_2), nitrogen (N_2), methane (CH_4), water (H_2O), and others in smaller amounts. A perfect cocktail to breath under normal pressure conditions on earth is generally proposed from various sources to be a mix of 21% oxygen, 78% nitrogen, 1% argon and carbon dioxide, 1% water vapour and other gases in trace amounts.[11] All space flight and other planetary conditions are discussed around these mixes.[12]

By designing interior spaces with low ventilation levels for their use, the mix of air starts changing and combines with other gases emitted through the various materials and products that are within it. These will range from carpet flooring, the adhesive and underlay it may be installed with, to a paint finish on the walls, the cleaning products used as part of maintenance, or perfumes and sprays used as part of day-to-day life. Human bodies perspire and exhale chemicals in addition to all the other materials around us too. A person simply speaking by themselves, practising a speech or reciting lines, in an empty room, can emit high levels of CO_2 and single handedly create a relatively toxic atmosphere for themselves. So ensuring there is healthy air for occupants at any time during their stay in an interior, a constant flow of 'fresh' air is required.

As air is not easily tested without sensors or technical devices, it is difficult to measure exactly for day-to-day users. A very simple test, which many might have experienced, is the effect of falling asleep or feeling heavy and tired, in a lecture theatre or meeting room. In under-performing spaces where the supply has not been designed for the number and length of use as required, the levels of CO_2 will raise through the number of people sitting in chairs and simply breathing. The ideal solution is to install air sensors in the room that link to either a ventilation supply system or to mechanised windows that can be regulated to open at a set amount and time for sufficient air to enter.

Where spaces do not have the ability to install or purchase such systems, adding a simple wall mounted or desk mounted air sampling sensor can provide enough information for occupants to take some action, and either open some windows or ask a central facilities team to increase ventilation levels.

There are cases where buildings are old and the occupancy of them is higher than they were originally designed for, limiting the amount of fresh air floors can be supplied with through centralised duct systems. Where this occurs, and if this were a corporate office or public building, a calculation of the balance between increasing the number of staff or occupancy on the floors against the loss of productivity and comfort through reduced stimulation and brain activity, should be calculated and a strategic decision for operation taken. Over time, it may become apparent that another building may be best suited for their culture and needs.

Designers are advised to consider the levels of occupancy in spaces by understanding what air quality can be provided and not rely on purely space plans and the

FIGURE 4: 11
Example of online monitoring dashboard indicating the energy, water and air quality levels on a trade show stand in Berlin, Germany

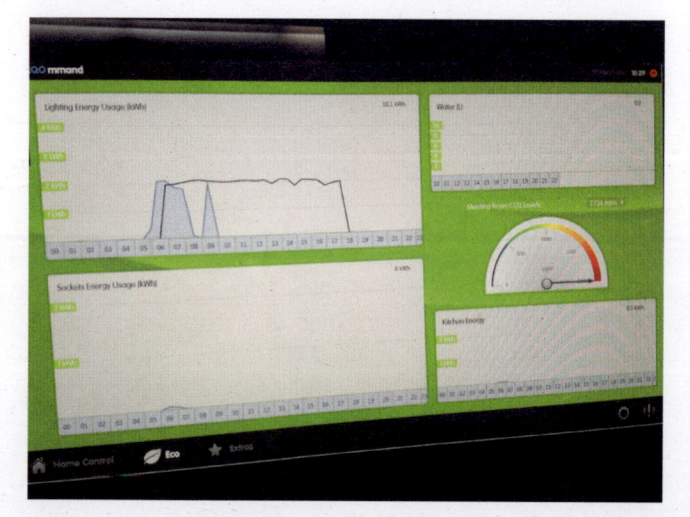

number of seats or standing places that may be able to fit within them.

The effect on performance of activities is more and more documented through studies, with one of the first and most clear based in a primary school setting standing out. The study gained prominence through the work of Clements-Croome but undertaken by Bako-Biro et al (2008, 2012), indicated how specific tasks as part of the learning and development of skills, were detrimentally affected when CO_2 levels went above 1000ppm (parts per million). Additionally, another study by UCL[13] shows that a correlation exists between increased levels of CO_2 and increased levels of pupil absence due to sickness. The study reported that for every 1000ppm the CO_2 was reduced by, there was at least 1.0% to 2.5% relative reduction in absence due to student illness. So performance is affected indirectly in addition to the direct effect through breathing in the moment.

Air health

The UCL study mentioned in the section above, which noted as side effects increased levels of classroom CO_2 linked with increased levels of student absence due to sickness, was a side effect of air flow rate and not due to CO_2 itself and its effects within the human body. The air we breathe has a physical composition which affects the human body due to its chemical effect when breathed or touches the skin, and due to the physical effect of small particles as they are inhaled into the lungs.

> *'Our sensitivity to particular components varies widely, for example carbon monoxide (CO_2) is a non-odorous but highly toxic gas at ppm (parts per million) concentrations whilst many volatile organic chemicals (VOCs) used for fragrance will be detected in the ppb (parts per billion) range. Particulate matter (PM) includes biological (e.g. fungal spores and fragments, bacteria, pollen, dust mite detritus) and non-biological types and is often described in terms of the concentration of particular size fractions e.g. <10 µm, <2.5 µm, and <0.1 µm, the latter being described as ultrafines, as size is an important determiner of suspension in the atmosphere and the sites of deposition in the lung when inhaled (Morawska and Salthammer, 2003).'*
> Dr Derrick Crump, Cranfield University

The toxicity of the air is due to VOCs and VVOCs (Very Volatile Organic Compounds) and they both create serious illnesses. The more of them breathed, the worse it is, and these days their contents in products and materials is reducing but they are still present. The less of these there are in products and materials the better, so the more designers and clients specify materials whose chemical effects are known and are minimal or removed the healthier indoor air is.

VOCs are emitted with air temperature change and long-term exposure to air as the materials basically dry. Cracked paint is cracked because it has been drying throughout its lifespan, the same with some vinyl floor finishes that curl at the seams; they do this because the material has been emitting gases and drying over its lifespan. Other sources of VOCs are cleaning products and also household items and personal toiletries. The more all these are removed and not purchased further the better the indoor air quality will steadily get. The list of sources and main toxins overleaf provides clarity on what to look for and ask manufacturers to remove or avoid these materials wherever possible.

Table 1: Sources and types of indoor air pollution

Source	Main pollutants[14]
Combustion of fuel	CO_2, NOx, organic compounds, particulates
Tobacco smoke	CO_2, organic compounds, particulates
Cooking	Organic compounds, particulates
People	CO_2, VVOCs, VOCs, water
Building materials	Organic compounds, formaldehyde, radon, particulates (including fibres)
Consumer products (e.g. cosmetics, clothing, air fresheners, candles, electrical goods, pesticides, toys, adhesives)	Organic compounds, formaldehyde, particulates
Furnishings	Organic compounds, formaldehyde
MVHR equipment	Biological particulates
Office equipment	Organic compounds, O_3
Outdoor air	SO_2, NOx, O_3, particulates, biological particulates, benzene
Contaminated land	Methane, CO_2, VVOC, VOC
Washing and cleaning	Water, organic compounds
Animals	Allergens (particulates)

As an example, many retail or hospitality interiors will install additional sources of smell through plug-in devices with the intent on creating a more stimulating retail or leisure environment. There are customers that will react negatively to these and feel ill to different degrees. One of these substances is salicylates and found both in natural foods and perfumes due to their method of harvest and supply. Although the research field is still thin on their presence as a secondary effect in indoor air, from the existing evidence in clinical settings there is a growing body of evidence which will lead to further work. Although the reaction may be commonly understood as an intolerance or allergy, it is a chemical 'oversupply' which acts like an overdose. Understanding the indoor air quality of a store and the side effects of the actual produce and features introduced also provides an opportunity to retailers and hosts to steadily remove these where possible or reduce to a manageable degree. When designing a store it is important to be aware that if the design team or the client's team wishes to introduce additional aroma devices that these will impact on the comfort and wellbeing of occupants. It is good practice to consider passive ways smell can be introduced through the authentic design.

To know what the air quality is within an interior, there are two ways right now; measurement devices can be purchased or rented by the week, and can read in the moment what the air mix is and report on-screen the results, and the other is to take air samples in test tubes which then can be taken to be tested in labs. This is all still a developing area, both technologically as well as on the harmonisation of common languages for the processes of measurement and testing standards, but one can find out quickly and in a cost effective manner, what an interiors Total VOC levels are (TVOC).

VOC: For actual benchmarks for each popular VOC refer to the WHO indoor air quality guidelines 2010 and ensure the exposure to occupants is part of the thinking, assuming the material or composition can't be designed out. An alternative source is the French agency ANSES who publish[15] the latest benchmarks and exposure times.

TVOC: Based on the latest available research and evidence, levels of TVOC that fall under

200μg/m3, are considered the lowest threshold to prevent sensory irritations although some environmental benchmarking systems accept 300 μg/m3. These are for readings over an 8hr period.

PM (particle matter) count: For particulate matter the WHO and ANSES recommend the following benchmarks:

- Over 24 hours:
- 25 μg.m^{-3} for PM2.5 and
- 50 μg.m^{-3} for PM10

- Over the long term:
- 10 μg.m^{-3} for PM2.5 and
- 20 μg.m^{-3} for PM10.

Specifying products and materials

Certain certification labels and standards are available currently that make the selection of interior products and materials easier for designers and specifiers. The main labelling schemes in existence throughout Europe are summarised below (further details available in Brown et al., 2013; ECA, 2012; ECA 2013):

- The **Finnish M1** scheme: materials that pass the emission criteria are given an M1 label.

- The **Danish Indoor Climate Label (DICL)**: specific criteria have been developed for a number of product areas including textile floor coverings and windows and exterior doors. This labelling scheme also includes sensory testing.

- The **German AgBB scheme** – it is a mandatory scheme requiring assessment of a product's composition and the emissions of its organic compounds.

- The **French** requirements for VOC emissions meeting specific levels by law since 2013 for flooring, paints, varnishes, wall finishes and building materials.

- **GUT** label for textile floor coverings.

- **EMICODE** system for low VOC emitting adhesives.

- **Blue Angel** scheme covers a wide range of materials and products used indoors.

- **Greenguard** certification programmes and those developed by the California Department of Public Health including the California Standard Practice Section 01350 – 'Cal01350'.

- **BIFMA** the American based furniture certification includes emissions.

- **Cradle to Cradle** product certification for all products and materials.

- **European Ecolabel (flower)** product certification for all products and materials.

- **CertiPUR** for foam insulation in furniture.

- **Natureplus** is a European product label for all building products including emissions.

- **Green Tag Label** is an Australian and New Zealand product certification that covers emissions for carpets, flooring, textiles and upholstery, and mattresses and bedding.

- **Green Label by Carpet and Rug Institute (CRI)** is USA based and covers the emissions from such flooring products, including underlays.

The EU INDEX project[16] undertook to appraise and harmonise the various country standards since 2004. Test standards or labels can be requested from manufacturers when looking at material specification, which provide information on the release of toxic gases. By requesting manufacturers for a product's Environmental Product Declaration (EPD) the design team is able to have most of the information on any product or material in one document. The quality assurance of these and the extent the EPDs

FIGURE 4:12
Extract from an indoor air quality test report indicating levels of survey points within a project for both TVOC and Formaldehyde. Report number 60348/1/CM

4 RESULTS

The test results are summarised in Table 2 and Table 3 for TVOC and Formaldehyde respectively. The full analysis report is provided in Appendix B for reference.

Table 1   TVOC Measurement Results

TVOC location number	Area of test	Measured value µg/m³	Value within limit
1-1034113	Front shop floor	7,900	No
2-1045451	Centre shop floor	7,500	No
3-1073540	Rear shop floor	5,400	No
4-1070646	Fitting room	8,800	No
5-1096232	Staff toilet	8,300	No

Table 2   Formaldehyde Measurement Results

Formaldehyde location number	Floor	Sample	Measured value µg/m³	Value within limit
1-6906408046	Front shop floor	1	38	Yes
2-6906408047	Front shop floor	2	39	Yes
3-6906408183	Front shop floor	3	57	Yes
4-6906408042	Centre shop floor	1	30	Yes
5-6906408043	Centre shop floor	2	35	Yes
6-6906408045	Centre shop floor	3	29	Yes
7-6906408184	Rear shop floor	1	53	Yes
8-6906408185	Rear shop floor	2	52	Yes
9-6906408186	Rear shop floor	3	40	Yes
10-6906408187	Fitting room	1	91	Yes
11-6906408188	Fitting room	2	120	No
12-6906408189	Fitting room	3	130	No
13-6906408190	Staff toilet	1	69	Yes
14-6906408191	Staff toilet	2	60	Yes
15-6906408192	Staff toilet	3	69	Yes

need to go in the research of materials impacts are guided by international standards, and specifically ISO 14025 which is a Type III environmental declaration. When provided with one of these, designers and specifiers need to ensure it states that it has indeed been produced using the ISO 14025 standard, this includes that it is third party verified and published. It also needs to state the Product Category Rules it has used to undertake the LCA, as each product and material needs a slightly tailored set of data to reflect its nature and impacts. The European Standard EN 15804 has also been developed to guide the content and form of EPDs for building products specifically. When specifying interior products and materials, designers and clients can refer to an EPD to investigate the impacts to air quality and compare between products to select the overall best fit.

In the UK specifiers of office retrofit projects are encouraged to use low emitting materials under the SKA rating scheme (RICS, 2013 and Higher Education, 2016). Internationally schemes for assessing the sustainability of buildings such as BREEAM (BRE, 2014) and LEED (USGBC, 2014) include recognition of the use of low emitting construction products.

Study highlights of indoor air quality testing outcomes in occupied spaces

Dr Derrick Crump, University of Cranfield (Crump D (2013) Investigating indoor air quality problems; Best practice and case studies. Forensic Engineering, 166, 2, 94–103.)

1 Missia et al., (2010) conducted IAQ measurements in five European cities (Athens, Nicosia, Dublin, Copenhagen and Milan). Measurements of VOCs and aldehydes were conducted in four buildings per city in the summer and winter period and on-site emission tests were conducted on selected materials. Indoor concentrations were varied and depended on the building age and type with approximately 40% of the indoor air levels originating from building materials.

2 Guo H (2011) measured 15 VOCs and formaldehyde in 100 homes in Hong Kong and concluded that on average 76.5% of the total VOC emissions was from offgasing of building materials, 8% from room freshener, 6% household products, 5% mothballs and 4% from painted wood.

3 Sinn and Jo (2014) measured indoor and outdoor air concentrations of 30 selected VOCs in 10 newly built apartments in Korea one month before and then every month over a 24-month period when occupied. VOC sources in new apartments during the pre-occupancy stage were mainly assigned to emissions from building finishing materials, whereas during the post-occupancy stage VOC sources were primarily assigned to emissions from household products as well as building finishing materials.

Putting design for wellbeing into practice

Based on all the above issues around the supply of fresh air and the composition of it, and considering how clients, designers and occupants can all work within their remit, the following high level strategy recommended by Nazaroff (2013)[17] can be adopted to achieve and maintain good indoor air quality, in order of priority:

1 Minimise indoor emissions – specify the right products and materials, review cleaning materials and look at occupant behaviours that may contribute.

2 Keep it dry – regulate the relative humidity of the spaces wherever possible.

3 Ventilate well – supply of fresh air to reflect the space needs and occupants' tasks.

4 Protect against outdoor pollution – install filters if external air is polluted or if occupants have high respiratory sensitivity.

Designers and clients need to consider how different decisions they make for other drivers, such as space planning effectiveness for psychological comfort, ensuring spaces have adequate storage capacity or minimising acoustic distraction, will work with or conflict with air movement and its quality. Placing walls, high level storage units and free standing privacy screens in the interior floor and close to the source of air, will change the way air will move within the space. Air will distribute according to the physical objects it comes across, just like light and sound will also reflect off a surface, air will do the same.

When pulling together an interior, note the following considerations or solutions:

• Consider where the openable windows are or the mechanical supply grills are, and make sure to avoid placing any long-term working or sitting positions directly in front of them. If using the space is a necessary requirement, consider if shorter term uses can be placed there or occupants who are less sensitive will be happy to use such areas.

• Placing active roles or places of work/play, in areas close to the ventilation or heating source is also another way of considering a suitable solution while integrating two requirements.

• If you are creating separate rooms within the space, and the interior strategy is working with natural ventilation movement, make sure the air can flow between spaces or through a ceiling plenum if that is a viable solution. Building walls or rooms will stop or significantly limit air movement in the required flow rates.

• High level storage units placed in front of windows or air sources will also create a physical block to air flows.

• Provide user adjustments visibly in all areas or ways occupants can request an adjustment to air quality features (temperature, air flow speed, humidity, CO_2 and VOC levels). Providing insight and clarity to users will reduce feelings of stress from discomfort.

• Consider how much stimulation the occupants need based on their User Profile. The more excitement or stimulation provided the more you can increase the sensual feelings derived from the movement of air, through increased feelings of 'freshness' and activity of their senses.

• Consider how important the cognitive performance of the occupants is in relation to other needs and ensure the levels of CO_2 and the amount of distraction through a sensory experience allows concentration and cognitive activities to work effectively.

• In the design and selection process of materials and products, consider what the materials are made with, or installed with, and how they will be contributing to the air quality occupants will live in and their state of health. Ensure the first aim is to introduce zero harmful substances.

• In the above material selection process, consider how the temperature and freshness levels being provided for the air quality will align and complement the emotional impact of the colours and textures selected. Selecting colours so they are a palette of very fresh colours such as a type 1 group, combining it with shallow hard textures, angular shapes and then adding high levels of freshness to the air quality, will suit a specific occupant group comfort style and climatic condition, or make for an uncomfortable space users may enter and exit promptly.

• As project budgets allow and technology evolves further, propose an indoor air modelling study to be undertaken. This can help predict how thermal comfort may result on proposed settings and flow and speed of movements expected in specific areas. The movement of building exhaust fumes is now a requirement for many in-town or city buildings to ascertain where toxic chimney fumes will settle and spread, based on their toxicity and weight. Similarly, on a smaller scale the modelling can assist interior studies when there are materials emitting high VOCs.

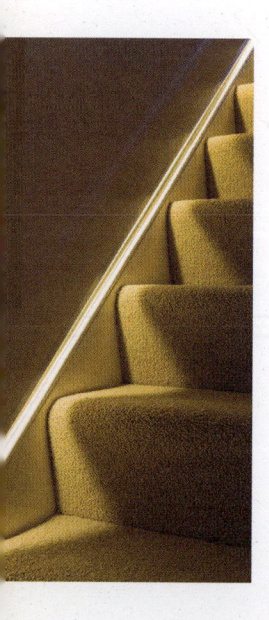

FIGURE 4: 13
Illumination and texture

CHAPTER 16
Illumination and light design

Visual and non-visual impacts on humans 137 • Lighting for meaning and emotional expression 138 • Working with daylight 139 Strategies to integrate in design 139 • Artificial light 142 Light source types 142 • Impacts to colour and texture 144 Task and ambient lighting 145

On most projects, clients and occupants get very excited when it comes to talk about colours, materials and furniture. A lot of time can be taken up to select, view, test and install some elaborate or unique products and materials. Yet, the richness or fine texture materials, the subtle colour combinations of fabrics and the way users are perceived themselves within these spaces, are fundamentally dependant on the quality of illumination provided. Vast sums of money and time by all involved can be spent on 'the fun stuff' but it is disproportionate to the actual perceived quality achieved in a space. Some of the more minimal interior spaces, or ornately designed interiors, can evidence the difference that a good or bad illumination approach can make.

The number one recommendation for where to spend time and money in an interior, assuming the aim, is to achieve a great interior space, is to spend it on achieving good quality lighting. After this is achieved, designers and clients can purchase one or one hundred objects, they will look and feel the best. A talented lighting designer, Roberto Serra, has referred to light's impact with 'the ability to see affects our ability to move, perform, relate to the world around us, to time and space.' This summarises succinctly the effects and scope of lighting on a project and why it should be placed high amongst all project impacts.

When we refer to 'light' we are actually referring to the amount of illumination that will touch a surface. The way this illumination is delivered and how it reacts on surfaces, is where we have many choices and ways to consider it as part of the design process. Light is in fact energy wavelengths which the human eye and skin can perceive, but it also affects the human body beyond what we perceive with these two senses. How this occurs and how light supports occupant wellbeing will be discussed in more detail.

The following aims and benefits of light in interiors are in short outlining how it can be used intentionally to support occupant comfort and wellbeing:

• The ability to link occupants to daylight, or daylight emulating light, provides both a way to support a Biophilic approach by linking to a natural feature, and also ensures occupant circadian rhythms are regulated.

• Illuminate surfaces in such a way that the textural qualities and impacts are perceived.

• Illuminate surfaces so the perception of colour and all its impacts are benefited from and there is minimum distortion.

• Support occupants' perception of space, the dimensional makeup of the volume, its depth, and remove or add complexity as required from tasks undertaken.

• Aid as a means of communication the way users will subconsciously understand how to wayfind or interact with information throughout an interior.

• Provide a specific atmosphere to an interior based on its use such as feelings of intimacy or openness.

• Enhance the user harmonised version of beauty and freshness that supports feelings of stimulation, comfort and safety.

• Support all types of tasks undertaken in spaces from going to sleep, viewing an artwork, eating food, attending a concert, reading a book and writing a report.

Skilled Lighting Designers are a strong addition to a design team. Traditionally, experienced electrical engineers have been allocated the task of planning lights into spaces and given fixed guidance on Lux levels to follow for generic types of spaces, but unless skilled in the fine art of illumination, this approach can't compare results as being equal. Apart from the issue of using light as an art form to sculpt an interior space and understand how it harmonises with the users and their needs, designing by Lux levels does not equate to the amount of light which users perceive in a space. Lux levels, used commonly as a means to regulate 'good lighting' can't tell us how well-lit a space will be perceived. A classroom or hospital corridor may be designed to what is recommended as good practice based on the Lux levels of light that hit the desks or the floor surfaces, but how occupants will *perceive* light walking down a corridor or sitting at a desk and looking at a teacher's gestures, are actually different results. And the difference in approach makes one support occupants' comfort and wellbeing and the other not.

There are many times when a design is developed without the electrical engineers asking what finishes and colours have been selected. What this means is that the lighting designed on a Lux level approach will be perceived completely differently if a wall or floor finish is dark or light. When using very light or dark colours we will need to ask for lower or higher Lux levels if no other design solution can be found to provide light without changing colours. Textures and surface reflections are also major influencers on how illuminated a space will be perceived by occupants. The smoother and harder a surface is, and the more acute the geometry is with the source of light, the more uncomfortable the experience of light will be.

Although many have written about the impacts of light, Dr Peter R Boyce summarised in 2009 three main paths that broadly describe the impact of light on human health and which we will touch upon 2 and 3 in this section:

1 impact of light as radiation

2 impact of light through the visual path or perception

3 impact of light through the non-visual path of perception

Visual and non-visual impacts on humans

When we say we need light in a space it is understood that we need light to enable us to see. This has been the only, generally understood need behind lighting interiors. Over the last few decades more research has been provided that demonstrates a much wider impact of daylight on the human body that goes beyond the visual perception of light. The non-visual effects on the human body are related to the amount of daylight we are exposed to and the light fitting colours and movement emulating aspects of this.

One of the effects daylight has through the human eye is commonly referred to as circadian rhythms. The exposure of humans to daylight and its change throughout the day from morning to evening has the effect of regulating systems in our body linked to a variety of bodily functions. The daily exposure to daylight has the effect of synchronising human bodies to natural and necessary patterns. These include our sleeping and wakefulness pattern, the release of hormones, good digestion and a regular pattern in waste secretion. It is also described as our innate body clock.

The effects of an un-synchronised body clock, unregulated circadian rhythms, can be clearly felt and understood through the experience of jet lag when travelling quickly to different world time zones. The daily quieter effects of an un-synchronised body clock can be harder to recognise but include fatigue, bad sleep, mental drowsiness and other chemical-based issues. Although we can expand on the negative effects of non-exposure to daylight by referring to lots of medical details, we will summarise it for the purposes of this book as a significant

FIGURE 4:14
Non-exposure to daylight is a significant negative issue for wellbeing

issue and urge all interior occupants and interior designers to ensure the availability of daylight exposure into an interior, and the ability to view out, are maximised. Ways of exploring its use through the way we design an interior will be elaborated further on.

Re-creating daylight with artificial light can be done but is still under-developed as an approach. Certain settings, amount and colour of light are known to emulate daylight, but these states are not comfortable for other reasons such as too bright light, or emotionally affecting occupants in spaces, as they feel too cold and such like.

Lighting for meaning and emotional expression

Using light to convey or instil very fine intellectual, emotional and spiritual human states is not new as a tool or acknowledgement of its impact. One has only to have visited a church or theatre performance once to experience strong emotions and intense states of being. Many religious spaces use a combination of natural light and spatial volume to generate feelings of awe, safety, emotional openness and mental stillness.

In public spaces, a clear crisp but neutral light supports an efficient way of using and interacting with the space and other fellow users. If we consider such spaces with very cold or very warm lighting, of which many of us may have experienced already, we can recall feeling and behaviour that generated fear, isolation, hardness and lack of empathy.

FIGURE 4: 15, 4: 16, 4: 17 AND 4: 18
Light can convey different states

Working with daylight

The amount of daylight available inside buildings will depend on the architecture provided, the climatic and geographic location, neighbouring features such as other buildings, trees and other natural elements, and the time of day and year.

If the project can afford it, undertake a daylight study on the pattern and movement of daylight that can be expected in the interior proposed. This will allow maximising its availability and understanding at which points it needs to dovetail with artificial lighting or may need adjusting to support the activities in the interior. A daylight study can be undertaken by a daylight modeller. If the building is relatively new there is likely already a daylight model for the architectural design. Further development of daylight modelling to include the exposure required for circadian regulation is becoming a growing body of research. A proponent for much of this has been Dr John Mardaljevic who with others in the field is promoting the development of daylight modelling for its maximum benefit on circadian rhythms, understanding the conditions from around the world and keeping the variety of architectural conditions too in mind with the quality of daylight provided. Two papers[18] that outline the approach and benefits for daylight modelling co-authored by Dr Mardaljevic provide many of the design approaches, which maximise daylight use.

It must be said at this point that daylight that is not designed into a building and its behaviour regulated, will in itself become a problem and remove comfort. Dr Mardaljevic is a proponent of a metric for buildings that have the required design properties to support circadian regulation and passively use daylight positively and with the minimal occupant interventions to manage its effects. He refers to such well-designed buildings as 'well-tempered daylit environments'.

Daylight as a source can't be regulated as such, and when buildings are not well-tempered, they introduce issues around shading, space planning and activity planning too. As with thermal comfort, daylight requires an adaptive approach to maximise its use for comfort when not designed into the building or a specific change of use, from the outset.

FIGURE 4: 19
Daylight in a private residence

Strategies to integrate in design

Strategies to increase the entry of daylight, beyond the introduction of vertical windows or glazed facades, are the following:

- Introduce sunpipes or suntubes through the roof.

- Add horizontal high level reflective shelves to reflect daylight onto the ceiling and deeper into the interior.

- Introduce internal atria or light wells where building floors are too deep and their ceiling heights too low, for the perimeter glazing to allow daylight penetration.

- Introduce rooflights with indirect reflections ideally to soften and spread the light into the interior.

- If possible, increase the height of windows up to the ceilings to allow light to wash the ceilings and travel deeper into the interior.

- Where possible create external sheltered spaces where interior users can venture easily.

Once you have maximised the amount of daylight that can enter into a building, there are several things to consider after that to maximise the amount and use of it in the best way possible. The following ideas are to be considered to ensure the design is working with the daylight provided and not conflicting with needs of occupants due to the activities they are doing:

• Consider the use of spaces, which occupy a north-facing or south-facing room. The presence of daylight in relation to the time of day and tasks being undertaken in spaces using daylight could be harmonised. North-facing daylight will be softer with little glare and reduced summer heat gain. If temperatures drop though, they will be most directly impacted. Spaces facing east and west will have direct daylight exposure only in mornings or evenings, and the light hue will affect the colours in these spaces. Morning light is cooler and evening light warmer. When selecting colours, considering the effect of daylight on them will ensure their perception in space will be more accurate and coordinated to harmonise with their User Profile needs. These suggestions though may not be relevant to a geography on the south hemisphere and advice should be sought locally and adapt the above principles.

• Direct daylight that is not softened through any reflectors can be quite harsh and create sharp contrasts creating discomfort or negating other spatial properties that support wellbeing such as the colours and textures introduced and which may not be viewed clearly. Introducing multiple sources of daylight or light to soften contrasts can help.

• Where walls and doors are introduced, consider how rooms are affected and have access to daylight directly or indirectly. Consider clear or opaque glass doors or wall sections.

• Consider if walls need to go full height or can the space benefit overall from mid-height walls and no doors.

• Mirrors can be used to reflect light and external images, resulting in amplifying their extent and bringing them into the interior.

• Consider the colours and textures used in relation to the sun-path inside the interior and how these need to be approached to amplify or subdue the effects of the daylight.

On occasions where too much direct daylight is present, it can cause discomfort through its intensity into the eye, through high levels of glare by reflecting on interior or even exterior surfaces, or overheating of the interior air. There is a series of actions that can be taken to eliminate or reduce the effect. They will depend on the architecture and location of the building, but include some of the following:

FIGURE 4: 20 AND 4: 21
Making the best use of daylight

- Consider adding external louvres, shutters or screens. Louvres can be horizontal or vertical and fixed or mechanised and synchronised with the sun's path. Patterned panels to external facades, either fixed or sliding. These can combine some patterns and further artistic details combining expressions of beauty and practicality.

- Frittering onto the glass surface designed to the sun's path and light intensity.

- Internal blinds, curtains or shutters. These have the ability to be controlled by users or be connected to a mechanised system that follows the sun's path through the day.

- Glass films and glass specifications that emit reduced and low amounts of ultra-violet light. The glass specification can support both the amount and type of light entering into the interior space, but also the amount of heat gain through the use of sunlight.

Certain recognised built environment standards which look to promote good practice in environmental and wellbeing issues of design, will recommend the following features or approaches be adopted when designing spaces around the use of daylight:

- When calculating the amount of window space in comparison to the amount of solid walls, aim for a balance between energy efficiency and use of daylight, and recommend that window areas form no more than 25% of a room's floor area.

- When space planning and considering user experiences, workplace areas or spaces where users stay for any extended length of time, should not be further than 8m from perimeter windows or a large internal atrium.

- Where glare control solutions are introduced, and they screen views that are used to relax occupants' eyes over long periods of time, these should not reduce the view in a way that negates the provision of the view itself. There is a metric provided that the screening should have a performance where its Visible Light Transmittance (VLT) is greater than 10%. What that means is that more than 10% of the light hitting the surface of the screen will travel through and provides the interior occupant the same opportunity to view through the screen openings to the views beyond/outside. The higher the VLT percentage the more the sun and views out can occur without restriction. So there is a balance to be achieved between the amount of cover and openness to regulate the light and views to support occupants' comfort.

FIGURE 4: 22 AND 4: 23
Deep corridors in old residential properties can benefit from the effect of daylight as a security and comfort effect. The main light switches off when no one is present and only 'daylight' effect lights are on in front of residence doorways

FIGURE 4: 24
Patterned panels to external facades can either be fixed or sliding elements

Artificial light

When natural light is not available or sufficient, we resort to artificial. We can also use it to create an abstractive setting, working to extract specific emotional responses and behaviours from occupants.

So as with the perception of beauty discussed in an earlier chapter, supporting occupants by either following a Realistic or Abstract approach, so with lighting the designers need to understand which approach of these two will be most comfortable and harmonise with the needs and drivers of behaviour in all spaces.

Lighting can be considered as the extra colour, texture, form or pattern that completes an interiors palette. The one you have up your sleeve or the one you can rely on to make all others work well and tie them together. The way you use it can be so versatile and sculptural that it's like a magic wand.

Light source types

Depending on what design look and feel has been defined as harmonious with the User Profiles, the lighting must align with the design characteristics agreed upon.

For example, if it is a bar, which wishes to drive users to feel esoteric and drive sensual experiences through the sense of touch, sound and taste, then the lighting will need to be low illumination, warm hue, so that seeing will be diffused. Shadows and indirectness will add wonder, depth, curiosity and intrigue. This is an 'abstraction' approach. In another example, in residential or hotel settings and specifically lounges, lighting needs to support relaxation, communication and contemplation. The lighting therefore needs to again work with the emotions and support a less alert state and one of safety. Placing lighting in discreet, diffused locations will achieve this, especially at mid height by introducing table lamps. The hue needs to be slightly cooler than the bar area though to support a degree of alertness yet maintain calmness.

If the design needs to include patterns, express balance and symmetry then lighting effects can be used as a tool to create these, as well as using the physical light fitting objects.

In a commercial setting such as a mid- to high-end residential development's marketing suite, the agency will seek to make potential residents feel valuable and reaffirm the value of their product. A sense of elegance needs to be integrated into a professional space to marry both characteristics.

FIGURE 4: 25 Daylight access to workplaces supports physical health

FIGURE 4: 26, 4: 27, 4: 28, 4: 29, 4: 30, 4: 31 AND 4: 32
In residential or hotel settings, and specifically lounges, lighting needs to support relaxation, communication and contemplation

Impacts to colour and texture

FIGURE 4: 33 AND 4: 34
Examples of the effects of patterned shades

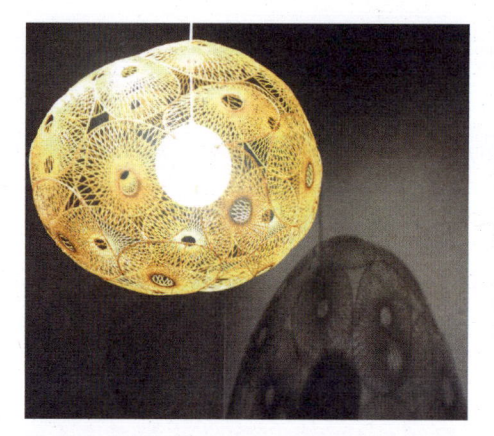

FIGURE 4: 35
Task lighting and freestanding lamps are design statements in themselves

All the issues raised under materials and textures, patterns and shapes apply to the effects lighting can make and how it is used. If a pendant has a patterned shade it will cast these shadows onto the surrounding walls. Those shapes will affect users, as would any wallpaper or other physical shape.

The other main consideration with lighting is the light fitting itself. Does the design's look and feel require the fitting to be seen and expressed as an object or to be invisible? This will be part of the design thinking and also part of the characteristics under the degree of elegance. The less one sees of a fitting and experiences the illumination in an effortless way, the higher its elegance will be.

Task lighting and freestanding lamps are design statements in themselves and although their effect in spatial illumination must be considered, they impact in their shape, colour and textures, which they embody and inherently add to the space.

Temperature of the light illumination itself will affect the final colours seen by occupants. If a very cool light is shone onto a surface with a warm hue colour, the effect of the material's warm hue will be neutralised and the colour will lose saturation. So apart from making sure that the lamp temperatures are in harmony with what occupants require and need, there is also consideration to be given to colours they also need to see. The cooler the colour of the lamp the higher is the effect on the non-visual effects.[19] Similarly with circadian rhythms, cool light that looks blue is known to depress the secretion of melatonin in the human body and extend the 'waking' part of the daily cycle. So if workplaces and schools wished to combat the sleepy effects after lunch they could increase the amount of cool (blue) light through their lamps. This will be going against the natural human cycle but if occupants have chosen to do this by extending working or learning hours then this technical approach will help their productivity levels for a period of time.

So in fact we have a conflict working with artificial lighting if we try to satisfy in one setting both good visual and non-visual effects of light, and how working with daylight can improve the conditions for both.

Task and ambient lighting

Beyond the design look and feel chosen as appropriate for a project, it is important to be clear that the lighting is serving particular purposes. Task lighting is generally referred to a narrow type of task which relates to close detailed work. This could be writing at a desk, reading in a chair, sewing or crafting at a workbench, repairing a dishwasher or a car in a large workshop. So lighting that is suitable to such manual tasks will ensure that occupants will not strain their eyes or, for instance, avoid any immediate physical harm such as cuts or burns from not seeing moving parts. So task based lighting is a basic health provision that then can allow wellbeing thereafter. There are many guidance references to be found in the professional lighting world from reputable organisations such as the SLL and CIBSE in the UK and

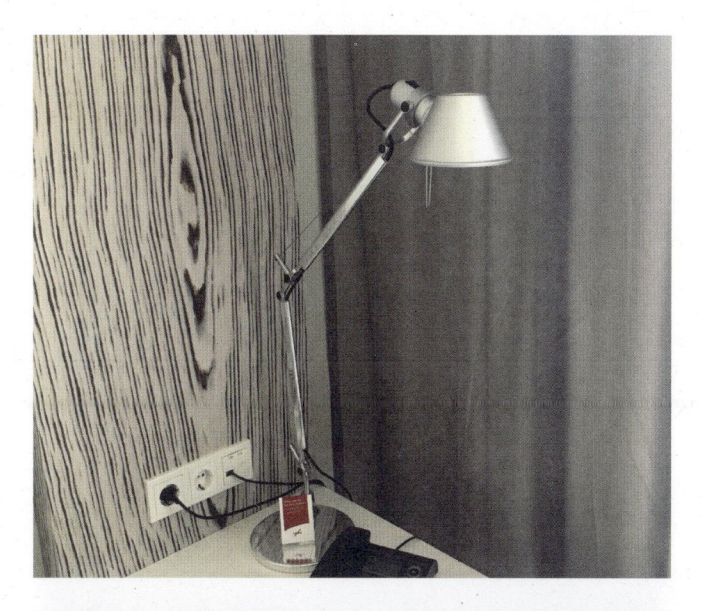

FIGURE 4: 36, 4: 37, 4:38 AND 4: 39
Examples of task and ambient lighting

ASHRAE in the US on the recommended Lux levels for different spaces based on the tasks occurring. As mentioned earlier in this section, the perceived light levels and the actual light levels are where the difference is found between good lighting that supports wellbeing and that which ticks a box.

The HSE in the UK has also published good work around the importance of good lighting at work and shows how close it falls to design lighting that meets legal requirements for safety and those that support wellbeing.

Some challenges in lighting for occupant wellbeing and task lighting for the space, can be seen typically in retail settings and public spaces such as stations. It is sometimes easier to highlight the 'don't' than the 'dos' in some cases and this is one of them. Guidance on how to deliver good lighting can be very wordy and generic in its well-intended aim to support a good result that captures such a wide variety of settings and requirements.

Putting design for wellbeing into practice

This chapter shares some insights on how lighting approaches can affect occupants and why it is important. Putting this information into our day-to-day practice can improve the way interiors will support occupant wellbeing. Below are some applications for clients and designers to consider.

1. Can the project team be strengthened with the appointment of a lighting designer?

2. Consider what style the lighting design needs to be in line with the needs identified in the User Profiles. Is it Realistic or Abstract?

3. Consider how the way light fittings are designed can support some of the Design Characteristics, such as balance, repetition, stimulation or calmness.

4. Consider how much daylight can be introduced into the interior spaces.

5. Consider the amount of daylight entering the interior and ways this may become a discomfort. Ensure glare control is provided in all cases where it is a problem.

6. Consider the lighting design as an experience by the occupants and take the design team meeting conversation beyond general benchmarks.

7. Consider how other design features such as material textures and furniture will impact on the way lighting will distribute and respond and ensure there is a two-way discussion on the space's materiality with the lighting designer or lighting specifier.

CHAPTER 17
Space planning

Contemplation and communal spaces 150 • Furniture 152 • Views out and lines of sight 154 • Harmonising interior layout with occupier culture or needs 155 • Security and interiors 157

Working with the space layout of interiors means a jostling of requirements. It is an obvious job of starting the design for any interior as designers try to test various ways to fit things in the space made available. So as a task itself it is very much a process but its impacts on wellbeing are also relevant to the overall success of a space.

We discussed ways to create a space's areas and features in an earlier chapter: discussing the effects of refuge and prospect for example which is a way of planning space and when people sit or use things within it.

The way a space is planned impacts on the following objectives which, done in an intentional way, can support occupant wellbeing:

1 Allowing daylight to travel deeper into the interiors of a building.

2 Encouraging or discouraging contact between occupants in a building.

3 Improving circulation and movement through buildings.

4 Improving security and safety either physically or as a perception.

5 Expressing a cultural style of an organisation.

6 Allowing design features to be experienced.

7 Supporting air movement and thus comfort through the air quality.

8 Supporting good views out and thus easing visual and mental strain.

9 Working to support good acoustic quality between and within spaces.

Quite a few of these issues have been discussed in earlier sections in this book. They are mentioned here as a summary of issues so the list can be used as a checklist during planning of spaces to consider and discuss with other project team members. It is currently typical practice not to associate what looks like flat shapes on a drawing with a 3D living space where occupants need to have a responsive relationship and one where they will be impacted.

Responding to objectives 2 and 3 above, work on the impacts of space planning on team relationships in workplace interiors specifically has been published by Dr Kerstin Sailer and colleagues in the industry and academia. Evidence indicates that there is a difference in the frequency and quality of interactions between occupiers of a building depending on the distance between them. Sailer raises awareness for planners to not assume that being seen means being connected, and thus assuming human relationships and connections are supported.[20] Planning to support the type of relationships that are appropriate for each space and organisational culture is what will support occupant wellbeing and productivity, so being aware of certain traditional assumptions can help planners to use designing for visual or haptic connection as a tool. Perhaps a university wants to allow students a feeling of belonging by making them all visible at any one time in a study hub, but making the physical connection just that bit longer will help them avoid study and assist their concentration for longer

FIGURE 4: 40
Circulation used for communication

periods of time. Whereas, in a workplace whose value lies in the knowledge-based economy, the innovation and problem-solving service they can generate for customers, will benefit from higher levels of collaboration and staff interaction so ideas are talked through and evolved. In these instances, making it harder to stay in your 'territory' and enable users to smoothly cross a floor or open void between two sides of a building, will encourage more interactions to flow.

Further work on the value of interactive quality includes a paper by Wolfeld in 2010 which succinctly outlines impacts on relationships by stating *'As defined by Reagans and Zuckerman (2001), network density is the "average strength of the relationship between team members" (p. 502). When employees meet face-to-face, cohesion is enhanced and they may understand each other better on personal levels. Effective collaboration relies heavily on face-to-face interactions, suggesting that the underlying characteristics of face-to-face interactions increase network density.'* [21]

A dominant issue around space planning and the formation of workplaces over the last few decades has been the move towards open-plan spaces rather than a series of cellular offices. There are good reasons to remove the cellularisation for the purposes of collaboration, increased connectivity, sense of belonging, staying informed on wider company issues and reduced physical requirements and thus costs. The big problem that comes with a decision to move open-plan without good design advice is the failure of open-plan spaces as effective workplaces. There are many examples of a company throwing a series of desks in a line and a meeting space in a corner, without considering how occupants will feel and perform. Although connectivity can go up because you can hear and see more of your colleagues talking and meeting, this can also go too far and become a complete distraction by constant stimulation. Acoustics and movement around the office requires effort for individuals to retain concentration on their own work. The way sound needs to support the balance between these requirements is where advice from an acoustician needs to be sought, which is discussed in another chapter in this book. If an acoustician is not possible then a healthy understanding of behaviours throughout typical uses of a space between the groups of people needs to be sought. This applies to workplaces as much as to turning kitchen and living areas into one space within residential developments or one-off flats. Combining any two differing uses needs consideration on the tasks being performed simultaneously.

The business case is relatively easy to make. Studies show that for each interruption a person requires about 15 minutes to re-engage with their task. If uncomfortable distracting sounds interrupt a worker for example once every hour of a day, this can be calculated at about 1hr 20mins of reduced productivity (based on 8hr day) and assuming an hourly rate of London's

FIGURE 4: 41
Plans, elevations and photos of the various life scene settings in the one open-plan space

living wage of £12 p/hr (2014) this will cost £72 a week and £3,240 a year. This is the estimated cost based on just one member of staff. Just one small team or group of occupants being impacted will provide a return on investment within the first year.

Planning-in the provision of spaces that support the various tasks is critical to multi-use spaces and recognising an understanding of a people centred interior. The inclusion of the 4Cs in the layout of all workplaces is a good start: these are spaces that will support Concentration, Collaboration, Creativity and Communication. Most workplaces, hotels or residences will require areas to support these activities and will vary from company to brand on the percentage of space allocated to each. This information should be identified in the User Profile.

The inclusion of the 4Cs in the layout of all workplaces is a good start: these are spaces that will support Concentration, Collaboration, Creativity and Communication.

Within residential interiors we can see some revolutionary planning in The Homewood. The interior plan of the Living Room is an example of design and planning mastery. The architect and owner of the house, Patrick Gwynne, planned it to serve his various activities through the day and evening, supporting contemplation, meetings, concentration workspace and entertainment. But the mastery lies in the way Gwynne has integrated all the functions quite clearly without one impeding on the other, or in any way looking at odds with each other. His use of space is excellent, leaving clear spatial breadths between the areas.

Contemplation and communal spaces

The need for privacy and physical and inner stillness are a big outcome of the move towards common spaces and combined spaces, in addition to the increase in population and its move to existing urban spaces. Also, the connection with technology which makes most users feel constantly 'on the go' has increased the need for quiet reflection. The proof of benefits related to mindfulness and meditation practices throughout the day on the performance of people and their quality of life, shows how valuable a tool space can become by providing dedicated spaces for these activities. A person can choose to fall still at a station or park bench, in a bathroom, at a cafe seat or a desk, but it is not conducive as they will be constantly fighting the work of their senses which will be naturally responding to the stimuli. To become mentally mindful, especially in the early stages of practice, it requires a quiet and calm environment to allow the body tension to ease and the mind activity and emotions to then be observed. For the practice of meditation, a space that allows a longer use is required, as it typically requires 30mins for a session. Mornings and evenings are the typical recommended times for meditation so understanding how many users a room needs to accommodate at peak times will be important.

It is worth making the point here that for anyone to achieve their wellbeing, in the fullest sense of the word, they need to practise regular meditation (not just mindfulness). The reason we present throughout this book the decisions and actions taken by the client or design team as them supporting wellbeing or enabling it, is because true enlightenment, self-knowledge, happiness and freedom of the self, come from within each human being. We can only achieve these through falling still and choosing to go to deeper levels of our consciousness systematically, which then affects the quality of our life throughout each day. The physical environment has the role of supporting our body and mind, the tools we use to exist, both during a meditation practice and during all other activities from sleep to 'wakefulness' in daytime. The wise across the ages say that wisdom, happiness and love are natural to all humans and we cover – see Figure 4: 44 up or block them through the way we live and limit the ability for these qualities to be fully expressed. Creating interior spaces we live in that support wellbeing, will mean they support our work towards behaving more wisely, lovingly and happily. For those still requiring science to provide evidence of realisation, the evidence is quickly being collated. The best way though is for them to try it out: real happiness is an experience and not something someone else can give you.

Meditation is known to reduce anxiety, blood pressure and depression, and to increase tolerance, empathy, learning, memory, creativity, self-awareness and goal setting.

The use of a separate breakout space in any interior occupied by multiple users such as hospitals, offices, restaurants or any leisure facility is very important for the purposes of social interaction and emotional wellbeing. We feel open to people when we can interact freely and express our personality and see that of a colleague or acquaintance. We are at our happiest when connected with the people around us. Small or larger details of an interior layout can help, for example the presence of a kitchen table has been seen to create the opportunity to hover and chat or even increase the amount of interaction between colleagues, friends or a family. It creates a place where it is acceptable to sit and talk rather than try and hurry a conversation in the middle of a corridor or open space.

Encouragingly, introducing workplace rest spaces has been a regulatory requirement since 2009 in Sweden.[22] This is a positive step that can discourage corporations from stuffing floor plates with desks when in need of more space without considering the impact of the removal of the social spaces on the whole team's productivity and retention.

FIGURE 4: 42 AND 4: 43
Common and community spaces

FIGURE 4: 44
A plan showing space planning in a workplace environment

The space planning itself should express an occupant's lifestyle or organisational culture. In a traditional corporate workplace scenario, where clients come first and then staff, or where a breakout space is placed in front of senior management offices or large client facing meeting rooms, staff are not likely to use it. Creating in fact a double problem where staff don't have a breakout space and visitors see an empty lifeless space.

In above plan shown in Figure 4: 44, originally the soft seating area outside the large meeting rooms was intended for staff breaks and lunch. After a discussion on how staff would feel if a large client meeting was gathering or finishing, it was decided that an alternative area within the non-public area would work with the culture and staff would make more use of it.

Furniture

FIGURE 4: 45 AND 4: 46
Informal seating

The type of furniture selected to populate interiors, to support and inform the activities of spaces, is core to a successful interior.

The way we sit will inform some of our mannerisms, way of communication and thus relationships, and even the way we think through our physical alertness or drowsiness. Placing lounge seating with soft sinking seat pads, with high arms and back will support a sense of cocooning and will lead the user towards daydreaming. Daydreaming is important as part of a creative process and problem-solving situations.

If communication is necessary between two professionals or people who may not know each other but wish to discuss personal issues, such as going to a health consultant, a school or social service space, then providing informal seating with a firmer seat and shallower sides will be supporting mental alertness yet emotional softness.

The arrangement of furniture can communicate openness and invitation to enter an undefined physical space or act as a soft barrier too as part of a way-finding system. This will support the communication style between such groups of users and support good communication and effective use of time and space.

The product designs themselves are a big part of expressing and articulating the identified design characteristics and design's look and feel. If patterns are needed, then the upholstery and furniture structure will add these features to the interior. If repetition or balance is needed, then numbers and layout of the furniture will express these characteristics strongly. If the space will support an organisation's need to have a fast change of users, such as school canteens, low cost restaurants or public transport waiting rooms, then the seating style needs to support the physical need to remove strain off the body for a short time yet firm enough to not encourage extended stays, allowing use for the large number of occupants.

Retail spaces have realised that couples will stay longer in clothing stores when there is seating provided for one of them as the other tries on garments. Considering the addition or exclusion of furniture will change people's behaviour in a very immediate and direct way.

Age, gender and physical ability are very important considerations when specifying suitable seating and tables. Understanding the needs of your primary users allows you to support some of the needs they may not talk about. Providing soft and low level seating in spaces where users are mostly elderly or have limited physical movement means they will not use them, or if they do, find getting up an uncomfortable and embarrassing moment. The same with tables and their relationship to people in front; if a female is using a desk or table there needs to be consideration as her clothing may include skirts or dresses which can make working at the desk a distracting and self-conscious experience or an unseemly one from a viewer's perspective. The same occurs with varying levels of physical mobility and the weight of some furniture, the ease in which they can be moved and adjusted. Understanding the ability for mobility is vital if designers are assuming spaces will be flexible and adaptable. Specifying a sledge base heavy metal framed seat on a deep pile carpet will restrict the ability to move furniture to support occupants' needs by smaller bodied or elderly users, or risk physical injury should they try to move them.

Ergonomically designed furniture is a very important example of design for health. Ergonomics is a better acknowledged issue, but many designers will still select based on design aesthetic and not physical comfort. Seating and sleeping furniture are the most important items for a healthy posture as they are used over long periods of time. Can you quantify the value of a good night's sleep? Similarly, if you are sitting over any lengthy period of time – typically at a work setting – seating should support the occupant's physical shape and also the activities they are undertaking. Where spaces are used by a large number of people of different shapes and structures, it is good practice to allow most of them to test a few and vote for the most popular ones. Hotels and restaurants can undertake this with focus groups and shared workspaces the same.

FIGURE 4: 47
Lounge area, including a variety of seating to meet a wide range of abilities and relationship dynamics

Views out and lines of sight

Humans are very inquisitive and also rely on sight as an innate safety tool. We use sight as a way of making sense of the world and our momentary position within it. We also need space and views of varying types for other purposes, one of which is to allow the eyes to physically relax and avoid strain. Having varying depths of sight around occupants of interiors, will allow them to refocus pupils over long periods of time, which avoids eye strain and increases comfort. This is especially important for intense visual work around computer screens, video media work, workshops or reading spaces.

If an occupant is in a space where they can hear but not see a source of sounds, this will increase their alertness, both from a sense of curiosity and security. Place this situation in their home, social or work setting and it will have comparable results. If the intention is to attract occupants' attention, as they are spending too long by themselves and not interacting with others, this can be a positive spatial performance, but if it's already adding to occupants' high alertness levels due to their nature, this will move into stress and a lack of wellbeing and productivity.

The quality of the view is also important, whether this be a view outside the window to another property or to a view of areas within the interior. Viewing the top of buildings' mechanical paraphernalia or waste bins tends to not be seen as desirable. The creation of green rooftops, window planters and internal courtyards can benefit not only the users of these spaces but also all others who are given views out to them.

FIGURE 4: 48 AND 4: 49
Sightlines and view quality

Although the discussion on open and accessible views tends to focus heavily on the provision of them, there are also needs which can require them to be limited. There are situations where privacy of space can support communication between people discussing a personal matter and introspection without feeling ogled at. Making sure this can be planned into the interior is vital to allowing for such moments in relationships or self-reflection, supporting occupant emotional needs. Schools, cultural spaces and workplaces can add great value to society by integrating these further.

FIGURE 4: 50
Privacy planned into an open interior

Harmonising interior layout with occupier culture or needs

The design's approach can impact a person's emotional wellbeing from a negative state to a positive state. For example, if a person is feeling they lack control over decisions in life, by being able to adjust to their liking their immediate environment, they will, for a limited time, feel a respite if they have this one outlet of influence. Also, being able to adjust and understand what can and can't be adjusted, is an important issue; transparency promotes understanding, which in turn increases trust and better communication.

The way a space is designed can also impact wellbeing if the approach does not harmonise with operational and ethical values. For example if an organisation is promoting transparency and trust but operates a 'closed door' policy for their executives, or has visible security and time-control monitoring around the work areas, staff will lose trust in advertised values. The physical environment needs to harmonise and reflect the values and priorities of the culture. In shopping centres and high streets alike, placing information staff outside and accessible to customers

FIGURE 4: 51 AND 4: 52
Museum of Happiness

has been valuable and part of an improved customer service experience. Similarly in public transport, over the last few years on the London Underground there has been a move to make station staff accessible to passengers by removing counters and screens, allowing a more personable transaction to take place. This is also seen in banks with the removal of counters for many services and introducing more informal and personable furniture settings.

An example of the way some public interior spaces can be and should be planned, designed and operated, is shown with the area around the London Southbank's Festival Hall Terrace Cafe. The space has existing parameters through the original architecture but recent work has improved its response to the various users throughout each day. It is one of those spaces that make public space add value to the wider society, as it is free to enter and occupiers are not hassled to purchase something but can enjoy contemplative or active use. The layout allows for flexibility in group sizes, ages, abilities and styles of gathering and activity. The overall ground floor layout allows for communication, concentration, creativity and collaboration. Whether one wishes to have a meeting or a quiet creative time, the seating and layout arrangements allow for them. In addition to the layout arrangements, the physical characteristics are well considered, including issues such as the connection to outside, daylight travelling as far back as the bar counter, good acoustic quality, visual design fluidity of the architectural details, ease of wayfinding with strong themes at the far ends combined with simplicity from a lack of visual clutter. Warmth and colour are added through the seats and seasonal graphics evolve to advertise the hall's programme. The indoor air feels clean and fresh with the air's temperature and velocity consistent. Refuge and prospect, as discussed part of environmental psychology, and territory marking characteristics, are slightly less covered but are dependent on the time of day and activities taking place and not a high priority for the space's main functional requirements. Lighting is basic and does not support a specific aesthetic approach of realistic or abstract, which would significantly add to this space's performance. The number of people occupying the space allows forgiveness for the lack of softness in texture, colour and shapes. The overall proportions of the space's volumes are comfortable and support the different types of activities taking place, although the arrival from the various sides may make the space seem top heavy. A low ceiling in a cafe actually increases comfort and the feeling of 'refuge', leading to longer, more relaxed use.

FIGURE 4: 53
London Southbank Festival Hall Front Terrace Cafe, view of seating area looking out to the terrace

FIGURE 4: 54
London Southbank Festival Hall Front Terrace Cafe, view towards interior seating area from the outside terrace

Security and interiors

We have already discussed how spaces considering material textures, colours, brand and user experience will show long-term success and are those that have shown, in the current market, a continuation of this approach throughout their operation. Following the events of 11 September 2001 in New York, a UK airline immediately responded to the new security level. Amongst other activities, the need to increase security in their own HQ in the UK was necessary. The adopted approach was consistent to the culture and not done through a physical security barrier, but done by maintaining the human touch, adding visible security guards in all the entrance lobbies. This approach ensured the continuation of their 'people friendly' approach but also the critical security requirements were met. By adding a physical barrier they would have given a 'closed doors' message and also compromised the fun-loving feel the company is known for.

Some recent approaches to 'securing' spaces and creating perceptions of safety actually does the opposite and through physical objects and design approaches can make public feel less secure.

A paper published by the new economics foundation, written by Jody Aked and Anna Minton '"Fortress Britain": High Security, Insecurity and the Challenge of Preventing Harm' published in 2012,[23] highlighted the approaches taken so far in residential settings, questioned the support overall to occupant wellbeing, and the benefit of the way security was being supported in Britain.

Another issue that impacts on our sense of security is acoustics. Noise generates

FIGURE 4: 55
Corridor acoustics

CHAPTER 17 • SPACE PLANNING

157

FIGURE 4: 56
There is a need for secure spaces that don't negatively impact wellbeing

worry and a knock-on effect on behaviour. This has been noted especially in school scenarios when classrooms become noisy and then teachers can lose control of behaviour. If we can be heard and can hear people without strain, we are calmer, and our stress levels are lower.

There is no question that physical security can be a real need, but at its core lies an emotional and cognitive issue, and we need to take a better look at how we 'secure' through physical design so that we don't only reduce emotional and mental wellbeing, but stop propagating it through divisions in the way we plan spaces. Removing the 'them' and 'us' as much as possible.

Putting design for wellbeing into practice

The act of planning the interior spaces, their layout and relationships is bringing together many of the issues discussed in previous chapters, and also has a few specific issues to consider beyond just 'fitting in' things like a shopping list. Placing the above issues into our day-to-day practice can improve the way layouts can support occupant wellbeing through the issues they enable or prohibit. Below we share some considerations and applications for clients and designers to consider:

1. Understand the lifestyle or culture defined in the User Profile and define what layout approach harmonises with user needs. Does the layout need to:

   a. Support communication by connecting people or provide privacy and reduce distraction?

   b. Reflect openness and trust or a hierarchical approach to relationships?

   c. Support specific tasks such as the 4Cs for workplaces (Concentration, Collaboration, Creativity or Communication)?

2. Propose the inclusion of a reflection space and/or breakout room as appropriate.

3. Consider how the layout is balancing physically or symbolically in messages, security and friendliness.

4. Consider what viewing paths are experienced at all areas of any longer term use task spaces and ensure there are long distances available for longer use periods.

5. Consider the furniture style and comfort and harmonise with user needs and preferences.

CHAPTER 18
Acoustic design

Designing for good acoustics 160 • Sound treatment and design thinking 163

FIGURE 4: 57
Fixed sound separation

Sound is as invisible to the human eye as air particles and gases can be – and interiors are full of all of these, impacting occupants on a constant basis. We must design spaces that are not removing health but allowing people's wellbeing to flourish. Wellbeing will be supported if audibility in spaces can occur without strained effort by occupants. Occupants should be able to hear each other without having to resort to straining their senses, either to hear properly or to block unwanted sounds. Wellbeing can also be impacted when the quality of sound is too quiet, as if in a vacuum as it feels abnormal and thus emotionally disconcerting. This is not typical but can happen and is discussed below.

The second most disruptive issue typically found in the experience of spaces, is noise; too loud, usually, but also the lack of it, which is reported as a 'lack of atmosphere', whether a space is occupied or not. If one has ever been left alone at home, they will know how unsettling a quiet house can be.

Designing for good acoustics

The distinction between sound and noise is important; noise being a sound that is a negative experience. Sounds can be a pleasant sensation and in many ways something we desire, but noise is an experience that is uncomfortable and we wish to avoid.

There are some very good and freely available technical guidebooks published on the design approach to create good quality acoustics. Some recommended reading includes:
- FIS guide to office acoustics, FIS, 2015.
- Acoustic design of schools: performance standards BB93, 2015.
- ANC good practice guide, 2014, which again is for school environments.
- BS 8233:2014 Guidance on sound insulation and noise reduction for buildings.
- CIBSE and ASHRAE good practice guides around acoustics in relation to building services are also available for a fee, as are many EN, ISO and BS standards.

All guides offer benchmarks on the reverberation and attenuation of spaces and between spaces for different uses, and types of experience. The acoustic benchmarks need to be aligned with the type of experience required for each space and project. Although the guidelines should be followed, and an acoustician should be wherever possible appointed to the design team, there are instances with or without an acoustician where the experience may fall outside guidelines and yet meets user preferences and thus comfort. This applies to many of the design issues and in acoustics it is no different. If the occupants find they produce through their use of the space and communication, very low levels of sound, they may require a higher level of reverberation of interior finishes and products to allow a higher bounce of sound. This needs to be done in an informed manner, otherwise the desire to create an 'atmosphere' can spill into noise very easily through lack of understanding of sound movement.

The way sound will transfer through building structure (vibration) is fundamental to the experience within interiors but we will focus mainly on the remit of an interior designer and scope of an interior fit-out for this book. We assume that good practice has been followed for the structure of floors, walls, external doors, windows and ceilings.

Under the issue of acoustics, the design process needs to consider the following issues that affect user experiences, these are:
- How the noise generated within spaces bounces around the interior surfaces in any given interior space.
- How the sounds of one space can be heard in another, or from an external area they enter into the interior.
- How mechanical services, now typically found in many buildings, create noise.
- How certain activities may require privacy or confidentiality.
- How an atmosphere of a space may require a specific design quality, which supports the behaviour of users, their personalities and way of expression.

Sound 'insulating' activities are looking to respond to sources that are:
- Airborne such as conversations or music, and Impactful such as falling objects, heels on the floor and thumping through a wall structure.

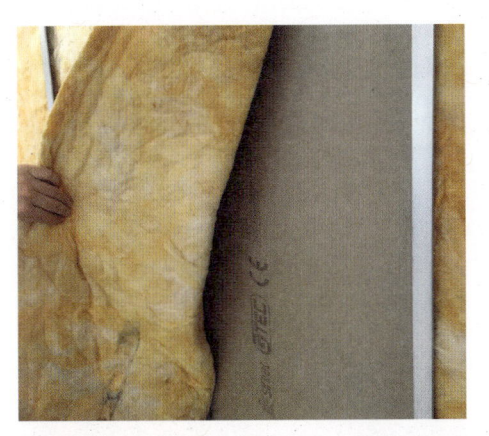

FIGURE 4: 58, 4: 59 AND 4: 60
Fixed and responsive sound insulation

CHAPTER 18 • ACOUSTIC DESIGN

161

As design teams, clients and occupants ourselves we can respond to these sources in three ways; these are:

Fixed: Through the specification of materials and type of construction.

Part-fixed and part-responsive: Through temporary screens and furniture types.

Responsive: Through changing activities or moving spaces.

If an acoustician is not appointed to the project, and you are working with an existing interior space, it is good to understand what sound performance there is already and use that as a benchmark, both for an understanding of the physical materials that are present right now and how users feel about the space. Sound meters are readily available on the market.

When space planning interiors, understanding the use of spaces, includes the amount of animation required in each or not, and relationships required between spaces. Sound is very much linked to activities being undertaken and ensuring the levels are designed to support comfort will ensure wellbeing is supported and productivity or rest is achieved. Depending on the project, there could be two strategic approaches to select from: the first is to define the spaces in acoustic zones based on the sound levels and thus cluster similar ones together, or if functions dictate specific adjacencies, work on the room/spaces performance individually and each to a higher performance than if they were clustered. There is no one ideal approach but one way which will suit most for each project.

As with daylight and temperature, so with sound; there can be a conflict between allowing openness between exterior and interior spaces and the transition between them. Adding large glazed areas within and between interior spaces to enable lines of sight and visual connection, can create higher transfer of sound. There are always solutions and when it comes to glazing it usually involves increasing the number of glazed panes, their joints performance and the extent of them in the space itself.

Openable windows are a preferable method for ventilation as outlined in the Air Quality section, but this can introduce an acoustic problem if outside there is a

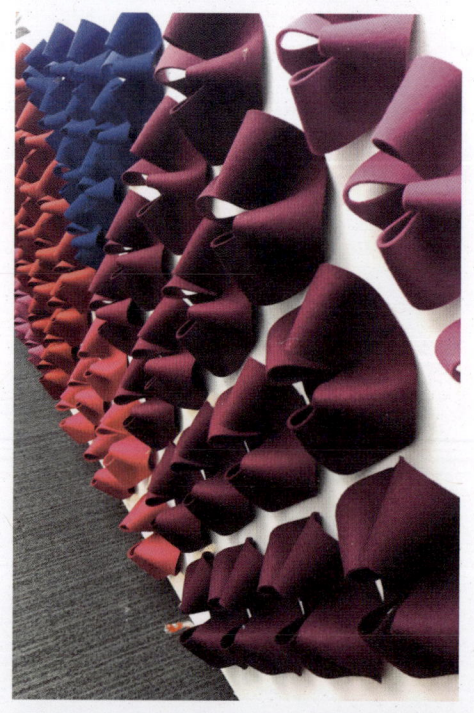

FIGURE 4: 61 AND 4: 62
Fixed materials support better acoustic quality

frequent source of noise such as a road, social space or even a school's playground.

Sounds from mechanical services or equipment used, as part of the interior activities, must be considered by the holistic design. If services engineers are on-board the project they will typically design the way mechanical equipment works so that it allows just a faint background sound, referred to as background or white noise. This is not a sound that generally stimulates attention but its lack is generally felt. We are not used to completely silent buildings, in urban areas specifically, and only notice this if there is a power cut. The sound from airflows moving in a high-speed ventilation system or the fans part of an air conditioning system are the sources of noise. Placing these away from sound sensitive areas to start with, is highly recommended.

Water flowing around the building, especially in vertical pipes, is another source of noise and discomfort for occupants. Where pipes are placed close to structural columns, they are recommended to be wrapped with insulation and cased in. Water services can also include water drainage or supply pumps when the falls are not sufficient for gravity. There are some quieter products on the market these days, but they still make a distinct humming noise.

Open soffits in many retail, leisure and workplace spaces have become popular over time, both from a reduction in cost, waste and due to energy efficiency actions. The soffit is usually a hard and reflective surface, so it needs good design thinking on reducing reverberation either vertically or lower down in the space. Ceilings are the most important areas to reduce reverberation within spaces.

FIGURE 4: 63
Pipework is often a real source of noise discomfort

Sound treatment and design thinking

When looking at the quality of acoustics within each room or space itself, we need to consider all surface finishes, the furniture and screen heights, operating equipment with extreme noise sources and the size and shape of the room's volume itself. This is after we understand how many people occupy each room, what activities they are doing and what acoustic quality they require for these.

Understanding how good acoustics are achieved is important but there is already a published[24] proposed hierarchy and list of issues recommended to follow, focused on workplaces, and it lists a number of features projects need to respond to in order of priority.

The first area to start at as a designer is to look at removing, reducing, or controlling the noise source itself wherever possible. Such an example is the food processing equipment in cafes following the growth of cold iced drinks and the barrister-based service. The blitz from blenders in cafes where most finishes are smooth and hard creates a sharp and very uncomfortable experience. Although customers will only experience it for one or a few instances, or the length of the queue they find themselves in, the staff are experiencing this through their whole shift. As designers and clients, we have the ability to design out or reduce the discomfort by changing equipment or moving this function to another back-of-house area

FIGURE 4: 64
Staircase runners can help create a relaxed feel in the home

not populated by all staff all of the time.

Hospital wards are other spaces that suffer in their purpose to heal patients yet there is conflict where medical staff need to perform their jobs and create noise and disrupt sleeping patients. The experience of trying to get uninterrupted sleep in a hospital when dealing with health issues is a big stress both physically on a recovering body and mentally when there is low emotional resilience. Simple and intelligent acoustic design could reduce the levels of disruption and support the objectives of everyone's role in these spaces.

As designers have the responsibility to select all the finishes and products in rooms, it is within their remit to include absorbency. This could be a visible feature such as colourful wall panels or blended with the architecture, such as a textured wall render that can look like paint from afar.

Caution should be raised on the use of too much absorbency and so making it hard to hear as sound does not travel. An example can be in boardrooms across tables when people can't hear each other, and between two retail colleagues communicating along a counter. We need sound to travel in such cases and smooth, hard materials need to be placed above to enable this to happen.

Providing dedicated media call and concentration rooms is a must for all workplaces these days. Ensuring the space planning integrates these is very important for the wellbeing of all occupants.

Aligning the acoustic design to the information available through the User Profiles can allow the design team to consider important details such as footwear and behaviour of users. It's vital to understand how they will interact within each space. If occupants are predominantly wearing hard and high-heeled shoes and the floor finishes are hard, they will be self-conscious of walking in any open space, for example a hospital corridor, residential corridor or hotel lobby. This is quite important in spaces such as long hallways, reception areas, cafes and lounges.

Putting design for wellbeing into practice

To respond to the above issues in our day-to-day projects, the design team can consider the following actions:

1. Appoint an accredited acoustician to the project team to design the way sound will behave based on the requirements.

2. Refer to the guidance listed, and the recommended performance levels relevant to each space type.

3. Decide what strategy will work best for each project; zoning acoustic types or working on specific room performances.

4. Consider which acoustic solutions between fixed, semi-fixed and movable are suitable for your project based on the activities and User Profiles.

5. When you need speech privacy, use appropriate insulation within walls, floors and ceiling cavities. When you need absorbency, ensure the materials meet the need and use the hierarchy suggested.

6. Ensure the design for the building services systems considers the acoustic quality required and engineers work with the design team to achieve this, including the water services.

7. Consider the placement of service penetrations such as power plugs, data cabling, air ducts and ventilation grills to reduce the amount of sound travel through spaces.

8. Consider the balance of absorbent and non-absorbent finishes and products used in the interiors and how they will affect the space's performance. Obtain the percentage of area required for absorbent materials and consider that these need to be based on the design look and feel and design characteristics information. Understand where deeper or smooth textures will work best, thus achieving both design objectives.

FIGURE 4: 65
Derwent London HQ, Savile Row, London. Acoustic ceiling panels support comfort during meetings

CHAPTER 18 • ACOUSTIC DESIGN

CHAPTER 19
Operational issues

Controllability 167 • 'Soft Landings' process 168
The landlord, facilities manager and tenant opportunities 168
Occupancy surveys 169

Although all the design and delivery issues discussed in this book are core for inclusion in spaces supporting occupant wellbeing, there are a few issues that fall under the way they are used by occupants or undertaken once spaces are occupied, so fall within operational issues. These issues include controllability, the 'Soft Landings' process and occupancy surveys.

Controllability

This is the ability to adjust any of the following items to the users' needs. The items include furniture styles, furniture features such as seat adjustability, task lighting, window shading, temperature, IT and AV aspects, personalising preferences of digital services and selection between privacy settings.

Providing control of immediate environmental features to occupants is known to reduce stress levels. The issue of controllability of mechanical features and lighting has been discussed in earlier chapters, but the place of work and its suitability to the task is also vital. Allowing clients a variety of control is usually part of current good service design, but staff requirements tend to be limited.

The occupant's User Profile done correctly will highlight all the opportunities where an interaction between the built environment and users exists. In certain situations, such as temperature control in multi-occupant interiors, the control provided may be minimal – this is still valuable and awareness of why should be communicated to users. The control method itself needs to be considered and aligned to the User Profile controllability skills and preferences defined as supportive to users. For example, installing a digital and highly capable software control system in a residential home of a retired couple, when they have expressed aversion for digital equipment, will not support their wellbeing and only serve in creating a stressful situation for them when they attempt to use it, or avoid it altogether.

The time users have available or are prepared to spend to control something is also typically very limited. Some mechanical control systems in commercial buildings, maintained by teams which change relative frequently, means that many technically minded professionals find them hard to use also and do not support the operation of buildings and interiors.

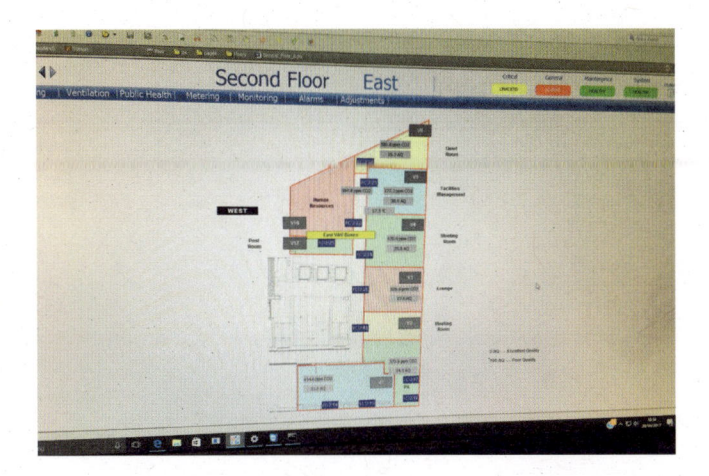

Although highly effective for residential interiors as much as commercial, providing user manuals for spaces is seen as a healthy step towards introducing new users to the general design principles and functions of an interior. All intentions behind certain design decisions get forgotten once occupancy happens or staff change, so having a written, short and concise, record of why something was designed in a certain way and how to use it, ensures harmony is executed as initially planned.

As noted in the ventilation section and research in this issue, giving more control to users by allowing them to open windows when they choose, makes them feel healthier and achieve higher personal wellbeing levels.

FIGURE 4: 66
Dashboard of a building BMS indicating air quality levels in each room, in addition to the energy and water consumption

'Soft Landings' process

'Soft Landings'[25] is the name given to a design and delivery process for projects with good practice guidance on the people it is right to engage with throughout the design, delivery and early operation of spaces. It guides teams on the types and timings for checks by stakeholders to ensure the space being designed will support all their needs and be as successful as it can. Stakeholders include the people going to occupy the spaces but also those visiting and maintaining them.

The process is guiding teams through what can be described as a collection of thinking and activities as good design. If a project engages thoroughly with people and understands the full impacts of the space's life cycle, it is going to deliver good design that supports occupant wellbeing. The other issue this process is safeguarding against is the sharp cut-off at the end of a project when occupants are left trying to figure out how to actually use spaces as intended. Naturally, the better designed spaces are the more they will reflect the user ability and understanding, but some issues still need gentle introduction and adjustment in the early days of occupation. The Soft Landings process is doing what it says on the tin, its landing users softly into their new space, giving a helping hand and technical support where needed. The Soft Landings process and supporting information is owned by the Building Services Research and Information Association.

The landlord, facility manager and tenant opportunities

There are issues that are solely in the control of either the landlord or the tenant when there is such a relationship of occupation and we are not dealing with an owner-occupier. Where there is such a relationship, which is the majority of commercial property around the world, there are some great opportunities for all parties to create value and support wider wellbeing. Residential environments for the rental and council markets are also affected and have the same issues at play with roles and opportunities.

Listing the main issues that are at play in a typical commercial building in the West and on current design styles and operation, we can see where all parties can proactively offer support for wellbeing. This list can offer both parties the opportunity to collaborate on the issues, especially where they require both parties to be participating at any time for a feature to support wellbeing. There are many industry stories of tenants not being able to adopt a certain practice as it relies on the property owner making an investment to their existing building. There are also instances where an informed property owner wishes to interact with their tenants but the tenants don't care or understand the issues as they are too busy running their business, or may find it a threat to their privacy.

The role of the facility manager (FM) is very important when present. This role can maximise and negotiate on behalf of both sides to improve the overall performance of issues. Their role could add further value by their informed and central position over the long-term relationship of the property owner and tenants. Ensuring the FM team is highly knowledgeable on wellbeing and how the building affects occupants and their performance and wellbeing is critical to them enabling and amplifying any efforts. It is also key to coordinating the knowledge and impacts a number of tenants can make in any one building around issues supporting wellbeing. For example, the supply and quality of air through centralised systems will be affected if tenants don't maintain their ducts found in their own premises.

Occupancy surveys

Asking occupants how they are and marrying up these with the quantitative measurements of the physical space, can provide a true and sustainable picture of how the built environment is supporting occupant wellbeing. In the wider industry the occupancy surveys tend to be referred to as Post Occupancy Evaluations (POE), which implies they are done after occupancy. As these occupants are still occupying these spaces it would seem appropriate to refer to them as occupancy surveys.

Surveys are usually undertaken for commercial projects but there is no reason these should be limited to one sector – they can become good practice and part of delivering good design.

Although they are good practice to do and project and design teams are in many cases willing to undertake them, they have steadily been removed over the years as clients have not wanted to pay for them. A short-sighted view and one that links to a bigger issue of identifying value, which is dealt with in the following chapter.

Unless one has asked what the users of a space actually think and feel about it, clients and design teams are guessing on comfort and wellbeing levels of occupants. This means clients, owners, managers or decisions makers, are in essence 'blind' to what works best or worst, and how the most valuable asset and issue, people, are feeling or performing when using the spaces.

Occupancy surveys can be done before a project, following completion and then at intermittent 6 or 12-month periods as spaces live on. They can be seen as

FIGURE 4: 67 AND 4: 68
End of project occupant survey by Spaceworks for Huckletree. Insights on what works and what can be improved

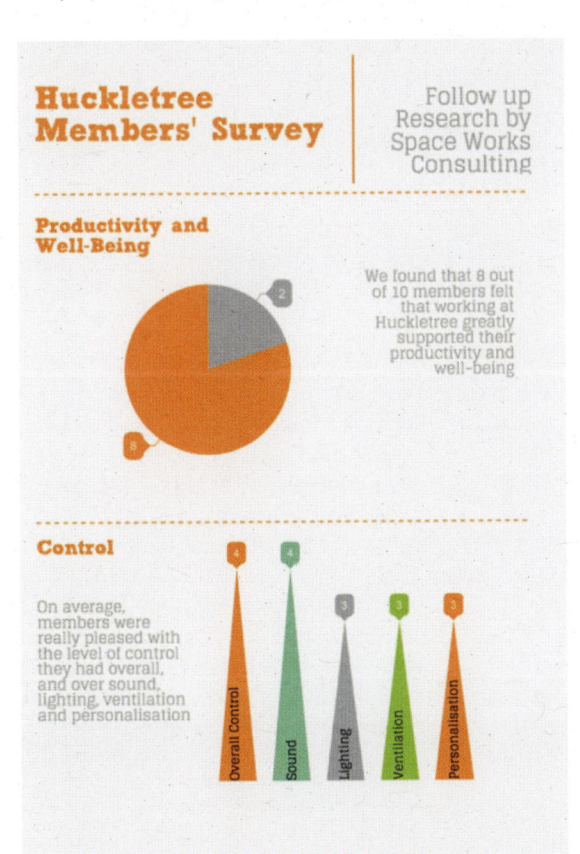

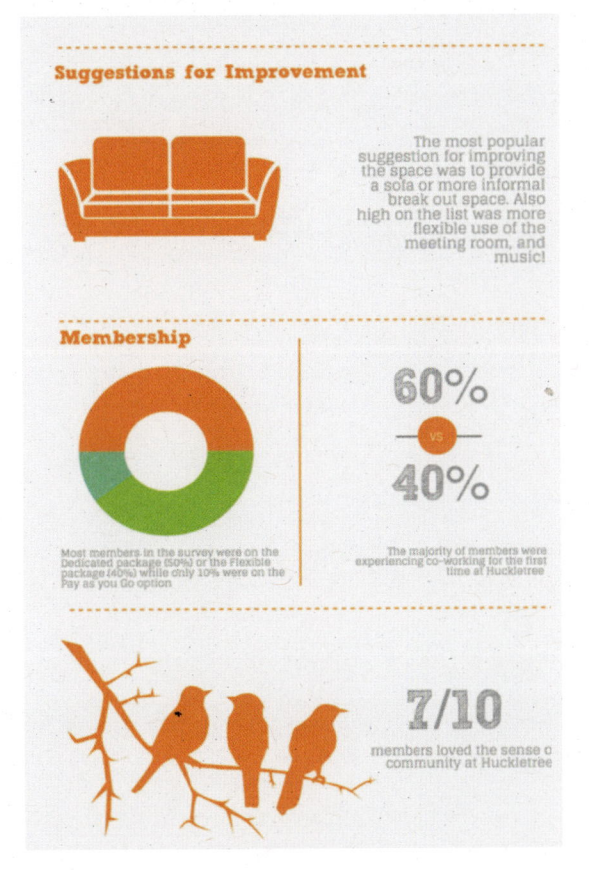

health checks for the use of space and the operation of a space. They assist in preventative planning and maintenance and support family lifestyles, personnel wellbeing or customer service strategies too in commercial organisations.

Occupancy surveys have one main purpose: to establish how well occupants are performing from their own experience. How space performance affects this, is our focus on the questions and insights we seek. Other questions help to answer organisational or home culture, management and relationship performance. If it is a home, how is it supporting the wellbeing and lifestyle needs of all residents? If it is a restaurant, how is it supporting all staff wellbeing and customer delight? If it is a clinical space, how is it supporting the wellbeing of staff, visitors and assisting in the recovery of the patients' health?

But let's start at the beginning and consider what scope these surveys need to cover. It's important to ask *all* occupants of a space how they feel about it; how they feel about the tasks they do in the spaces they themselves use, how they feel about the organisation or home unit as is relevant, and reflections on how they observe their own behaviour and performance. What we are looking to establish is an understanding of the impact of space on users, and frame other issues that will also affect their wellbeing and performance. For example, someone having a disagreement with their spouse and then coming into work, or going out for a meal together at a restaurant, may report distorted impact of the space on their reported levels of happiness, wellbeing and performance, but it was not because of the space itself.

Once the occupancy surveys have been undertaken, an analysis of them can provide space owners or managers with insights of how the operation, management, maintenance or use of the spaces can be refined or changed altogether to better support the user experience and support their wellbeing. Including a feedback loop and setting up lessons learned meetings with the design teams and stakeholders is also vital for the constant improvement of spaces.

Some existing occupant survey questionnaires to reference, and adapt to suit with expert contribution, include the EPIEQ TOBUS, and BUS questionnaire methodology which are relatively 'open', and there are also commercial questionnaire systems that offer benchmarking. All of these are easily found with a web search or by referral from a knowledgeable wellbeing consultant, HR professional or psychologist.

There is a very rich database of building assessments, some of which include occupancy questionnaires, undertaken mostly using the BUS methodology, found in the Digital Catapult's Building Data Exchange. This is an online searchable platform where after registration users can read and download case studies with insights and recommendations around buildability, energy efficiency and systems, including occupant feedback. Summary and detailed reports for both non-domestic[26] and domestic[27] buildings have been created following years of work, with highlights of recommendations below affecting directly wellbeing.

Domestic Building Performance recommendations highlights which impact wellbeing:

• Designers and Contractors to not use innovative systems without checking installers have used them before in similar settings.

• Designers to select simple systems as occupants do not have the knowledge or desire to learn complex systems.

• Developers and contractors to take time for handover of homes to residents, explain how to operate in different seasons and maintenance requirements. Provide clear and simple instruction manuals.

Non-domestic Building Performance recommendations highlights which impact wellbeing:

• Complicated controls 'alienate' users, as do Building Management Systems, and do not support efficiency targets as they are misused or overridden to meet user needs.

- When Passive House design is adopted, using natural ventilation or a mix mode supplemented with mechanical ventilation for some spaces, designers and contractors to make sure there is specialist knowledge on-site and at handover with users to enable them to deliver and use the spaces successfully.

The insights, which touch upon the impact to users or the interaction of a successful scheme with its users, in both types of projects, relate to getting right the User Profiles and knowing the occupants' preferences and abilities.

Putting design for wellbeing into practice

The best time to apply the Soft Landing's process and recommended actions is at the beginning of a project but whenever it does get applied it will start benefiting all concerned. The amount of controllability that is best to integrate in the design to ensure it is present during occupancy will be understood through the occupant surveys and integrated within the User Profiles. Any one of these operational delivery topics will more or less overlap with the others. Whatever the stage of the project consider if any of these issues can be integrated, but best considered at commencement and undertake the following:

1. Integrate the Soft Landings actions in the design programme. Brief the rest of the design and client team on the approach and delegate tasks they are to undertake.

2. Brief the occupants on the approach and provide clarity on what they can expect and how they can get involved through the process.

3. Decide who and how the User Profiles will be created.

4. Discuss the best approach on undertaking the occupancy surveys and follow the recommendations on good practice in undertaking them.

5. Discuss insights with the client and design team and ensure through the project the design checks refer back to the User Profiles and occupant insights agreed for the design to respond to.

6. Integrate the relevant levels of occupant controllability throughout the design features and within the decision-making process of the project itself.

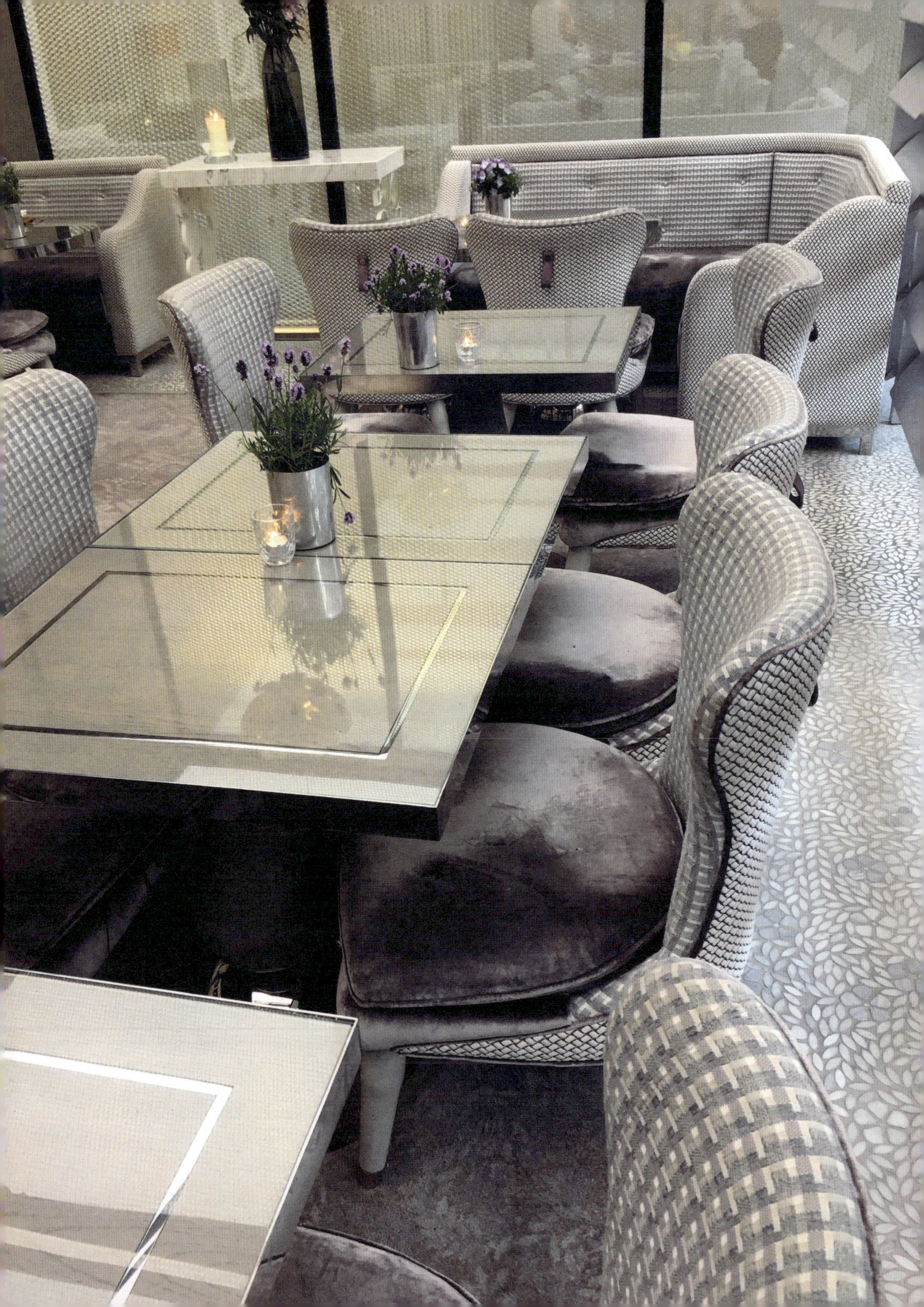

PART 5
Value in practice: Measuring Wellbeing

Chapter 20: Identifying and managing value 174
Chapter 21: Measuring value 186

CHAPTER 20
Identifying and managing value

Measuring wealth 176 • A better place 177 • Defining project KPIs and UPAs 178 • Performance of space 184 • Strategy, clarity and measurement of value 184

Wealth and prosperity are not just monetary and physical values. If we are seeking to create a life for ourselves and others around us, near or far that is rich, happy and full, we must rebalance what it is we add value to, what we measure as valuable and what makes us truly rich in life.

Economics is discussed narrowly in the mainstream as the measurement of monetary value, which misses out the things that really do have what it takes to make us truly rich. Just like plumbing is the name we give to the work dealing with the way we get water to a point of consumption without losing it along the way, so economics is a term to describe the process of managing value from source to consumption. Neither the plumber nor the economist can say they know what makes the value, but that they offer a method of dealing with a transaction process. Most important is to have clean water that goes to where it is needed so someone can drink it and live well. So with economics, they should not be telling us what is valuable but help us measure the things that are. But, we seem to have made the water pipes and process of adding connections to the design more important than the water we are seeking to run through them. The person is still waiting to get some water at the other end and when some do get it these days, it can be rather toxic as no focus is paid to the quality of the water itself, or such a small supply is provided that the person is left parched. The current way of discussing economics has taken away the ability to flow the value to the actual people we are meant to serve and care for, expecting economics to tell us what is valuable, and as an industry and society, we are more absorbed with the pipe we may have in front of us rather than how it works with those of others to allow goodness to flow and grow. The financial cost of the design and delivery of a space is equated as being the only value to measure, and the real impacts to those related to the space do not enter the discussion, or only in extremely rare cases if they do.

How do we create spaces that enable real wealth of spirit? Spaces that foster rich relationships and enable a happy life existence for all. Many current interiors offer mean spirited and lifeless spaces, aspiring to such a narrow image of what life can offer and be.

Now, to the mammoth issue of measuring this full value, although it would be ideal to not have to undertake such justifications for good instinctive life behaviours to be enabled, it is still a valid need to understand and balance these as part of a cognitive approach to designing for wellbeing. If the world was occupied by perfect virtuous people then this would not be necessary, but as we are frail and learning in the process, we necessitate the need for a cognitive method to justify adding the value of the only things that truly matter to life.

FIGURE 5: 01
Sometimes we need reminding of the most important aspects of life...

Measuring wealth

It is admirable to see efforts worldwide where measurement of happiness and wellbeing are already commenced, and where new systems thinking is encouraging new ways. In Europe we have had an effort by the UK government the Office of National Statistics since 2012 to measure national wellbeing and happiness related performance in addition to GDP as markers of progress. In 2001, the French government introduced a law on economic reporting to account as a triple bottom line with monetary, environmental and social performance. The implementation of this reporting shows a steady improvement of all data and practices with some leaders clearly standing out as highlighted in the study of Wolff et al.[1] In Asia, the Gross National Happiness (GNH) index has been established in Bhutan to measure their prosperity, with global comparisons ranking the country as one of the highest.

International collaborative efforts on reported global happiness that are worth noting include:
- The Global Happiness Report,[2] with Richard Layard and Jeffrey Sachs involved amongst other good economists and thinkers, measures six key indicators which are freedom, generosity, health, social support, income and trustworthy governance.
- The Happy Planet Index by NEF[3] goes a step further and calculates a score for each country that involves indicators for wellbeing, life expectancy, inequality of outcomes and ecological footprint.

Similarly, we are starting to see socially and environmentally responsible companies publish reports opening up and reporting against social and environmental targets. Work undertaken by the World Green Building Council around wellbeing within offices (2014), retail (2016) and residential (2016) spaces has also proposed ways of thinking about it and a high level methodology to start discussing an inclusive value metric and wellbeing. The actual comparison is still not clear between the value achieved to the cost incurred, but with similar approaches to the one discussed in this chapter being adopted in the future, there is hope efforts can move further.

Dealing with the value of our projects means looking at the value interior spaces provide to three distinctive groups:
- the people who own these physical spaces and property
- the people who occupy them either once or for a lifetime
- and the wider society and humanity of which they form part of and are dependent on.

We need to enable the measure of value from the design and delivery of the interior spaces in such a way that it does two things:
- ensures the project can be delivered sustainably from a cost transaction perspective
- ensures that the project identifies and drives real value to the lives of all involved and affected.

Projects typically undertake only a calculation of the monetary cost to design and build a space and then compare it with the monetary allowance allocated at the project's inception. This tends to create a very short-term view of a monetary transaction and value gain. There are some project briefs that describe how project selections need to be based on fair value, but there is no guide or understanding for how to do this, so clients and teams are usually driven to still select the lowest cost. There are a few parties that try to create better thinking around value but this can only be done for owner-occupier spaces and if they happen to be in the industry themselves to have insight on a building's life cycle and value retention.

Many clients are trusting that they are being given good and true advice, which would be achieved if they are given a transparent, informed conversation on value. Purchasers are also guilty of shopping for the cheapest service, which is again an outcome of societal and business practices that makes for poor economics and lives. Clients must take part in their own way towards improving the value of what they buy and consider their purchasing based on true value and not just lower cost.

A better place

The following stages and sections of identifying, measuring and managing value form part of 'a better place' study. This is a methodology created and researched by Grigoriou Interiors with industry partners that can be used to inform the *what*, *why*, *whom* and *how* for every project. A methodology that offers clarity and reasoned, calculated thinking towards achieving the real value for each user group.

'*A better place methodology*' comprises of four stages which are:

1 People: understand the occupants and create User Profiles for each user group.

2 Space: survey the physical space against good practice benchmarks.

3 Insights: analyse the findings of stages 1 and 2, and extract insights to identify how the space can support occupant wellbeing and performance.

4 Value: measure the values, including financial value, and strategic importance of improvements in the space.

Performance targets for the effective environmental operation of an interior are more widely available in the industry through environmental benchmarking and labelling tools such as SKA rating, BREEAM, LEED, Estidama and others that are country specific. These are updated at regular intervals and also pick up a portion of wellbeing issues of space design. A few wellbeing measurement and benchmarking systems are now on the market and more developed constantly, so in addition to '*a better place*' by Grigoriou Interiors, the US based WELL building standard and the Australian NABERS IE are amongst a few. They are not measuring or benchmarking similar things, so careful examination of each system's scope is important by clients and consultant teams based on what information and incentives are needed. Some systems measure only indoor air quality, others include layout and facilities, and others operational and building wide issues.

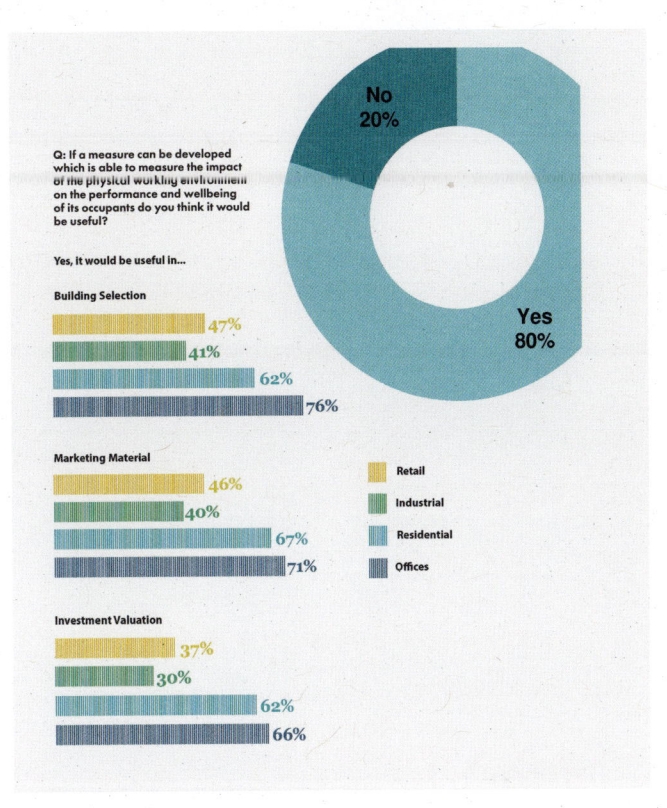

Knowing how people feel or react to certain situations in interiors is vital to providing the best source for informing the occupant User Profiles. Staff and customer/user behaviour need to be expertly surveyed before and after a project. How does a client or the design team know what measure of change they are seeking if the start line doesn't exist? A budget figure, a date in a programme and a line on a plan, all provide a framework to measure recognised issues, but currently the most important element, the wellbeing of users, has not been measured.

FIGURE 5: 02
A Better Place by Grigoriou Interiors

FIGURE 5: 03
Extract from *Wellbeing Matters* report, published by the Feeling Good Foundation

177

There are many approaches that consultants can adopt to obtain the information, which is best selected on a case-by-case basis due to the nature of the occupant. This was covered extensively in the previous chapter on occupancy surveys. The other important consideration is to frame all other variables, which impact on the results. Knowing what percentage of an organisation's budget should be split between manager leadership training and refurbishment works, for example, can be informed by such surveys.

The earlier occupancy survey sections, and the following aspects of design thinking and assessment, form part of *'a better place'* methodology and inform the majority of the principles and thinking around it, on defining, identifying and comparing measurable value of the design and its outcomes.

Defining project KPIs and UPAs

At project commencement there are typically two targets set as good practice: delivery timescales and the cost associated with the project's design and delivery process. The environmental impacts of projects are increasingly being added as a key target following decades of championing for their inclusion. What we have been missing is a metric to enable us to measure the comparable impacts of real value for and to people; to our happiness and wellbeing, to our prosperity as a species.

Setting Key Performance Indicators (KPIs) for all the important things on a project is core to setting common project targets that the client and all teams can drive towards, and be informed by. Out of sight, is out of mind, and this has been increasingly true with the fast pace we have convinced ourselves is good business and life over the centuries. So having targets and guides spell things out for all involved can ensure value thinking will be considered, integrated wherever and as much as possible, and enable its measurement that supports further growth. Setting targets and measuring them is not of course necessary to enable real value in projects to be achieved, but for most projects it has become a reliable approach to at least start with. The targets and systems we use are only enabling frameworks and it must be remembered that they are not the end goal itself. They are the pipes and connections that allow the water to flow, not the water itself.

Every project will have performance indicators that relate to the purpose of the space itself so will vary based on the building and service the space is performing for clients and occupants. In addition to the space specific indicators, there are core measurements for occupant wellbeing and social value that apply to all projects and space.

As an example of project KPIs the following could be considered for a commercial space:
- High staff morale and satisfaction
- Low sickness / high wellbeing levels in staff
- Attraction and retention of staff
- High performance levels of staff
- Staff like and support the brand and culture
- High customer visits due to experience
- Site of social connection for local community
- Cost effective operation.

For a residential space the project performance indicators could include:
- Living happily in this house with my spouse
- Enjoying conversations with my children in the living room
- Being able to support a family member or close friend over long periods of time
- Support the local community
- House children healthily.

To enable the achievement of any KPI listed above, there will be a number of activities that need to be undertaken by each involved party, which done to their highest performance, will support the achievement of the KPI. So understanding what is required from each involved person and what 'good performance' looks like in their role and behaviour, gives us the ability to start talking about performance.

FIGURE 5: 04
What is the value of colleagues getting along and enjoying coming to work?

This information will be included and expanded within the User Profiles as discussed in an earlier chapter. The documents need to include what it is the profiled persona will be doing in the spaces they will occupy and what high performance behaviour looks like. Once the teams understand that, they can analyse all the physical features and behaviours the space needs to ensure support of the people and that they can perform to the best of their ability.

For example, asking someone to write a report that has depth and be on time, but then place them in a highly distracting environment or an extremely relaxing environment, you will find they will struggle to perform.

The activities which reflect 'high performance' of occupants are referred to as User Profile Activities (UPAs). These will be as few or as many as each project and each user group requires. There will be a few which will form the predominant activities of each User Profile and which are possible to design for. Once a list is defined, this needs to be informed as to the occurrence and impact of the activities towards the project KPIs.

Clarifying the weighting of impact

Weighting of features: Different occupant activities will be affected by a different impact weighting of the space's features. For example, the wall finishes will have a higher impact on a young person's ability to think or relax than the textural variation of the finishes in the room. If the person is older, say around 50 years old then the amount of texture will be more important as it is linked with use of memory and the ability to use their depth of knowledge more effectively. Depending on the User Profile of the space and the operational strategy on which user is more impacted by it, the textural variation of the finishes should be higher or lower to support performance and wellbeing.

Time duration: Different users occupy spaces for different times and will be impacted in a relevant amount. The apportioned impact and priority of design decisions should be relevant to the time and users.

The full impact of issues on a person's wellbeing is highly intricate and at this stage of development not fully possible to undertake, and its relevance can only ever be really to that one point in time it is undertaken. What we are able to undertake is a self-declared understanding, by each

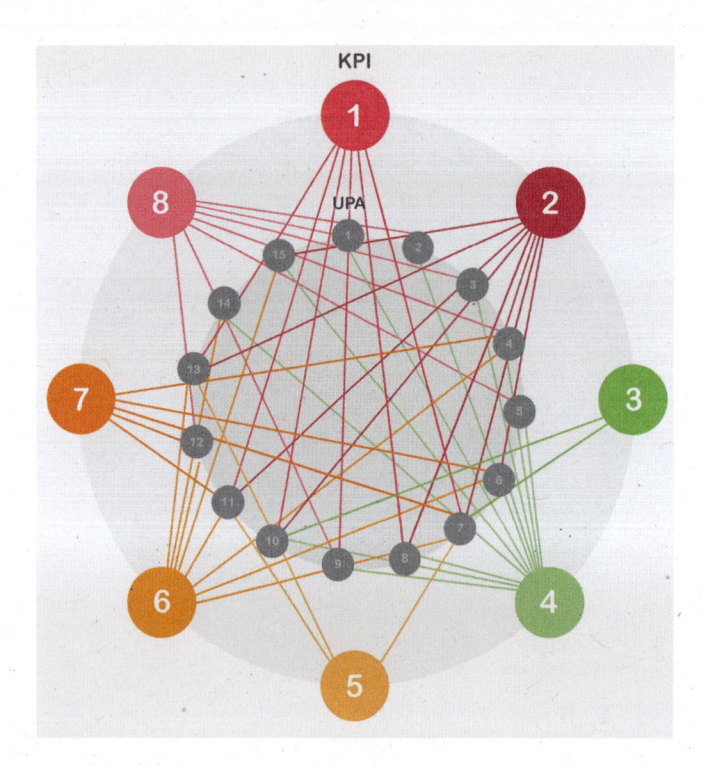

FIGURE 5: 05
Each UPA will contribute in part towards a number of KPI's

occupant, on their perception of impact by the space in relation to other known issues as part of the bigger picture. For example the case study by Dr Bridget Juniper (see Chapter 21) provided further on highlights the other issues that weigh in on the overall performance and wellbeing of a person in a call centre. To ensure occupiers are well, happy and fulfilling their needs and those of their job, all impact issues need addressing.

The links and co-dependency between management approach for example and space can be demonstrated in the following food retail case study undertaken by The Pioneers, a company specialising in workplace management innovation. The brief's objective was to assist their client, a popular high street food retailer, to provide fantastic customer service. They were looking to understand how management behaviours affected customer experience. One activity that stood out was around shift staff briefings, their location and how this changed the behaviour of staff with the customers during that shift. They observed that having the shift's brief near the grill and behind the counter meant the staff treated this area as their 'home base' for the rest of the shift and would huddle and return back to that space between specific jobs. If

the shift brief was undertaken within the restaurant floor, using one of the customer tables or standing amongst them, then the staff spent more time around customers during the shift and increased interaction with them. This case shows how use of the interior in two different ways and management approach produced a very different result. The ability to host the briefings in either location was a bonus and did not incur in this instance a physical change, but it did demonstrate the strong hold on people by the space, whether they are conscious of it or not. It is territory marking at its most basic form and part of environmental psychology.

Decisions in management will be enabled by space or resisted by it culminating in inefficient or value-added results. Making it clear to clients that space design, management culture and all other variables are not a 'hero solution' in their own right, can manage expectations and use resources more effectively. Knowing the importance of the co-dependence can help them plan in adjacent actions and phase the works to suit their organisation. This can apply to home settings of course with lifestyle changes, as the principle is applicable to all scenarios.

Whatever the client strategy, it is important to allocate the relevant impact proportion of the space to the end performance of occupants to enable correct allocation of value return and expected impact. If a school wishes to improve its performance and the concentration levels are identified as the top priority, we can work systematically towards narrowing down the design issues that can improve these. In addition, their nutrition and physical activity will also likely have an impact and could be concurrently tackled.

Within an academic study[4] the value impact will allow for deadweight, displacement (not considered relevant in space design) and attribution. Deadweight is a portion of a result that would have occurred irrelevant to the actions the project has taken and attribution is the impact that is attributed to the action integrated into the design, delivery or occupancy behaviour.

Between the physical features of a space there is also a hierarchy of impact. For different users and activities this will adjust but the minimum issues to deal with as a priority will be those features that measure below the occupants' current average wellbeing state. This can be understood by using Maslow's Hierarchy of Needs[5] pyramid. In relation to occupant engagement in a management scenario and in wider design context as a scale of functionality up to creativity enabling. In Maslow's Hierarchy in Interiors Table (Figure 5:05) the allocation of all the physical issues against each level shows how they can be weighted as a start. If an occupant is found to be mostly in the Belonging level, all features which are below this level will not be harmonising performance, undermining the state they are mostly falling within. Following this 'catching up' action, then priority needs to be given to the issues that fall within the next level and so on.

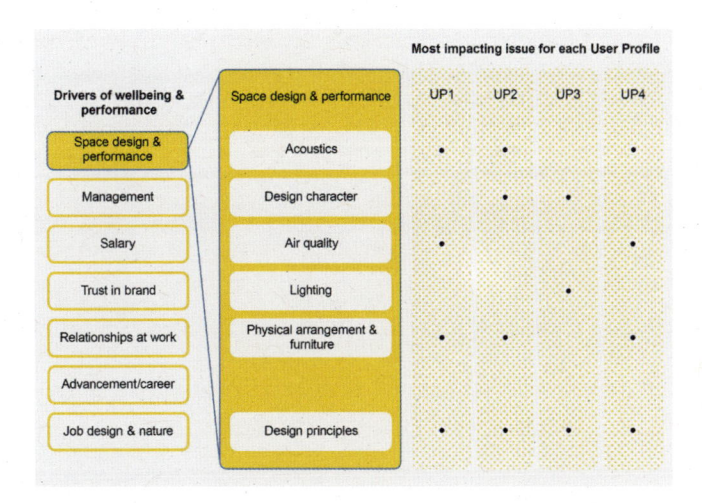

Understanding which level of the hierarchy each User Profile is at can be established through the one-to-one interviews or survey questions, asking questions around the understood behaviours that fall within each level of the hierarchy. In a very simplified example, if someone does not feel like they belong within a team or organisation, their behaviour will not be engaged. If their behaviour is not engaged what aspects of the space will be 'enough' for them and which features would lead them to start engaging? Engagement is one of the strongest indicators of an organisation's performance, according to a Gallup Consulting (2010) worldwide study. Organisations that had higher levels of engagement outperformed those with low levels, showing an average of 18% higher productivity and 16% higher profitability between the higher and lower performers.

The following example of general groupings of design features are allocated against each level of Maslow's hierarchy (overleaf).

FIGURE 5: 06
Each UPA will contribute in part towards a number of KPI's

FIGURE 5: 07
Understanding the engagement of staff or students or other users and overall sense of belonging to a space is very important in the way the design needs to cater for their comfort and wellbeing, but also support performance

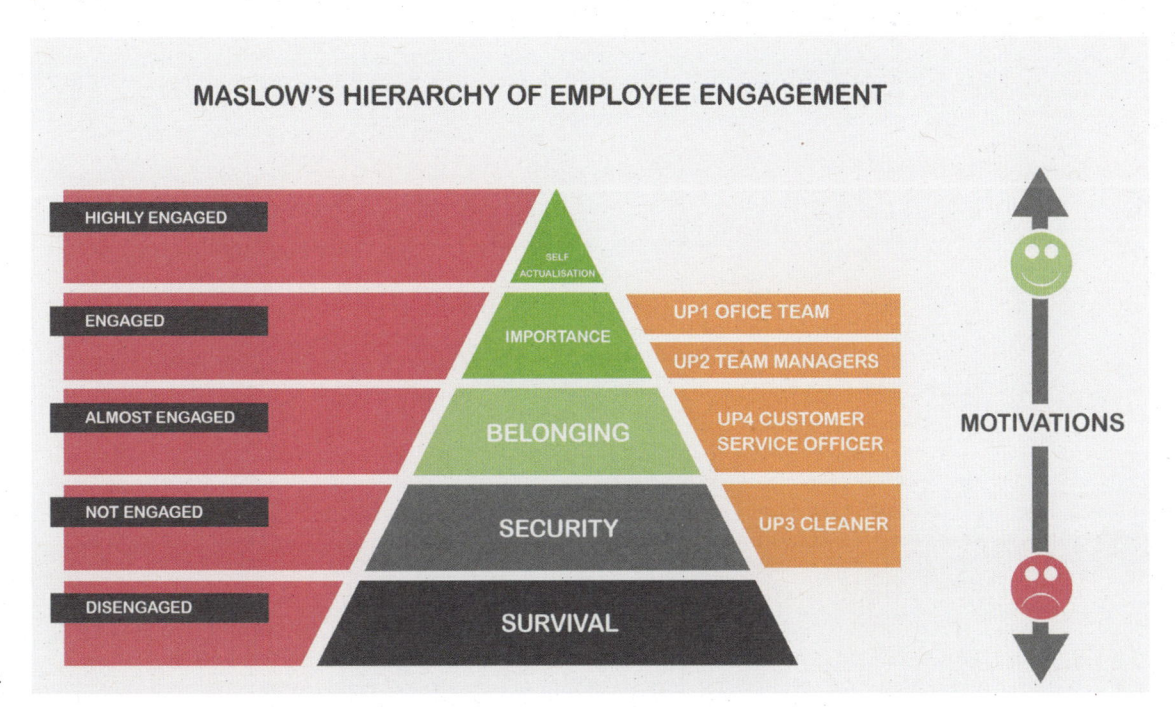

Maslow's Hierarchy in Interiors Table version 1

	Basic/ Survival	Security	Social/ Love Belonging	Esteem / Importance	Self-actualisation
Lighting	Glare diffusion	Sense of control	Lighting quality		
		Lighting levels			
IEQ	Formaldehyde and air particulates	VOC levels	Source of ventilation		
		Air temperature	CO_2 levels		
		Sense of control			
		Air humidity			
		Air movement			
Layout and furniture	Views out	Refuge and prospect in space layout	Layout of space for teamwork	Overall sense of control	Quiet room and meditation space
	Access to good daylight	Personal territory	Minimum distances between team locations within floors and buildings	Variation in ceiling heights	
		Connection and transparency between spaces	Large kitchen table and separate breakout space	Task-based spaces	
		Density of occupancy.			
Design character	Colour use for visual comfort	Curve bias	Ceiling height above 2.8m	Points of interest: aesthetic-usability effect.	Consistent design language
		Biophilia effects on space features.	Colour harmony with users and tasks	Level of textured difference between materials	Art and culture features
Acoustics	Reverberation	Attenuation	Absorption and background masking		
		Sense of control			

FIGURE 5: 08
Maslow's Hierarchy in Interiors Table

The expectation of a design from users has been framed in Maslow's hierarchy in the book titled *Universal Principles of Design* by Lidwell, Holden and Butler (2010), outlining that the most basic need of a user is that a design must be functional; if it's not working it's of no value which most of the world will agree with. Reliability in use is the next step and knowing that a design can be trusted. The third level in hierarchy is the usability of the design and how easy something is to use by different user abilities. The fourth level is how the design enables proficiency by users and allows them to do things they hadn't tried before. Finally, the top indicator of success for a design is when users start being creative with it, innovating beyond its original use.

Within each feature we then have an impact within each room or type of intervention. From a study by Barrett and Zhang (2009) on schools and the allocation of colours for example, the study revealed the different impact they had placed on walls, floors or ceilings. So assuming that the need was to

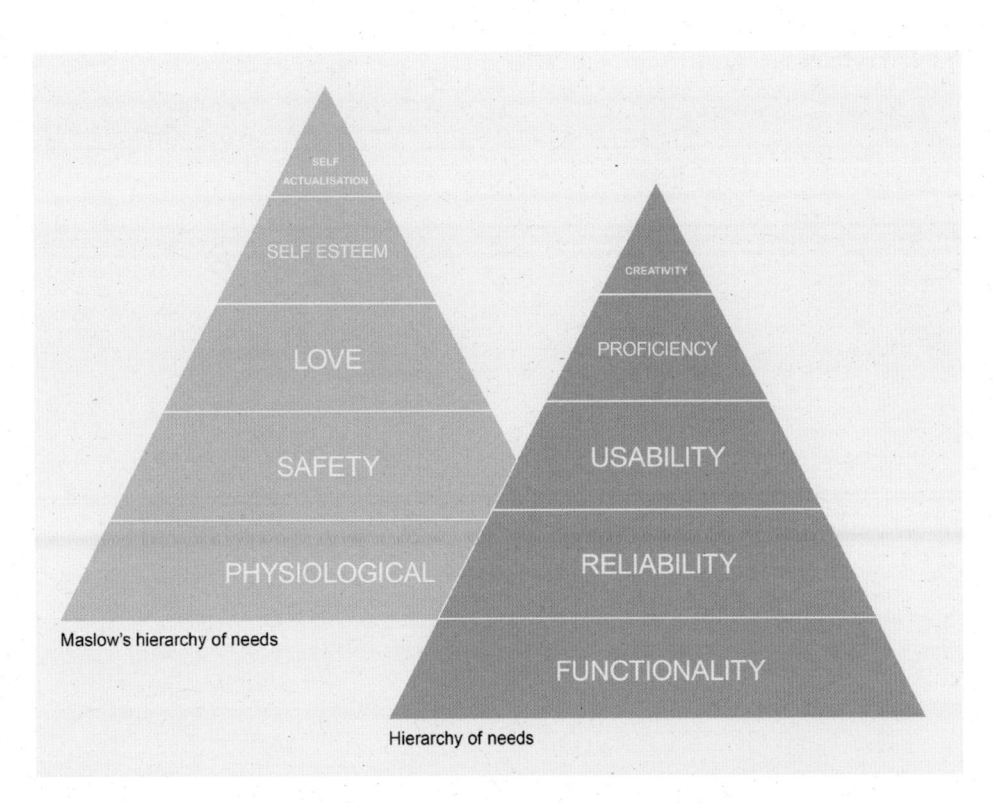

FIGURE 5: 09
Maslow's original hierarchy of needs and the Universal Design Principles application in the performance of a design

Maslow's hierarchy of needs:
- SELF ACTUALISATION
- SELF ESTEEM
- LOVE
- SAFETY
- PHYSIOLOGICAL

Hierarchy of needs:
- CREATIVITY
- PROFICIENCY
- USABILITY
- RELIABILITY
- FUNCTIONALITY

add colour in a space, and that was deep blue, it will harmonise with a calming and introverted activity if it is placed on the ceiling, a sedate, regulated and serious atmosphere if applied to the floor finish. The ceiling, colour selection and allocation will have a positive impact and add value if the location is harmonising with the colour location, and remove value if there is disharmony.

In the acoustics guide by the FIS (AIS) and work by Professor Bridget Shield of London's South Bank University, the recommendations include the hierarchy of impact of improvement for different interventions. These are as follows:

1 Ceiling absorption

2 Screen/panel height to desks

3 Screen/panel absorption to desks

4 Workstation plan size dictating the space around each person

5 Floor absorption

6 Screen transmission loss

7 Ceiling height, recommending good practice at 2.7m high

8 Light fittings and their ability to have openings through their own body to allow sound through

9 Speech level and adopting respectful behaviour and a responsive relationship to the way a space is occupied

10 Masking noise

Performance of space

Undertaking a space survey is vital in understanding where levels of performance are currently if in occupation, or if new spaces are being designed or prospected for purchase or tenancy.

Up to now the property agents marketing details will include the number of car park spaces, lifts, air conditioning and accessible floor and ceiling features, but do not refer to the most important impacts on occupants. Based on the hierarchy of issues earlier and an understanding of what sellers or property owners wish to attract, it would make business sense to market to prospective occupants the most important features that will impact the most valuable aspects of their occupancy. Air quality levels and design objectives for wellbeing need to form the basic listing details so that we have harmony between the buyers and sellers.

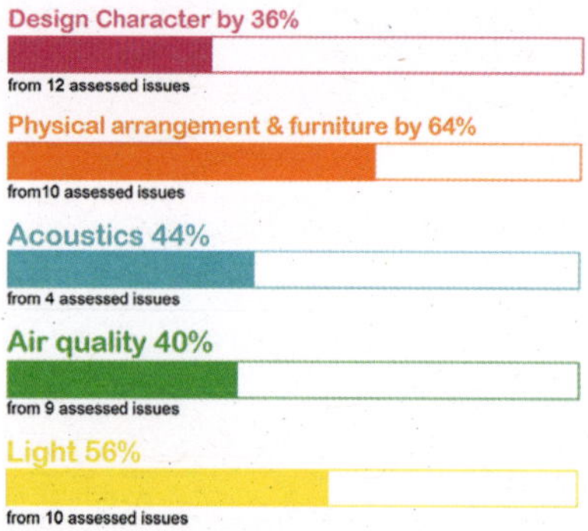

Undertaking a space survey to evaluate its wellbeing performance means doing a series of measurements with handheld meter readings, visual evaluations, distance or length measurements, colour assessments and layout evaluations. These can be done at different quality levels and scopes currently and will improve significantly over the next few years as industry knowledge, technology and skills improve.

FIGURE 5:10
Example of survey results from an interior. Detailed metrics and evidence is collected to verify scoring and support the following analysis with User Profile needs

Design Character by 36%
from 12 assessed issues

Physical arrangement & furniture by 64%
from 10 assessed issues

Acoustics 44%
from 4 assessed issues

Air quality 40%
from 9 assessed issues

Light 56%
from 10 assessed issues

The five main categories interior features fall under are Lighting, Air Quality, Acoustics, Design Character, Physical Arrangement and Furniture. Spread between these there are around 40 sub-issues where researched benchmarks define current good practice levels, allowing a measurement of how each performs.

Strategy, clarity and measurement of value

It would not be right to aim for anything less than 100% wellbeing levels in each space for the whole time each is used. This must be our aim and accept that by aiming for this, our projects will achieve closer results to this than if this is not the aim. The performance of occupants in a space, whether that is a school, retail unit, cinema, gallery or residence, and their activities may be eating, learning, watching or sleeping, will be completely individual in each case and comparable within their own situation, so a mixed result is practically likely.

Once the User Profiles and the KPIs have been completed, and the team has undertaken a spatial survey for each space occupants' use, and benchmarked against user's needs hierarchy, the team can see which UPAs will need supporting by the top impacting physical features. So the design team will know which occupants they wish to support, for the most needed activities, through the most impacting spaces, and which exact features within these spaces will need prioritising. From the previous chapters and the information contained in the User Profiles, the design team will know how each interior feature needs to be approached to support occupant comfort, wellbeing and performance.

Space, people and performance analysis with hierarchy

	Primary space	Top 3 spatial issues impacting comfort	Affecting these UPAs	Affecting these KPIs
UP1	Individual offices	• Acoustics • Colour, pattern and shapes of finishes and furniture • Task and collaboration based space	UPA1 UPA2 UPA4 UPA5	KPI 8 KPI 4 KPI 6 KPI 7 KPI 2
	Reception area	• Acoustics • Air quality • Views out	UPA1 UPA2 UPA4 UPA5	KPI 8 KPI 4 KPI 6 KPI 7 KPI 2
UP4	Living room	• Lighting • Layout of space and furniture • Colour, pattern and shapes of finishes and furniture	UPA2 UPA4 UPA8	KPI 8 KPI 4 KPI 6 KPI 7 KPI 8 KPI 1 KPI 2
	Breakout space	• Lighting for use • Colour, pattern and shapes of finishes and furniture • Layout and quantity of furniture	UPA10	KPI 1 KPI 2 KPI 3 KPI 4
	Kitchen	• Layout, facilities and space fittings • Colour, pattern and shapes of finishes and furniture • Air quality	UPA3 UPA6 UPA9	KPI 8 KPI 4 KPI 7 KPI 6 KPI 2 KPI 1

FIGURE 5: 11
Following the User Profile and spatial survey analysis, and in mind of the value KPIs targeted, the physical features which need work done to support occupant wellbeing can be understood

Identifying the value of the KPIs and linking it to a physical feature can help us link the real value of all the small things that actually achieve the greater. Once we identify the design features that fall under the harmonised User Profile needs, we are able to understand what more can be done to fully support their needs and therefore wellbeing.

The space performance also must be surveyed and clarity needs to be obtained on the level of performance it may have as existing. If it is a space that is being moved into then measurements are looking at the space's potential and limitations.

If an organisation is looking to move into a building and the floor to ceiling height is 2.4m it will impact the occupants differently and give them relevant value. If the occupiers will be doing concentration tasks and sequential type of thinking then this ceiling height will support the occupant tasks and provide relevant value. If they are doing relational thinking tasks and creative communication then high ceilings will support them and give higher value.

It is very important to identify what is of value to an organisation or family to inform their search and brief for a space design.

CHAPTER 21
Measuring value

Measuring wellbeing 187 • CASE STUDY: Measuring wellbeing in a call centre 187 • Measuring productivity and SROI 190

Measuring wellbeing

As mentioned in the book's Introduction, and it is not an exaggeration to say, that the aim for occupant wellbeing is the highest value output of a project. That it may on occasions conflict with the perceived wellbeing of other people beyond the space demise, such as an investor, developer, the neighbours or local society is an example of wrong thinking and unwise approaches. The fact we are living in a society whose economy is built on making money from customers' ill-being will cause problems in our aim to achieve full wellbeing support for our occupants, but it is the right aim.

The measurement of wellbeing is still in an age of puberty but some examples have been around for some time now. One of the early proponents of measuring wellbeing and productivity is Dr Bridget Juniper, who has worked with various organisations and provides the following case study.

Case Study: Measuring wellbeing in a call centre

by Dr Bridget Juniper

This case study involved a national call centre with over 30 sites and 2,200 call centre agents. We were asked to measure the wellbeing of staff as this was a prime concern to management; there was high sickness absence (17%) and attrition was 29%. Costs of sickness absence alone were estimated to be in the region of £12 million a year. An Impact Analysis was carried out. The remit was to consider all elements of the call centre operation including, but not limited to, the actual physical workspace. This serves as a useful case study because it shows, certainly for this company, the impact of workspace on wellbeing in relation to other more conventional areas such as a management and physical health concerns. Following the Impact Analyses, the confirmed number of questions was 34 spread across 8 domains including workspace (Facilities) with 4 items. See Figure 5:12.

The analyses showed that employees considered workspace (Facilities) issues to be very important to their overall wellbeing. In fact, workspace was second only to Rostering concerns. See figure 9

Call Centre Assessment – 34 Confirmed Questions

Domain	Number of Items	Description
Advancement	5	Impact of advancement on wellbeing
Facilities	4	Impact of facilities on wellbeing
Job Design	3	Impact of job design on wellbeing
Managers	4	Impact of managers on wellbeing
Physical Health	5	Impact of work on physical wellbeing
Psychological Health	5	Impact of work on psychological wellbeing
Relationships	5	Impact of social relationships on wellbeing
Rostering	3	Impact of shift work on wellbeing

FIGURE 5:12
Call Centre Assessment – 34 Confirmed Questions

below. Mean scores ran from 1–5 where 1 indicated very little impact on wellbeing while a score of 5 indicated a great deal of impact. As a guide, a score of 3 or over is considered to be significant and indicate a call for action. In Figure 5:13, it can be seen that the mean score for FAC was 3.75.

In this study, we also examined the relationship between wellbeing and business outcomes. The outcomes in question were sickness and attrition. Our Key Driver Analyses showed the important impact of facilities on these performance indicators. Figure 5:14 shows that the Facilities Domain had a larger impact on people's intentions to quit (16%) compared to the other seven.

Similarly, Facilities was shown to be the largest contributor to sickness absence patterns amongst call centre agents as shown in Figure 5:15.

These results, when shared with the client, were counterintuitive. No one on the management side had anticipated the impact of the workspace on staff wellbeing and behaviour. Armed with this independent and comprehensive set of results, the company was able to set about delivering a programme to address the wellness of its staff. With regard to the workspace specifically, they upgraded the kitchen facilities as these were shown to be a big issue for call centre people who only had 30-minute breaks from their shift to prepare meals and refuel before returning to the phones. Some furniture items were replaced and seating arrangements were changed to promote more social interaction between agents; the results indicated that people were experiencing isolation and loneliness because of the seating layout. As a consequence of this programme of improvements, absence dropped by 1% over the following 12 months. Attrition was also down by 3%. Savings made through these improvements were estimated to be in the region of £250,000 per annum indicating a satisfactory return on investment of 1:2.5.

Practical actions

- Never presume you, as a practitioner, know the interior design answers based only on your experience and knowledge. Always bring the employees' perspective into the room by asking them directly their views and needs. Wellbeing is subjective and dynamic; its makeup will vary hugely between different workplaces.

- The most effective way to do this is through the approach described above so there is a rigorous process and a clear direction of travel.

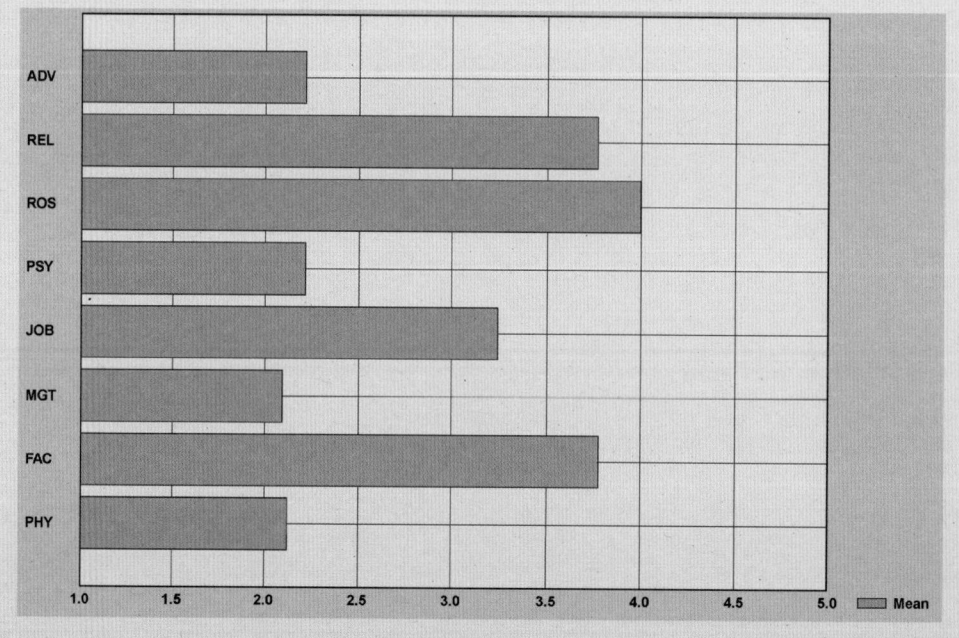

FIGURE 5: 12
Overall domain scores for call centre wellbeing

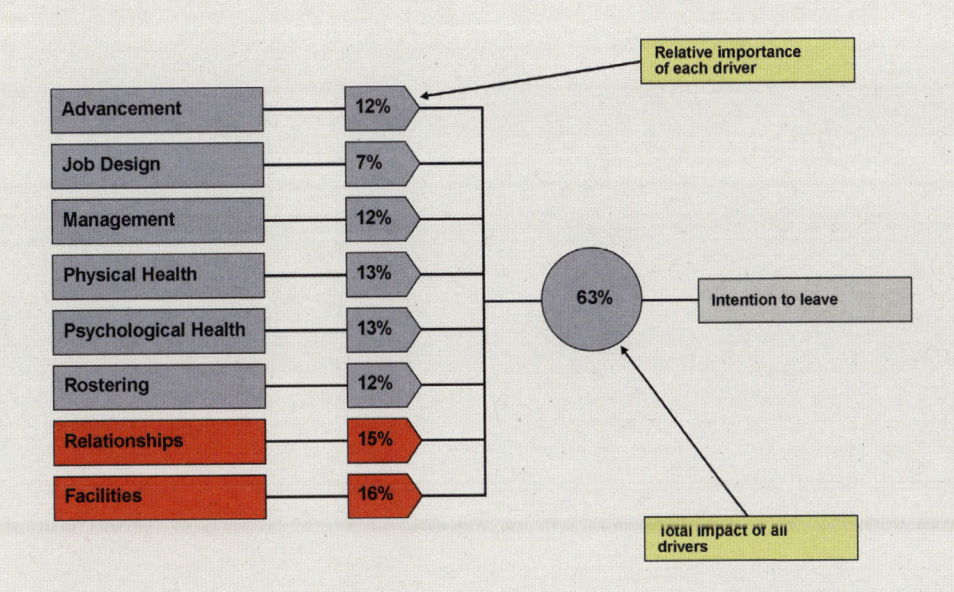

FIGURE 5: 14
KDA for intentions to quit

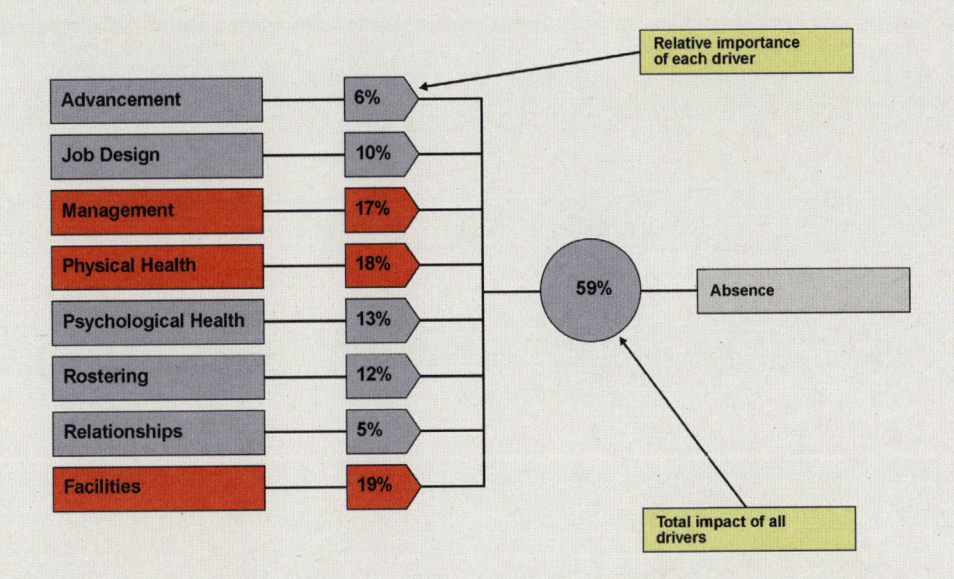

Driver	Relative importance
Advancement	12%
Job Design	7%
Management	12%
Physical Health	13%
Psychological Health	13%
Rostering	12%
Relationships	15%
Facilities	16%

Intention to leave: 63% (Total impact of all drivers)

FIGURE 5: 15
KDA for sickness absence

Driver	Relative importance
Advancement	6%
Job Design	10%
Management	17%
Physical Health	18%
Psychological Health	13%
Rostering	12%
Relationships	5%
Facilities	19%

Absence: 59% (Total impact of all drivers)

- If this is not possible because of practical reasons, then at least, set up focus groups with some staff and facilitate discussions on what it is about the workspace they think is working and what is not. This will at least give you some insights that can be factored in.

- Bring other stakeholders in the organisation with you. HR professionals are critical as there is so much crossover between property and HR disciplines when it comes to employee behaviour and performance. Involve them in the measurement process from the outset. Generally speaking, they will not understand the role that the workspace can play. Remember Maslow's Hierarchy of Needs and how the references to the most basic of needs (physiological) have all but been forgotten in most HR textbooks today.

Measuring productivity and SROI

The measurement of what constitutes productivity will be relevant in each context and what occupants are doing, how they effectively conclude an activity they intended. In the case of a shop it will form the productivity of staff to serve and of customers to relax and eat well. In the case of a home, occupants will be productive if they can sleep in the bedroom, read and socialise in the living room and so on.

Measuring productivity tends to use monetary values in addition to growth of new customers and attraction to talented people, return or not of customers, retention of staff. We add as a metric the performance of occupants in the completion of the tasks they intend to do in any given space at a recognised standard of good performance.

The effects of all activities will also impact the Social Return On Investment (SROI). How the space and the way occupants use it will impact the wider society. The KPIs originally set for the project are important to recognise the impact the project will make on a social scale, so this must be understood at that time and enabled through the way the project has been designed and delivered and occupied through its life. Issues could include air toxicity, the social interactions and emotional support a retail store may offer, the way a school supports mental health locally etc.

There are a number of methodologies around measuring both the above issues and then converting them to a monetary value for ease of strategic decisions. Productivity could be measured in number of customers per year, average spend per person, average time a school is interacting with the local community, the social interactivity a housing development offers – these are just a few examples. Measuring the social return is not in itself a problem.

Monetising it to compare project spend or to help choose between two SROI targets for example if they happen to need phasing in delivery, is where there are various methodologies now slowly arising.

Further reading and guidance on SROI can be found through the New Economics Foundation (neweconomics.org) and Social Value UK (www.socialvalueuk.org).

'SROI measures change in ways that are relevant to the people or organisations that experience or contribute to it. It tells the story of how change is being created by measuring social, environmental and economic outcomes and uses monetary values to represent them. This enables a ratio of benefits to costs to be calculated. For example, a ratio of 3:1 indicates that an investment of £1 delivers £3 of social value.'
A guide to Social Return on Investment, UK Cabinet Office 2009.

If we look at 'productivity' in the various contexts interiors serve, the measurement values will be relevant to them. For example, in healthcare interior spaces will be productive when they support the patients' procedures and recovery. To demonstrate how patients respond to a design supporting their wellbeing through recovery, a 1984 study on how views out on greenery impacted patients' recovery time demonstrated value through number of days and healing. Having views out to greenery sped up recovery time against those facing a brick wall by 8.5%.[6] In education settings where aims include amount of knowledge, new skill acquisition and development of interpersonal skills, assessment stages of acquired knowledge are an acknowledged metric. Here air quality has been shown to impact student skills and performance, so when the air quality levels (CO_2) were low, exam results were low also.

Although projects usually refer on how much more value can be added by improving the spaces we live in, it is equally true that the same exact spaces are slowly losing their existing value if no interventions occur.

Value metrics that relate to a monetary equivalent value are required to inform the KPIs and for this to be undertaken accurately the team should appoint a social value consultant. Data on the cost to society and corporations of wellbeing not being supported is available nationally in the UK. As organisations start developing their own internal data around wellbeing and ill-health these metrics can be developed to finer proxies. Some of the KPIs related to an organisation's staff salaries or maintenance costs or a family setting will be personal and uniquely relevant to each case. Obtaining for example staff salary averages for each User Profile or the cost for maintaining a school can be obtained by the client or their suppliers.

FIGURE 5: 16
Measuring the things that matter

Conclusion

You arrive at a hotel and are directed to the lounge to meet a friend. You approach the doorway and hover at the entrance. You now know that you are scanning for the best seat based on the innate need for refuge and prospect, on sound quality and seat comfort. You sit in a curved shaped chair, covered in dark soft textured material and pull the round table closer to you to place a pad on. Your friend arrives and you enjoy a happy evening of conversation and refreshments, feeling relaxed physically, open and light emotionally and mentally clear and stimulated. You will be back and wish to meet up again sooner rather than later.

If this book has clarified that wellbeing is not given but enabled, through 'good' interior design that is personal to each occupant, then a primary objective will have been achieved.

The content is aimed at establishing a solid base for design thinking and a design approach to support wellbeing which can be built upon on an ongoing basis. A few core messages that the chapters have communicated include: the idea of harmonising the needs of occupants with the design; there is no one perfect design, but one perfect fit; and knowing who clients and designers are designing for in real factual detail, which is vital to remove blind guesses and aesthetic favouritism by teams.

Some main design decisions that affect multiple issues throughout the project will relate to the design being more *realistic*, thus emulating and supporting a biophilic link, or *abstract* by providing clarity and powerful stimulating environments for occupants to flourish further. Whichever chosen strategy, it will inform approaches from the building systems and controllability all the way to materials and shapes, ensuring there is design fluidity that leverages the effects of each individually.

It is not anticipated that projects will contain all the required benchmarks most of the time, but aiming for occupant wellbeing will ensure a good and right project aim, a 'good' design. Aiming for spaces that create rich and rewarding atmospheres that support a life that counts, is up there in the reasons why one would get up on the toughest day and be part of such a team.

Over time, the standard design benchmarks will become those which support occupant wellbeing. The inclusion of evidence for the design characteristics and aesthetic issues needs to be picked up by institutions and discussed more openly and informed with further and developing evidence. There has been over the centuries an attitude that has prohibited questioning and a healthy discussion around an aesthetic approach, resulting in a number of unsuitable spaces that still somehow are awarded accolades. We need to start awarding at industry ceremonies and featured projects (and products) the projects which have clearly aimed at wellbeing and have positive occupant insights following at least one year's use.

In the main, client teams don't work on many design and delivery projects through their lives so the design team's role is important in steering and nudging behaviour where it may not already be in line with good practice value thinking. Using evidence of impacts from design that supports wellbeing will make the specific ideas more approachable.

FIGURE 5: 17
Seating layouts in cafes and restaurants can be designed following evidence, with an intent to support people's comfort and wellbeing

Good design is that which supports wellbeing and the real values for a wealthy life. We can do better in the way we use our built environment and live in interior spaces. They are tools for life so let's make them work for us, for a good life worth living.

As this book concludes, the discussion around wellbeing is increasingly on the agenda, our understanding of it on the rise – it is very encouraging.

Seeing the interest and enthusiasm to now take action around the world on wellbeing, and act for the good of humanity, makes one feel like a rich person. If you have reached this part of the book and along the way it has given you hope that you can make a difference too through a small or large impact, and that you are not alone in caring, then I am indeed the richest person there is, standing beside you.

'...every time you make a choice you are turning the central part of you, the part of you that chooses, into something a little different from what it was before. And taking your life as a whole, with all your innumerable choices, all your life long you are slowly turning this central thing either into a heavenly creature or into a hellish creature...' C.S Lewis

We all have the ability to choose one way or another in every decision we make. I hope you use all of yours intentionally to design for everyone's wellbeing.

Elina

FIGURE 5: 18
Granary Square, King's Cross

FIGURE 5: 19
'Botanical Mandala'

CONCLUSION

References

Introduction

1. Design Council, 2015

2. Preamble to the Constitution of the World Health Organization as adopted by the International Health Conference, New York, 19-22 June, 1946

3. School of Philosophy and Economic Science

Part 1. Philosophy: Prerequisites and Outputs of Wellbeing

1. In Proceedings of AIC -(International Colour Association) Interim Meeting 21-24 October 2014, in Oaxaca, Mexico Theme: 'Colors, Culture and Identity: Past, Present and Future'

2. Sir Christopher Wren, *Parentalia*

3. A design standard that awards buildings which are not just limiting negatives but being a positive influence to the environment and occupants: www.living-future.org

4. Alasdair White, *From Comfort Zone to Performance Management*, White & MacLean, 2009

5. P. P. Bluyssen, 'The healthy indoor environment: How to assess occupants' wellbeing in buildings', 2014

6. BSRIA Soft Landings methodology, https://www.bsria.co.uk/services/design/soft-landings/

7. Alain de Botton, *The Architecture of Happiness*, London, Penguin, 2007

Part 2. Design in Practice: Delivering a Design for Wellbeing

1. User Centred Design Guide, The Circular Design Guide, Ellen Macarthur Foundation and IDEO 2016, How to conduct user interviews, Interaction Design Foundation (2017), and Nick Babich, The Art of the User Interview, Springboard (2017)

2. Taub, M., Clements-Croome, D. J., Lockhart, V., 2016, BCO Report on The Impacts of Wearables on Designing Healthy Office Environments: A Review (BCO Report see www.bco.org.uk)

3. Extract from 'The Synthesis of Empathy, Abstraction and Nature in the Work of Kandinsky, Steiner and Mendelsohn' by Fiona Gray, Deakin University, Geelong, Australia 2008

4. Vischer, J. (2008). Towards a user-centred theory of the built environment. Building Research & Information, 36(3), 231-240.

5. Appleton, J. (1975). *The Experience of Landscape*. London: Wiley

6. Lidwell, W., Holden, K., and Butler, J. (2010). *Universal Principles of Design, Revised and Updated*. Rockport Publishers, Gloucester, MA

7. Hildebrand, G. (1999). *Origins of Architectural Pleasure*. University of California Press: Berkeley, CA

8. Hase, B., & Heerwagen, J. (2001). Phylogenetic Design: A new approach for workplace environments. *The Journal for Quality and Participation*, 23, 27-31.

9. Becker, F., & Steele, F. (1995). *Workplace by Design: Mapping the High Performance Workspace*. San Francisco: Jossey-Bass

10. Sommer, R. (2008) *Personal Space: The Behavioral Basis of Design*, Updated. Bristol: Bosko Books

11. Mehrabian, A., & Diamond, S.G. (1971) Seating arrangement and conversation. *Sociometry*, 34(2), 281-289

12. Stryker, J.B., & Santoro, M.D., (2012). Facilitating face-to-face communication

in high-tech teams. *Research-Technology Management*, Jan-Feb (2012), 51-56

13. Griskevicius, V., Cialdini, R.B., & Goldstein. N.J. (2008). Social norms: An underestimated and underemployed lever for managing climate change. International Journal of Sustainability Communication, (5)13

14. Levine, J.M., & Moreland, R. L. (1990). Progress in small group research. *Annual Review of Psychology*, (41), 585-634.

15. Brown, K. W., & Kasser, T. (2005). Are psychological ecological Wellbeing compatible? The role of values, mindfulness, and lifestyle. *Social Indicators Research*, 74, 349-368

16. Compton, T. (2010). Common Cause: The Case for Working with our Cultural Values. Woking: World Wildlife Fund

17. Turner, B., Clements-Croome, D., and Pallaris, K. (2018) The Multi-Sensory Experience in Buildings. In Clements-Croome, D., (Editor). *Creating the Productive Workplace: Places to Work Creatively*. Third Edition. Taylor & Francis, 2018

Part 3: Design in Practice: Aesthetic Issues Affecting Wellbeing

1. Mark Rothko, *The Artist's Reality: Philosophies of Art*, Yale University Press, New Haven, 2006

2. Alain de Botton, ibid.

3. Noethers Theorem by Emmy Noether 1915 – Today's theoretical physicists are following Einstein in their search for the beauty and simplicity of Nature through the rules of symmetry. Emmy Noether established the connection between the forces of nature and the abstract notion of symmetry; 'For every continuous symmetry of the laws of physics, there must exist a conservation law. For every conservation law, there must exist a continuous symmetry.'

4. The Cognitive Symmetry Engine: An Active Approach to Knowledge, http://www.iros2011.org/WorkshopsAndTutorialsProceedings/SW7/henderson.pdf

5. S. Douady and Y. Couder, 'Phyllotaxis as a Dynamical Self Organizing Process, Part I: The Spiral Modes Resulting from Time-Periodic Iterations', 1996

6. Miranda Lundy, *Sacred Geometry*, London, Wooden Books, 2018

7. A. Yoto A et al., 'Effects of Object Color Stimuli on Human Brain Activities in Perception and Attention Referred to EEG Alpha Band Response', *Journal of Physical Anthropology*, 2007

8. H. Dalke et al., 'Colour and lighting in hospital design', *Optics and Laser Technology*, 2005

9. Kaida Xiao et al., 'Colour Appearance of Room Colours', *Color Research and Application*, 2010

10. Bar and Neta, 'Humans Prefer Curved Visual Objects', *Psychological Science Journal vol 17*, 2006

11. www.patterninislamicart.com

12. Represented and named with a 'phi' after the Greek sculpture Phidias

13. James Joseph Tattersall, *Elementary number theory in nine chapters* (2nd ed.), Cambridge University Press, Cambridge, 2005

14. Myers and Zhu, 'The Influence of Ceiling Height: The Effect of Priming on the Type of Processing That People Use', *Journal of Consumer Research*, 2017

15. M. Nikravan Mofrad 'The Impact Of Floor-To-Ceiling Height On Human Comfort', *Asian Journal Of Civil Engineering* (Bhrc) Vol. 14, No. 5, 2013, Pages 277-287.

16. Michael Hann, *Symbol, Pattern and Symmetry: The Cultural Significance of Structure*, Bloomsbury, London, 2013

17. Mark Rothko, ibid.

18. Alain de Botton, ibid.

19. Alain de Botton and John Armstrong, *Art as Therapy*, Phaidon, London, 2013

20. Mike White, interestingly, has discussed 'Flourishing' as 'a more dynamic concept than 'wellbeing' – it implies resilience and emergence, and it presumes inter-dependency; one cannot flourish at the expense of others.' In M. White (2011), Arts in Health – A New Prognosis (Ixia: online: http://ixia-info.com/new-writing/arts-in-health-%E2%80%93-a-new-prognosis-mike-white/)

21. 'CABE's experience is that the vast majority of PFI buildings commissioned to date have not been designed and built to a high enough standard and public service delivery suffers as a result.' In CABE (2005), Design Quality and the Private Finance Initiative (CABE: online: http://webarchive.nationalarchives.gov.uk/20110118095356/http://www.cabe.org.uk/files/design-quality-and-the-private-finance-initiative.pdf)

22. Arts and health work is sustained by a number of regional fora and organisations around the UK – for more information see http://artshealthandwellbeing.org.uk

23. J. Tusa, Art Matters (*Guardian*: http://www.theguardian.com/artanddesign/2005/dec/13/art), 2005

24. rb&hArts (2013), unpublished interview

25. H.J. Trappe (2010) (abstract for) 'The effects of music on the cardiovascular system and cardiovascular health', (Pubmed.gov: http://www.ncbi.nlm.nih.gov/pubmed/21062776)

26. B. Rhodes (2006) 'When art is in the right place' (*The Times*: accessed online via http://www.globalaging.org/elderrights/world/2006/art.htm)

27. Bar and Neta, 'Visual elements of subjective preference modulate amygdala activation', Neuropsychologia, vol 45 issue 10, 2007

28. For more information see http://streamresearchproject.blogspot.com/

29. The King's Fund take for granted that generating 'ownership of the environment' is one of the key benefits of their 'Enhancing the Healing Environment' programme. See, for example, http://www.kingsfund.org.uk/sites/files/kf/field/field_gt_document_link/enhancing-healing-environment-2012-brochure.pdf

30. Anon. (2011), Chickasaw Medical Center (Page Southerland Page, Inc.: online: http://pagethink.com/v/project-detail/Chickasaw-Nation-Medical-Center/34/)

31. Smith, R., (2002) 'Spend (slightly) less on heath and more on the arts', (*BMJ*: online: http://www.bmj.com/content/325/7378/1432).

32. R. Staricoff & S. Clift (2011) Arts and Music in Healthcare: An Overview of the Medical Literature 2004-2011 (Chelsea & Westminster Health Charity: accessed online via http://www.lahf.org.uk/sites/default/files/Chelsea%20and%20Westminster%20Literature%20Review%20Staricoff%20and%20Clift%20FINAL.pdf)

33. R. Staricoff & S. Clift, ibid.

34. M. de Tommaso, M. Sardaro & P. Livrea (2008) Aesthetic value of paintings affects pain thresholds (Conciousness & Cognition: online, accessed via http://www.artshealthandwellbeing.org.uk/resources/research/aesthetic-value-paintings-affects-pain-thresholds)

35. The Long-Term Health Benefits of Participating in the Arts (Manchester Metropolitan University Arts for Health: online, via http://longitudinalhealthbenefits.wordpress.com/)

36. Mark Rothko, ibid.

37. Barrett and Zhang, Salford Centre for Research and Innovation in the built and human environment (SCRI), Optimal Learning Spaces, Design Implications for Primary Schools, 2009

38. Valter Afonso Vieira, Claudio Vaz Torres, Rogerio Gava, 'Haptic Information Processing: Assessing the Need for Touch Scale', 2007 XXXI EnANPAD

39. Peck and Childers, 'Individual Differences in Haptic Information Processing: The 'Need for Touch' Scale', *Journal of Consumer Research*, Volume 30, Issue 3, 1 December 2003, Pages 430–442

40. BRE Bookshop, Information Paper 10/12, Measuring the wellbeing impacts of interior materials, Research Programme WISER

Part 4: Design in Practice: Physical Issues Affecting Wellbeing

1. Rehva.eu *REHVA Journal* 2013, Issue 4, page 8

2. British Council of Offices, 'What Workers Want,' 2016

3. Clemets-Croome D J, Denzero Project report, 'Sustainable Intelligent Buildings for Better Health, Comfort and Well-Being', 2014

4. Office Angels and the Union of Shop, Distributive and Allied Workers (USDAW) (USDAW, 2006)

5. Derek Clements-Croome, *Intelligent Buildings: An Introduction*, Routledge, London, 2014

6. Indraganti M., Ooka R., Rijal H.B., Brager G.S, 'Adaptive model of thermal comfort for offices in hot and humid climates in India', 2013

7. de Dear, Richard J; Gail Schiller Brager; Reardon, James; Nicol, Fergus; et al., 'ASHRAE Developing an adaptive model of thermal comfort and preference', 1998

8. James Atkinson, Yves Chartier, Carmen Lúcia Pessoa-Silva, Paul Jensen, Yuguo Li and Wing-Hong Seto, 'Natural ventilation for infection control in health-care settings', WHO, 2009

9. Cartwright Pickard and MEARU, , 'Are our homes making people sick?', *Architect's Journal* online, 7 August 2015

10. Rehva.eu *REHVA Journal* 2013, Issue 4 page 7

11. NASA.gov Earth Planetary Fact Sheet, Terrestrial Atmosphere

12. Comparison tables can be referenced at www.e-missions.net/ssa/CH4-breathingonthespacestation.htm

13. Chatzidiakou L, Mumovic D, Dockrell J, 'The Effects of Thermal Conditions and Indoor Air Quality on Health, Comfort and Cognitive Performance of Students,' UCL, 2014

14. ZCH (2012) Mechanical ventilation with heat recovery in new homes. Interim report, Ventilation and Indoor Air Quality Task Group, Zero Carbon Hub, Milton Keynes, January 2012

15. Anses (2014), Indoor air quality guidelines. French Agency for Food, Environmental and Occupational Health & Safety. Available at: https://www.anses.fr/en/content/indoor-air-quality-guidelines-iaqgs

16. Kotzias D, Koistinen K, Kephalopoulos S, Schlitt C, Carrer P, Maroni M, Jantunen M, Cochet C, Kirchner S, Lindvall T, McLaughlin J, Molhave L, de Oliveira Fernandes E and Seifert B, 'The INDEX project: Critical appraisal of the setting and implementation of indoor exposure limits in the EU', Report EUR 21590EN, European Commission, 2005

17. Nazaroff, W. W. 'Four principles for achieving good indoor air quality', Indoor Air, 23, 2013, pages 353–356

18. M Andersen, J Mardaljevic, and SW Lockley, 'A framework for predicting the non-visual effects of daylight – Part I: photobiology-based model', *Lighting Research and Technology*, 44(1):37–53, 2012, and J Mardaljevic, M Andersen, N Roy, and J Christoffersen, 'A framework for predicting the non-visual effects of daylight – Part II: The simulation model', Lighting Research and Technology, 46(4):388–406, 2014

19. Najjar RP, Wolf L, Taillard J, Schlangen LJM, Salam A, et al., 'Chronic Artificial Blue-Enriched White Light Is an Effective Countermeasure to Delayed Circadian Phase and Neurobehavioral Decrements'. PLoS ONE 9(7): e102827. doi:10.1371/journal.pone.0102827, 2014

20. www.spaceandorganisation.org

21. Wolfeld, Leah R., 'Effects of Office Layout on Job Satisfaction, Productivity and Organizational Commitment as Transmitted through Face-to-Face Interactions', *Colonial Academic Alliance Undergraduate Research Journal: Vol. 1*, Article 8, 2010

22. Swedish Work Environment Authority AFS 2009:2 Design of the workplace, Occupational Safety and Health Administration's regulations on the design of the workplace as well as general advice on the application of the regulations

23. J Aked, A Minton, Nef, '"Fortress Britain": high security, insecurity and the challenge of preventing harm', 2013

24. AIS A guide to office acoustics, page 65, 2015, and Bradley J.S, 'The acoustical design of conventional open plan offices', 2003

25. The Soft Landings process and supporting information is owned by the Building Services Research and Information Association. www.bsria.co.uk

26. Innovate UK, Building Performance Evaluation Programme: 'Findings from non-domestic projects, at a glance', January 2016

27. Innovate UK, Building Performance Evaluation Programme: 'Findings from domestic projects, At a glance', January 2016

Part 5. Value in Practice: Measuring Wellbeing

1. Wolff, Dominique & Bendick, Marc & Egan, Mary & Mauléon, Fabrice, 'France's Mandatory 'Triple Bottom Line' Reporting', *The International Journal of Environmental, Cultural, Economic, and Social Sustainability: Annual Review. 5*, 2009, pages 27-48

2. www.worldhappiness.report

3. www.happyplanetindex.org

4. Dr Kelly Watson, University of Manchester, study on non-clinical healthcare centres, 2016

5. Abraham Maslow, *Motivation and Personality*, Pearson, London, 1954, 1987

6. Roger S. Ulrich, 'View through a window may influence recovery from surgery', *Science*, 1984

Index

A
'abstract' approaches 6, 52, 193
acoustics 47, 160-165
   distracting sounds 149-150
   hierarchy of impacts 182, 183
   security and 157-158
   space planning and 149-150
aesthetic issues 56
   balance 51, 61-62, 66, 88
   ceiling height 92-93
   elegance 51, 58-59
   hierarchy of impacts 182
   materials 109, 115
   physical issues and 118
   repetition 51, 78-79
   symbolism 84-86, 95-96
   symmetry 51, 61-66, 88, 91
   textures 110-115
   volumes 91, 92-93
   see also artwork; colour; patterns; proportion; shapes
air conditioning/ventilation systems 42, 123, 126, 163
air quality 121
   air composition and occupancy 128-129
   air filtration 42, 126
   air sampling sensors 128
   carbon dioxide levels 128, 129
   design considerations for 134
   health and 129-131
   hierarchy of impacts 182
   material emission standards 131-132
   particulate matter (PM) 42, 126, 129, 131
   pollutant sources and types 130
   test outcomes 132, 133
   volatile organic chemicals (VOCs) 129-131, 132, 133
see also ventilation
Aked, Jody 157
Albers, Josef 75
Allchurch, Emily 104
ambient lighting 145-146
amygdala 82
angles 81-83, 86
anxiety zone 10, 11
Appleton, Jay 33
Armstrong, John 98
artificial lighting 142-146
artwork
   in hospitals 100-107
   value of 98-99
asthma 127
authenticity 52

B
balance 51, 61-62, 66, 88
Baumgarten, Alexander 56
beauty 3-7
'a better place' methodology 177-178
Billger, Monica 75
biophilia 48-49, 51
   colour 68
   humidity 127
   lighting 136
   proportion 87, 90
   shapes and patterns 87, 88
   symmetry 63
Blake, Quentin 102
blue 71
Bluyssen, Philomena 10
Bradley, Paige 103
brain activity
   colours and 69
   contours and angles and 81, 82
BRE Trust 115
Brown, Brené 28

C
call centre case study 187-189
canopied entrances 46
carbon dioxide levels 128, 129
Cartwright Pickard 126
ceiling height 92-93
Chiba University 69
Chickasaw Nation Medical Center, Oklahoma 104
Childers, Terry L. 115
circadian rhythms 69, 137, 139, 144
Clements-Croome, Derek 122, 124, 125, 129
Clift, S. 105
clothing, thermal comfort and 8, 121, 123-124
collaboration, designing for 34-35
colour 3, 13, 68-76, 182-183
   applications of 70
   brain activity and 69

colour groups 70, 74, 111
impacts of 69
lighting and 70, 140, 144
psychology of 68, 70–72
selection process 73
shape and 75, 83
symbolism 95
textures and 111
comfort 7–8
performance and 10–12
see also thermal comfort
comfort zone 10, 11
communal spaces 151–152
contemplation spaces 150–151
contours 81–83, 86
controllability 34, 42, 167
Couder, Y. 65
co-working spaces
environmental stressors 34
Huckletree case study 36–37
occupant control and 34
prospect and refuge principles 32–33
sociopetal design 35
Crump, Derrick 129, 133
curves 81–83, 86

D
Dalke, Hilary 69
dance programmes, hospital-based 103
danger zone 10
daylight 41, 42, 137–138, 139–141
daylight modelling 139
de Botton, Alain 5, 13, 58, 98
de Dear, Richard J. 125
Deller, Jeremy 106
design characteristics 51–52
design issues 52–53
distractions, costs of 149–150
Douady, S. 65

E
elegance 51, 58–59
Emerson, R.W 5
empathy 25, 28–29
entrance design 46–47
environmental benchmarking tools 177
Environmental Product Declarations (EPDs) 131–132
Environmental Psychologists (EPs) 30–31, 38

environmental psychology
defined 32
Huckletree case study 36–37
prospect and refuge principles 32–33
sociopetal design 34–35
territory and personalisation 34
environmental stressors 34
ergonomics 153
existing buildings 40–41

F
facility managers (FMs) 168
Fibonacci sequence 65, 89–90
Fischer, J. L. 96
Fisk, W. J. 127
fluency 51, 52, 78
formaldehyde 130, 132, 133
fresh air 13, 41–42
see also ventilation
functional 6
furniture *see* seating/furniture

G
glare control 141
Global Happiness Report 176
golden ratio 65, 78, 87, 89–90, 93
Gray, Fiona 29, 30
green 71
grey 73
Guo, H. 133
Gwynne, Patrick 89, 148

H
Hann, Michael 96
happiness measures 176
Happy Planet Index 176
harmony 12–15, 51
Hat Factory, Germany 59
healthcare environments
acoustics 164
artwork in hospitals 100–107
contours and angles 82–83
lighting and colours 70
natural ventilation 125
The Homewood 89, 148
Huckletree 36–37
Hume, Victoria 100–107
humidity 127
Hunter, Emma 103
hypothalamus 69

I
indigo 71
interviews, one-to-one 20–25
Islamic art 86–87

J
James, Andrew 104
Jo, W. K. 133
Jung, Carl 84–85
Juniper, Bridget 180, 187–189

K
Kandinsky, Vasily 30
Kennin-ji temple, Kyoto 85–86
Kepler, Johannes 89–90
key design considerations 42
Key Performance Indicators (KPIs) 178–179, 184–185
Kilner, Philip 103
Klarén, Ulf 3

L
labelling schemes, emissions from materials 131–132
Layard, Richard 176
Le Corbusier 13, 89
Lewis, C.S 194
Lidwell, W. 182
lighting 136–137
   aims and benefits of 136
   artificial 142–146
   colour and 70, 140, 144
   daylight 41, 42, 137–138, 139–141
   design strategies 139–141
   glare control 141
   hierarchy of impacts 182
   impacts on emotions 138, 142
   impacts on health 137–138
   light fittings 144
   Lux level approach 136–137
     task and ambient lighting 145–146
lines of sight 154–155
Living Building Challenge (LBC) sustainability standard 6–7
London Southbank Festival Hall Terrace Cafe 156
London Underground 156
Lundy, Miranda 65
Lux levels 136–137

M
Mackintosh School of Art & Design 126
Manchester Metropolitan University Arts for Health 105–106
Mardaljevic, John 139
Maslow's Hierarchy of Needs 12, 181–183
materials
   aesthetic issues 109, 115
   emission labels and standards 131–132
   textures 110–115
   thermal comfort and 124
measuring value and wellbeing 175
   'a better place' methodology 177–178
   call centre case study 187–189
   happiness measures 176
   hierarchy of impacts 180–183
   Key Performance Indicators (KPIs) 178–179, 184–185
   occupancy surveys 169–171
   productivity measurement 190–191
   Social Return On Investment (SROI) 190
   space surveys 184–185
   User Profile Activities (UPAs) 179, 184–185
   weighting of impacts 179–183
mechanical air conditioning/ventilation systems 42, 123, 126, 163
meditation 150–151
Mendelsohn, Erich 59
Meyers-Levy, Joan 92
Minton, Anna 157
Missia, D.A. 133
Mofrad, Nikravan 92
Mudarri, D. 127
multi-sensory design 47
music
   in hospitals 102–103, 105, 106
   musical intervals 65

N
National Alliance for Arts, Health & Wellbeing 101
natural light 41, 42, 137–138, 139–141
natural materials 109
natural ventilation 42, 125–126
Nazaroff, W. W. 127
Nicol, Fergus 124
The Nightingale Project 102
noise *see* acoustics

O
observing users within spaces 20, 25
occupancy surveys 169–171
occupant controllability 34, 42, 167

one-to-one interviews 20–25
open-plan offices
   distractions 149–150
   environmental stressors 34
   occupant control and 34
   sociopetal design 35
operational issues 167–171
optimal performance zone 10, 11
orange 71

P

particulate matter (PM) 42, 126, 129, 131
patterns
   Fibonacci sequence 65, 89–90
   golden ratio 65, 78, 87, 89–90, 93
   lighting and 144
   proportions 51, 86–88
   repetition 51, 78–79
Peck, Joann 115
performance and productivity
   air quality and 129
   comfort and 10–12
   measurement of 190–191
personalisation 34
personality profiles, colour 68
phyllotaxy 65, 90
physical issues 118–119
   aesthetic issues and 118
   controllability 34, 42, 167
   humidity 127
   operational issues 167–171
   see also acoustics; air quality; space planning; thermal comfort; ventilation
plants 48, 127
Plato 7, 86–87
pollution, air *see* air quality
Post Occupancy Evaluations (POEs) 169–171
prioritising issues 41–42
productivity *see* performance and productivity
proportion 51, 86–88
   golden ratio 65, 78, 87, 89–90, 93
   symmetry and 65
prospect and refuge principles 32–33
psychology
   of colour 68, 70–72
   contours and angles and 81–83, 86
   textures and 111–112
   see also environmental psychology
Pythagoras 86

R

'realistic' approaches 6, 52, 193
red 71
refuge and prospect principles 32–33
repetition 51, 78–79
resilience 8, 11
Riddle, Mark 95–96
Rothko, Mark 5, 56, 98, 110
Royal Brompton Hospital 102, 104

S

Sachs, Jeffrey 176
Sailer, Kerstin 148
school environments
   acoustics 158
   carbon dioxide levels 129
   ceiling height 92
   comfort 8
   proportion and patterns 88
   textures 113–114
seating/furniture 152–153
   ergonomics 153
   hierarchy of impacts 182
   prospect and refuge principles 32–33
   sociopetal design 34–35
   thermal comfort and 123
security 157–158
sensors, air sampling 128
Sensory Toolkit 47
Serra, Roberto 136
shapes 81, 93
   colour and 75, 83
   contours and angles 81–83, 86
   Fibonacci sequence 65, 89–90
   golden ratio 65, 78, 87, 89–90, 93
   lighting and 144
   proportions 51, 86–88
   repetition 51, 78–79
   symbolism 84–86, 95–96
Shield, Bridget 183
Shin, S. H. 133
Silver, Harry R. 96
smart technology 20, 25
   thermal comfort and 124
Smith, Richard 104
Snell, Sue 104
social norms 4, 35, 44, 70, 84, 95
Social Return On Investment (SROI) 190
sociopetal space 34–35
Soft Landings framework 12, 40, 123, 168

sound *see* acoustics
space planning 148–150
  acoustics and 149–150
  communal spaces 151–152
  contemplation spaces 150–151
  hierarchy of impacts 182
  lines of sight 154–155
  occupier culture and needs and 155–156
  prospect and refuge principles 32–33
  reducing distractions 149–150
  security 157–158
  sociopetal design 34–35
  user experience design 44–45
  views out 41, 154–155
  see also seating/furniture
space surveys 184–185
Space Works Consulting 32–37
standards
  acoustics 160
  daylight design strategies 141
  emissions from materials 131–132
  humidity 127
Staricoff, R. 105
Strauss, Levi 96
surveys
  occupancy 169–171
  space 184–185
symbolism 84–86, 95–96
symmetry 51, 61–66, 88, 91

T
task lighting 145–146
territoriality 34
textures 110–115
  lighting and 144
  psychology and 111–112
thermal comfort 3, 8, 121–125
  air conditioning systems 123
  air velocity and 125
  clothing and 8, 121, 123–124
  openable windows 42, 122, 125
Thompson, D'Arcy Wentworth 91
Tommaso, M. de 105
touch *see* textures
Trappe, H. J. 102
trickle window ventilation 126
Turner, Briony 47
Tusa, John 101, 107
TVOC (total volatile organic chemical) levels 130–131, 132

U
UCL 129
user experience design
  biophilia 48–49
  entrances 46–47
  multi-sensory design 47
  spaces 44–45
User Profile Activities (UPAs) 179, 184–185
User Profiles 12–15, 19–27, 31

V
ventilation 41–42, 125–126
  air composition and occupancy 128–129
  air filtration 42, 126
  air sampling sensors 128
  air velocity 125
  design considerations for 134
  mechanical 42, 123, 126, 163
  natural 42, 125–126
  openable windows 42, 122, 125, 162–163
  trickle window vents 126
views out 41, 154–155
Villa Savoye 13, 89
violet 72
Vischer, Robert 29
Visible Light Transmittance (VLT) 141
volatile organic chemicals (VOCs) 129–131, 132, 133
volumes 91, 92–93

W
Wade, David 7, 86, 90
wearable technology 20, 25
  thermal comfort and 124
wellbeing, defining xii–xiii
White, Alasdair 10, 12
windows
  openable 42, 122, 125, 162–163
  trickle ventilation 126
Wolfeld, Leah R. 149
Wolff, Dominique 176
World Green Building Council 176
World Health Organization (WHO) xii, 122, 125, 130, 131
Worringer, Wilhelm 6
Wren, Sir Christopher 3
Wright, Angela 68, 69, 70–72, 73, 74

X, Y, Z
Xiao, Kaida 75
yellow 71
Zhu, Rui 92

Image credits

pxiii Grigoriou Interiors; pxiv Grigoriou Interiors; p4 all Grigoriou Interiors; p6 all Grigoriou Interiors; p7 Grigoriou Interiors; p10 Alasdair White/Grigoriou Interiors; p11 Alasdair White/Grigoriou Interiors; p12 Grigoriou Interiors; p14 Derwent London / © Hufton & Crow; p15 top Grigoriou Interiors, bottom Derwent London / © Hufton & Crow; p16 Grigoriou Interiors; p19 left Grigoriou Interiors, right Agnese Sanvito; p20 Grigoriou Interiors; p21 all Grigoriou Interiors; p23 Grigoriou Interiors; p24 Grigoriou Interiors; p26 top Grigoriou Interiors, bottom and right FutureGov; p28 all Grigoriou Interiors; p29 Grigoriou Interiors; p30 Creative Commons CC0 1.0 Universal; p31 Museum of Happiness; p33 Grigoriou Interiors; p34 Grigoriou Interiors; p35 top left and bottom Huckletree, top right Grigoriou Interiors; p36 Huckletree; p37 Huckletree; p40 all Grigoriou Interiors; p41 Agnese Sanvito; p44 all Grigoriou Interiors; p45 all Grigoriou Interiors; p46 Grigoriou Interiors; p47 top Grigoriou Interiors, bottom Bryoni Turner; p48 all Grigoriou Interiors; p49 all Grigoriou Interiors; p51 left Starwood/Marriott International, right Grigoriou Interiors; p52 left Agnese Sanvito, right Grigoriou Interiors; p54 Grigoriou Interiors; p56 Grigoriou Interiors; p58 all Grigoriou Interiors; p59 all Dario J Laganà Norte Photography http://www.norte.it/ ; p61 all Grigoriou Interiors; p62 all Grigoriou Interiors; p63 top PDP, bottom left and right Grigoriou Interiors; p64 Grigoriou Interiors; p65 all Grigoriou Interiors; p66 Grigoriou Interiors; p68 Grigoriou Interiors; p69 Grigoriou Interiors; p71 top PDP, top middle Starwood/Marriott International, all others Grigoriou Interiors; p72 top and middle Grigoriou Interiors, bottom Huckletree; p74 all Grigoriou Interiors; p75 Grigoriou Interiors; p76 Museum of Happiness; p78 Grigoriou Interiors; p79 top Grigoriou Interiors, bottom Anni Callaghan, Ivo Prints; p81 all Grigoriou Interiors; p82 all Grigoriou Interiors; p83 all Grigoriou Interiors; p84 all Grigoriou Interiors; p85 top Jeffery Courtney, bottom left and right Grigoriou Interiors; p86 Grigoriou Interiors; p87 top Grigoriou Interiors, bottom Dave Wade; p88 all Grigoriou Interiors; p89 all Grigoriou Interiors; p90 all Grigoriou Interiors; p91 Grigoriou Interiors; p92 all Grigoriou Interiors; p95 Brodie Neill, photography credit Angela Moore; p96 Grigoriou Interiors; p98 Grigoriou Interiors; p99 Grigoriou Interiors; p100 Grigoriou Interiors; p103 Emma Hunter; p104 all Emily Allchurch and Sue Snell; p105 all Emily Allchurch and Sue Snell; p106 all Grigoriou Interiors; p109 all Grigoriou Interiors; p110 all Grigoriou Interiors; p111 all Grigoriou Interiors; p112 all Grigoriou Interiors/Maria Popova; p113 all Grigoriou Interiors/Maria Popova; p114 top Agnese Sanvito, bottom Grigoriou Interiors; p115 © Bob Johnston; p116 Grigoriou Interiors; p118 Grigoriou Interiors; p119 top PDP, bottom Grigoriou Interiors; p122 Huckletree; p123 Grigoriou Interiors; p124 Grigoriou Interiors; p125 all Grigoriou Interiors; p126 all Ductbusters Ltd; p127 Grigoriou Interiors; p128 Grigoriou Interiors; p132 BSRIA; p134 Agnese Sanvito; p137 Grigoriou Interiors; p138 bottom left Agnese Sanvito, all others Grigoriou Interiors; p139 Agnese Sanvito; p140 all PDP; p141 top left and right Agnese Sanvito, bottom Grigoriou Interiors; p145 Agnese Sanvito; p143 middle right Starwood/Marriott International, all others Grigoriou Interiors; p144 top left and right Grigoriou Interiors, bottom Agnese Sanvito; p145 middle right Huckletree, all others Grigoriou Interiors; p148 PDP; p149 RIBA Collections; p151 top left and right Grigoriou Interiors, bottom TSK; p152 Grigoriou Interiors; p153 Starwood/Marriott International; p154 left Grigoriou Interiors, right Agnese Sanvito; p155 top Grigoriou Interiors, bottom left and right Museum of Happiness; p156 Chris Jackson, p157 top Chris Jackson; bottom Agnese Sanvito; p158

Grigoriou Interiors; **p160** Grigoriou Interiors; **p161 top left** Grigoriou Interiors, **top right** Starwood/Marriott International, **bottom** Huckletree; **p162 all** Grigoriou Interiors; **p163** Grigoriou Interiors; **p164** Agnese Sanvito; **p165** Derwent London / © Hufton & Crow; **p167** Derwent London / © Hufton & Crow; **p169 all** Spaceworks; **p172** Grigoriou Interiors; **p175** Grigoriou Interiors; **p177 top** Grigoriou Interiors, **bottom** Elina Grigoriou; **p179** PDP; **p180** Grigoriou Interiors; **p181** Grigoriou Interiors; **p182** Grigoriou Interiors; **p183** Grigoriou Interiors; **p184** Grigoriou Interiors; **p185** Grigoriou Interiors; **p187** Dr Bridget Juniper; **p188** Dr Bridget Juniper; **p189** Dr Bridget Juniper; **p191** Grigoriou Interiors; **p193** Grigoriou Interiors; **p194** Grigoriou Interiors; **p195** Lucy Morley